CW01091066

HAFEZ

GEOFFREY SQUIRES

MIAMI

UNIVERSITY

PRESS

HAFEZ

TRANSLATIONS

AND

INTERPRETATIONS

OF

THE

GHAZALS

LIBRARY OF CONGRESS CATALOGING-IN-PUBLICATION DATA

HAFEZ, ACTIVE 14TH CENTURY.

[DIVAN. SELECTIONS. ENGLISH]

HAFEZ : TRANSLATIONS AND INTERPRETATIONS

OF THE GHAZALS / [PREFACE AND

TRANSLATION BY GEOFFREY T. SQUIRES].

PAGES CM

ISBN 978-1-881163-54-1

1. HAFEZ, ACTIVE 14TH CENTURY—TRANSLATIONS INTO

ENGLISH. I. SQUIRES, GEOFFREY, TRANSLATOR. II. TITLE.

PK6465.Z32S68 2014

891'.5511—DC23

2013049056

DESIGN AND COMPOSITION BY QUEMADURA

PRINTED ON ACID-FREE, RECYCLED PAPER

IN THE UNITED STATES OF AMERICA

MIAMI UNIVERSITY PRESS

356 BACHELOR HALL

MIAMI UNIVERSITY

OXFORD, OHIO 45056

PREFACE
VII

I

LOVE

3

II

THE GARDEN

39

III

THE TAVERN

67

IV

THE LOVER

115

V

THE AGE

167

VI

THE BELOVED

231

VII

THE FAITH

285

VIII

THE MYSTIC

319

IX

THE MORALIST

363

X

THE POET

367

NOTES

423

BIBLIOGRAPHY

506

ACKNOWLEDGMENTS

514

PREFACE

This brief preface is intended simply to help readers approach and begin to find their way around the text. Detailed notes can be found after the poems.

The fourteenth-century poet Hafez (sometimes spelled Hafiz) is a paradox. He is probably the best-loved of all the great Persian poets, and people in Iran, young and old, rich and poor, conservative and liberal, still refer to him and quote him daily. Yet he is also the most complex of those poets (one Persian edition even gives a paraphrase after each poem) and has generated by far the largest literature of any of them, both in his own country and abroad. The reason has been put succinctly by Bürgel (1991:7): "There is hardly any single verse of Hafiz posing a problem in itself. However, there is also hardly a ghazal not posing a problem of meaning and, consequently, of interpretation."

Moreover, there is a widespread view that Hafez is untranslatable. This does not mean that people over the last two centuries have not managed to render particular ghazals skillfully or beautifully but that no one has succeeded in bringing him across as a whole. It is partly a problem of scale. The Divan or collected works includes nearly 500 ghazals, of which I have translated just over half. These ghazals— short lyric poems not unlike the sonnet—are simply in alphabetical order and since it is difficult to date many of them we cannot put them in any kind of autobiographical sequence. Besides, even though Hafez was famous in his own times, we know relatively little about his life. So, understanding him, let alone translating him, is a daunting challenge.

Given these difficulties, I have done a number of things. To begin with, I have chosen short extracts from some poems to act as a kind of overture, opening up some of the main themes, before plunging into the full complexity of entire ghazals. I have broken up some of the more disjunctive poems into shorter pieces, which, besides making them more manageable, offers some variety of pace and dynamics. The poems are grouped in ten sections which help to bring out the various facets of the originals, although these divisions are by no means watertight. I have interspersed the poems with brief prose comments (in bold type) that both punctuate them and provide some pointers for the reader. And I have added brief explanations of new names and terms at the ends of poems where they occur. I suspect that as readers get to know the text they will be able to dispense with this scaffolding, or if they wish ignore it from the beginning: the sheer momentum of the poems should carry them through.

Readers who prefer to place all this in context should turn first to the Notes, which provide a general introduction. Persian speakers may want to go directly to the section on Sources so that they can relate the translations to the originals. There are detailed notes on each of the ten sections and on many of the individual poems. There is also a substantial bibliography in Farsi, English and French.

The French have a saying: *traduire c'est trahir*: to translate is to betray. I think it is impossible to produce a translation that is wholly authentic and faithful to the original. Each translator inevitably brings something of his or her own time and place to the process, if only in the language used. And there are particular hazards involved in translations by westerners of oriental literature. I have tried my best to get a true sense not just of the original text but the context in which it was produced, but it is a case, I think, of what Beckett once described as "failing better."

All this may sound rather negative, which would be a pity. There is so much to enjoy in Hafez: the sheer energy, virtuosity and beauty of his writing, the way he plays with, not just words, but thought itself, the constant element of surprise. And the mountain of scholarly literature is there for a reason: this is a poet of multiple levels, facets and meanings. Several times I thought I was finished, only to find something else, another seam and even now I have no real sense of a conclusion.

The second, happy paradox, for the English-speaking reader, is that this poet who lived so long ago and in such different circumstances, who wrote within such different conventions and belonged to such a different tradition, still somehow speaks directly and immediately to us about the human condition, about our hopes, doubts, joys and fears: all those things that bind us together across place and time.

I

LOVE

Boy   bring round the wine
and give me some

for love that at first seemed easy
turned difficult

3

It is important to preface a book of Hafez' ghazals with the reminder that these poems were initially performed, often with music, in a court gathering or some other social circle, rather than read on the page. We need therefore to be alive to the drama of their presentation: the voice, the audience, the occasion.

Heart   where are you going
and in such a hurry
where are you taking me

    friend
    with Hafez you must give up
    all hope of sleep   all prospect of repose

    the very idea of stability

Even if you abuse me   God forgive you
yet you speak well

harsh words turn sweet on your lips

What scent is this

dark curls   smelling of musk
the dawn wind loosening your tresses

hearts fill

    what chance do I have to enjoy
    the pleasures of your caravanserai
    when at every moment the camel-bells cry out
    time to load up   move on

stain your prayer-carpet with wine
if the Master tells you to
for the pilgrim should observe the customs of the way

What would I give   what would I not give
whole cities

      Samarkand   Bokhara

for that one dark Indian mole

Mouth so small
no sign of it at all

waist like a strand of hair so fine
I cannot tell which one

a lifetime has elapsed
since I first caught a waft of your hair
yet my heart still scents its fragrance

I am surprised
that your image remains in my eyes
since they continually rinse themselves out

I have wronged you and yet persist
in hoping for your indulgence

indeed I have wept so much that passers-by
on seeing my tears inquire

what stream is this

My pain comes from my beloved
     and the remedy too

my heart has been sacrificed to my beloved
     my soul too

this that people say
     surpasses beauty
my beloved has this
     and that too

all this I have whispered privately
     behind the curtain
and will cry out in public too

heaven lies in the glory of your face
     and earth too

It is only recently that the word "conventional" has come to have a rather negative ring. For many centuries, it meant the agreed, best way of doing or saying something: the Latin root signifies a coming or bringing together. Much English and indeed European art and literature was conventional in this sense, and so is Hafez.

O dawn wind kindly say to that nimble gazelle
you have led me a merry dance
over the waterless plains and barren hills

    I wish the sugar-merchant
    long life and prosperity
    but why does he neglect his sweet parrot so

        O rose it is surely vanity
        that does not allow you
        to inquire after your doting nightingale

courtesy and kindness
are the only ways to win over
men of vision
the bird of wisdom is not trapped or snared

    when you sit with your beloved and a measure of wine
    drink a cup in memory of your erstwhile lovers
    who labored under an illusion
    and now have no measure but the measureless wind

I do not know why one is not accorded
even a hint of recognition
by those who are erect   dark eyed   bright cheeked

no one can fault your beauty   except insofar as
neither love nor trust find a place in your good looks

    it is no wonder that in the storeyed heavens
    Christ himself is drawn into the whirling dance
    at the sound of Venus' harp and Hafez' lines

On the road of love there is no such thing as distance
I see you clearly   and so send you my greetings

each morning and evening
the caravan of my prayers sets out
accompanied by the north and the east winds

and so that the forces of my grief
do not lay waste the kingdom of my heart
I dispatch my own precious soul as hostage to you

O you that are hidden from me
yet sit next my heart
I offer a prayer for you   and send my blessings

in the beauty of your face   admire God's handiwork
in the mirror of my heart   behold the divine

and so that your minstrels may proclaim
my passion for you
I send you now this song   these words   these lines

If reason knew how happy my heart was
to be bound by your curls
the wise would go mad in search of my chains

and since your face revealed one Verse of kindness
my exegesis has been concerned
with beauty and with grace

wind-blown your hair obscured the world
turning it dark
and for all my passion that was all
I ever gained from it

O that just once   upon your stony heart
my burning sighs might leave their mark
my searing cry   when night is taken away

If I follow you   you complain
but if I hold back   then you turn on me

and if   as you pass
overcome by longing
I crumble to dust at your feet
then like the wind you are gone

if I ask for even half a kiss
from your mouth pour out a hundred sickly excuses

how many reputations have been dragged through the dirt
by those seductive narcissistic eyes

the wilderness of love
is full of mountains to climb   valleys to cross
O where is the lion-heart
that does not shrink from these

pray for long life and resilience
for the fickle wheel of fate
has a thousand worse tricks to play on you

    Hafez lay down your head   on the sill of submission
    for if you resist   time will in time insist

The cheek

the chin

the dimple on the chin

the eyes

the eyebrows

the eyelashes

the lips

the mouth

O wind   like a bird   to Sheba I send you
look   from where   to where   I send you

it grieves me to see you   in this wasteland of sorrow
to the skies of true love   therefore I release you

you who took messages from Solomon to his Queen
O hoopoe   like the wind   to Sheba I send you

One rose from the world's rose-garden is enough
the cool of one swaying cypress is enough

may I be spared the society of hypocrites
of all the world's burdens   the burden of a cup is enough

good works are rewarded with castles in heaven
for us down and outs   this Magian ruin is enough

sit on the river-bank and watch life passing
for we who are free from care
this symbol of transience is enough

look at the profit and loss of the world's bazaar
and all life's tribulations
if that does not convince you
for us it is quite enough

a companion beside me   what more could I want
the blessing of that soul-mate is enough

let me not be sent to heaven just yet
away from your gate
for in all the world   the end of your street is enough

　　Hafez it is wrong to complain about your fate
　　a way with words   a flowing ghazal   is enough

Magian: one of many references to the ancient Zoroastrian religion of Iran
and its priests (magi)

Do not ask
do not ask me to say

how I have suffered the pangs of love
or drunk the dregs of estrangement

do not ask how I searched the world and at last
found my heart's desire

do not ask how it is that
in my yearning for the dust at your door
the tears poured down from my eyes

do not ask what I heard from your very mouth
last night with my own ears

      why do you bite your lip
      as if to say   do not say

      I have chosen these ruby lips and that is it

do not inquire about the sorrows I have endured
here in this wretched place
without you

or like someone who has lost his way
on the road of love
what stage I have reached

do not ask me to describe
do not ask me to say

do not ask

Like a candle I laugh and sparkle
with my love for you

like a candle
my patience has melted away

my devotion to you shines out like a candle
among the fair

like a candle I burn through the night
for those who like candles risk their heads
in the backstreets of desire

like a candle I have become soft as wax
because of my suffering
like a candle my being
dissolves into water and fire

like a candle tears roll down my cheeks
like a candle my secret
is exposed to everyone

my days are dark without
your beauty which adorns the world
the more I love you   like a candle
the less there is of me

at dawn I have only a moment
to hold you in my sight
show me your face my beloved
so that guttering   I may go out

O light my porch like a candle
spend one night by my side
or I shall shroud the whole world
in the black smoke of my sighs

The nearest English equivalent to the ghazal is the sonnet. Both are short lyric poems with regular meters and rhymes, but there are three key differences. Like the sonnet, the ghazal often comes out at fourteen lines, but by no means always. Secondly, whereas the final couplet in the Elizabethan sonnet usually clinches the poem, in the Hafezian ghazal it often seems like an addendum, naming and praising the poet himself or his patron, and functioning perhaps as a copyright mark. Most importantly, each couplet in the ghazal is complete and self-contained, raising questions about the structure of the poem as a whole; if it is a whole; if we should even think of it as a whole.

Halfway through the night you came to the side of my bed
wine in hand   blouse torn   and your hair all over the place

skin glowing with sweat   lips playing with a smile
more than a little tipsy   reciting a ghazal

with mischief in your eyes   and wistfulness in your voice
you leaned down by my pillow   and whispered plaintively

asleep   my old love   are you

the Lover who is offered that cup   which banishes night's sleep
must be love's heretic   if he does not swear by it

do not grumble at those who drain the dregs   O Reverend Puritan
for this is all we were given   the day the world began

whatever He put before us   we downed and didn't care
whether it was the draught of paradise   or made us the worse
    for wear

O Hafez many a vow like yours   has been broken beyond repair
by a laughing cup of wine   and the tangles in someone's hair

23

Cool wind of dawn   amber-laden
faint scent of heart's desire

which rises early seeking where you are

    O hoopoe   happy bird   be my guide on the road
    for my eyes are filled with tears
    of longing for the dust at that door

behold the crescent moon and the sunset glow
and think of my wasted form
drowning in my heart's blood

without you I continue to breathe   to my great shame
unless you forgive me   how can I be forgiven

from your friends
the sun in its unfailing course has learned
how to tear open the black bodice of night
at dawn

on the day I depart this life   from love of your face
the red rose will grow on my grave instead of grass

    and let your tender heart
    not tire of hearing me so soon
    for saying *bismillah*   Hafez has just begun

bismillah: the initial invocation of God at the beginning of a speech or address, in full "In the name of God the Merciful the Compassionate"

The image of the looking-glass, the pure reflection. The heart as a mirror that is polished so carefully, so assiduously that in the end it is nothing in itself or by itself, has no nature or substance of its own, no content or inherence, but serves—and the word is advised—simply to show.

O theophany of beauty   who lifts your veil
O bird of paradise   who gives you seed and water

sleep deserts me   at the consuming thought
of in whose arms you find your nest of repose

the road of lovers' hearts has been cut
by your languid gaze
from this we know that the drink you serve is potent

be on your guard that in these waterless tracts
the desert ghouls do not fool you with some mirage

you who do not ask after this poor mendicant
have you no thought of reward or punishment

even in error the arrow of your glance
found my heart
so how will it be then   when your aim is true

if you do not respond to my cries it is because
your threshold is so lofty as to be out of earshot

O castle of my heart   yet intimate dwelling
may time's dereliction never befall you

        Hafez is not a slave to desert his master
        return   for your reproaches cast him down

My soul dissolved
so that my heart could set about its work
    but to no avail

I kindled foolish hopes   to no avail

in the eyes of the world I became a vagabond
searching for my deeds to the treasure
    but to no avail

seeking the bounty of your presence
I importuned noble men   to no avail

laughing you said
that you would come and lead our gathering
selfishly I became your humble servant
    to no avail

you sent a message to say
you would join in the debauchery and drinking
I became famous for being bibulous
    to no avail

hoping that I might kiss those ruby lips
I poured out my heart's blood   as if into a cup
    but to no avail

surreptitiously
I devised a thousand stratagems to entrap you
    all to no avail

    O do not set foot on love's road without a guide
    for I have done so a hundred times   to no avail

What language can Hafez use
to describe your beauty

since like the divine attributes
you are beyond comprehension

Love is a boundless ocean
nothing for it   but to drown

each time you give up your heart to love
is a moment of true joy
such good deeds have no need of divination

follow the path of unreason   look for the signs
for like the road to the treasure
it is not obvious to everyone

bring wine   and do not try to scare us
with reason's prohibitions
for such authorities hold no sway
in this jurisdiction

the clear eye beholds you
like the new moon in the sky
but not every eye perceives that crescent beauty

O you who are my very soul
ask of your own eyes who is slaying me

it is not in my horoscope
it is not the fault of the planets

    Hafez' cries have no purchase
    leave no mark on you

    I am astonished at this heart of granite

My one who is like the moon
a week ago left town
to me it seems like a year

    what do you know of separation
    how hard it is to bear

in the favor of your cheek
the pupil of my eye
mistook itself for a mole
seeing its reflection there

milk flows from your sweet lips still
although each of your eyelashes
is a dastardly murderer

O you whom everyone points out
for your largesse in this city
how strange your indifference to strangers

    from now on I shall harbor no doubts
    about the existence of the atom
    for your small mouth proves the point

they brought me the good news
that you might be passing
do not alter your plans
for truly that would be a blessing

    how can Hafez succeed
    in moving this mountain of grief
    for he has become so emaciated with weeping
    that his body is as thin as a reed

Hafez' poetry assumes an audience that would have understood what he was saying. Often this would have been the court circle, or that of some senior official, but it would be wrong to think of Hafez simply as a court poet: the rich intellectual and artistic life of Shiraz at the time would have comprised various "assemblies" (*majles*) which were a kind of cross between salon and forum, and which provided sociable venues for intelligent conversation and entertainment of various kinds.

Last night   all night   we told the tale of your hair
in our gathering   we discoursed on the chains of your hair

my heart   though bloodied by the darts of your eyelashes
yearns still for the double bow of your brow

if the dawn wind   God bless it   had not brought news
we would have heard from no one in your quarter

the world was at peace   knowing nothing of love's turmoil
till one glance of yours triggered an insurgency

and I   who have now gone mad   lived a quiet life
till your dark Indian hair laid a snare in my path

O open the tie of your garment so that my heart may open
since all the happiness I have known lies at your side

and if you remain true to me   visit my grave
for hoping to glimpse your face   I leave this world

The eye

the pupil of the eye

the gaze

the glance

the look

sight or insight

vision

Let me remember you who in parting
did not remember me
who did not soothe my sore heart   with your valediction

you who are in the prime of youth
and had the power to set me free
who did not grant this old slave his liberty

I shall wear a petitioner's shirt stained with my blood
before the indifferent heavens
who would not show me the way
to plant myself beneath the banner of justice

my cries outdo even those of Farhād
here on this mountain-side
in the hope that their distant echo might reach your door

and since you withdrew your shadow from the meadow
the dawn-bird no longer nests in the boxwood tree

creation's artist will not delineate
the lineaments of desire
of he who does not confess your God-given beauty

if the wind has brought some message quickly from you
it must have learned something of your agility

O change the tune   play a Hejāzi mode
for without taking leave   my beloved took that road

Farhād: the doomed lover of Shīrīn in the story of the king Khosrow and his
beautiful queen Shīrīn

Hejāz: the part of Arabia where Mecca is situated but also one of a number of
Persian musical modes

34

Flaunting their charms   they dance to the sound
of Hafez' poetry

the dark-eyed Kashmiris   the Turks of Samarkand

II

THE GARDEN

A Persian miniature. Stylized clouds in the sky. A tree leaning, overhanging, its branches reaching out, perfectly disposed to protect, give shade. Flowers of various kinds, including roses. Several figures, dressed in long robes, some with books or instruments (what looks like a stringed tar and a daf, a tambourine or hand-held drum) seated on carpets; one holding a cup or bowl for another to drink.

A walled garden
the company of friends

how delightful it is
how contented we are

the time of the rose
is the time to carouse

breeze teasing the nostrils
at every breath

pleasing not just the senses
but the very soul

while the air fills
with heart-felt sighs

and the tongue of the lily
whispers in my ear

that in this old world
it is best not to care

At dawn   with the scent of flowers   I took the garden air
so that like the broken-hearted songster   I could find comfort there

I looked at the show of the red rose   that lights up the dark like a
    lamp
so arrogant that it robs   the nightingale of repose

the elegant narcissus opens   filled with tears of regret
at the sight of the tulip's scars   the black bile in its heart

the lily's tongue threatens me   like the keen blade of a sword
and the open-mouthed poppy   gossips to everyone

sometimes like wine-worshippers   they raise their goblets up
sometimes like a serving-boy   they refill the drinker's cup

    take after the flowers and enjoy   the booty that comes to you
    so that Hafez may not be one   whose message does not get
        through

A garden   in spring-time
what better way to pass the day
than in the company of friends

where's the serving-boy   why the delay

treasure each moment you have
for no one knows what the end will be
life hangs by a single hair
look to your own troubles
and don't worry about the world's pain
for the world won't worry about you

what is the Water of Life
but an agreeable wine
and the gardens of paradise
but the banks of a small stream

drunk or sober
we are all of the same tribe
to whose fetching glance should we give away our hearts
what choice have we anyway

and what do even the heavens glean
of the mystery behind the curtain
be quiet   know all
don't pester the chamberlain

if a servant is to be held accountable
for his shortcomings and his sins
what price mercy then

the puritan looks forward to the elixir of heaven
Hafez opts for the pitcher

we shall see in due course the preference of our Maker

Resolving to repent first thing today
I said to myself   I shall consult the omens
but spring which shatters all good resolutions
has now arrived   so what is to be done

I tell you straight   I cannot sit by and see
my friends drinking   and me just looking on

    examine my head
    if I abandon the festivities
    when the tulip is in full bloom

since that countenance has led
to the burgeoning of my passion
I entrust my enemy's head to the care of a stone

I shall set my king upon a flowery plinth
like an idol
decked with bracelets and necklaces
of jasmine and hyacinth

I may be a beggar in the tavern   but see when I am drunk
how I strut before the heavens   and order the orbs around

with lips smiling like a bud   in honor of the king's court
I shall raise the cup
tearing open my shirt in celebration

I who depend for my livelihood   on hallmarked royal gold
how can I censure those whom wine sets free

Hafez has had enough   of drinking secretly
let him come out to the sound of the lute and the *nei*

nei: ancient reed flute from which the sound is produced by blowing across
the open end, giving a haunting, breathy quality

The lily

the anemone

the rose or wild-rose

the narcissus

the violet

the tulip

The garden is refreshed
by a breeze from another world
and I am blessed with a joyful wine
and my paradisal love

why should a tramp not boast of being a king
on such a day
with a cloud for his pavilion
and the field his banqueting-hall

to me this vernal month of May
points a moral
take cash in hand rather than relying on credit

    and do not place your trust in enemies
    for no illumination will result
    if you light the candle in your cell
    from the lamp of the synagogue

restore your soul with wine
for this ruined old world has it in mind
to make of our dust   bricks

    O do not enter my inebriation
    in the black ledger of my actions
    for who knows what the hand of fate
    has inscribed upon our brows

and when finally the time comes
do not draw back from my cortege

for though Hafez is steeped in sin
surely he is on his way to heaven

If we look for development in many ghazals we do not find it. They seem like a more or less random collection of self-contained images or ideas, each of which may be beautiful or striking in its own right, but which do not form the kind of linear progression that we are used to in the western lyric. Perhaps our expectations are at issue here. We expect poems to go somewhere. But what if they are there already?

One morning I went to the garden to pick a rose
when suddenly to my ear
came the sound of the nightingale

wretched like me
it was afflicted with love for a flower
and across those lawns gave voice to its plangent cry

I wandered along the paths
my mind preoccupied with these two
the rose   companion to beauty
the nightingale   bound to love
she unchanging   he unwavering

when the song of the nightingale had pierced my heart
I could bear it no longer

the garden sees many roses come into bloom
but no one has ever picked one
without suffering the pain of the thorn

Hafez   expect no happiness
from this turning sphere
for it has a thousand faults   and does us no favors

Breath of dawn   thin film of cloud
dew trickles   down the face of the tulip

a breeze from heaven   stirs on the lawn
alongside the paths   lie beds of green

so drink   my friends   to the new day
for the wine glows   like a burning ruby

If you sleep my little narcissus
    it is not without reason
if your hair is awry
    it is not without reason

if I spoke of the milk of your lips
their saltiness and sweetness
    it is not without reason

may long life be yours
though I know for sure
    not without reason
that your eyelashes are like small darts

I am overcome with grief
at separation   abandonment
O heart your lamentations
    are not without reason

last night the wind came down from the hills
and swept through the garden
O rose this torn collar of yours
    is not without reason

Hafez if your heart hides from others
the pain of love
when I see your tears I know
    they are not without reason

Hardly has the rose lifted its veil
than it prepares to depart

lament   O nightingale
sweet is the song of the wounded heart

From the branch of the stately cypress tree
the long-suffering nightingale again cries out
        may the evil eye spare the face of the rose

O rose
you who are privileged to be
the empress of beauty
do not treat the nightingale with disdain
for love's frenzy has seized its heart

        I shall not lament your absence   since without it
        how would I know the pleasure of your presence

if others are blithe and gay in their well-being
yearning for my love is the leaven of my joy

if the pious hope for *houris* and castles in heaven
the beloved is my *houri*   my castle the tavern

drink up to the sound of the harp
and drown your sorrows
and if someone chides you   say it is alright
God is forgiving

Hafez   do not complain of the pain of absence
for in separation there is union   and in darkness light

houris: the beings, sometimes described as maidens, promised to the virtu-
ous in the Muslim paradise

The falcon

the hawk

the hoopoe

the nightingale

the parrot

the raven

the small bird of the fields

The garden has all the lustre of youth again
and news of the rose
has reached the melodious nightingale

O wind if once more you should pass through that arbor
with its young saplings
convey my greetings to the cypress   rose   sweet basil

    if that young serving-boy
    would only parade his charms like them
    I would sweep the tavern steps with my eye-lashes

        O you who draw across the moon of your face
        the amber polo-stick of your plait
        do not strike my spinning head with it again

    I suspect that those who mock us revellers
    may at the end of the day
    ruin their faith in this place of ruination

be a friend to men of God   for Noah's ark
contained the dust of Adam for whom
the deluge was only a drop in the ocean

and leave this turning world
without asking for even a piece of bread
for that miserly black-hearted host
ends up murdering his guests

in the end all that is left
is a parcel of ground where we lie
so tell me what the point is
of raising palaces to the sky

O my moon of Canaan now the time has come
to bid farewell to prison
for dominion over Egypt is yours

Hafez   drink your fill   indulge   feel free
without as others do turning the Koran
into a snare of hypocrisy

Moon of Canaan: an allusion to Joseph

At break of day the nightingale said
to the newly awakened rose
do not play games with me
for the garden has seen many a one like you

laughing the rose replied   it is true
so I am not hurt
but a lover should not speak curtly to his beloved

if you want to sip ruby wine
from the bejewelled goblet of those lips
you must string together with your eyelashes
the carnelians and pearls of your tears

he who has not abased himself
and swept the tavern steps with his cheeks
will never know love's fragrance
in all eternity

last night in the garden of Iram
when the dawn wind brushed the curls of the hyacinth
I cried   O Throne of Jamshīd
where is your visionary cup
he said   alas that providence
which always watched over us
succumbed to sleep

Iram: an ancient Arab garden of legendary beauty

Jamshīd: the mythical original Iranian king who could see everything in his
magical cup

the language of love is not
that which comes to the tongue
boy bring us wine   cut short this verbiage

the river of Hafez' tears
has swept away his wisdom and sense of decorum
what can he do
for he cannot now hide the extremity of his devotion

Of the five senses, it is sight and smell that predominate in the Divan. Sight is associated with comprehension and understanding and, as in English, functions as a metaphor for knowing. Smell is associated with the scent of the beloved, as an intimation of presence or hope. In Hafez' time perfumes were not only an important part of personal adornment but were often used to create a fragrant environment for public festivities and gatherings.

Obsessed with your face
my heart couldn't care less about the garden
for like the tulip it bears
the marks of its own black brand
and like the cypress is rooted in one place

    my head does not bow
    before any arched eyebrow
    for the true recluse cares nothing for this world

how could I find my way in the darkness
through the twists and turns of your curls
did not your face illumine them like a lamp

    I am angry with the poppy
    for it claims to surpass your tresses
    marvel at what brains this cut-price slave possesses

it is right that both the candle and I
should weep for ourselves at dawn
for we each burn up and our idol doesn't care

Hafez' sore heart
applies itself to love's curriculum
indifferent to nature or society

    wander along the walkways of the garden
    and observe among the flower-beds there
    the tulip standing cup in hand
    like the king's bosom companion

The rosebush of pleasure is in bloom
where is the rosy-cheeked boy
the spring breeze gets up again
where is the pleasing wine

each new rose reminds us
of those with a rosy hue
but where is the ear to listen now
where are the eyes to see

missing from our congress of pleasure
is the fragrance of those we desire
O sweet-breathed morning air
where is the musk of that hair

I cannot show off like the rose
be patient then O breeze
I have plunged my hand in my heart's blood
O where has that vision gone

get up   for the morning candle
boasts of outshining your cheek
my enemy's tongue grows too long
where is my tempered steel

you said that you would give me
a kiss from your ruby lips
I said I shall swoon with passion
but where is my free will

Hafez may be the custodian
of the treasure-house of wisdom
but who now has the words
to portray these woeful times

Last night on the branches of the cypress tree
the nightingale sang sweetly in Pahlavi
giving instruction on the Stages of the Way

saying   see
the rose displays the fire that Moses saw
so that from this bush you might understand
the complexities of unity

the birds of the garden deploy their verbal skills
so the master can drink to the sound of old ghazals

happy the beggar's mat and his peaceful rest
for Khosrow himself did not have such luxuries

all that was left to Jamshid
was the story of his visionary cup
be wary   heart   of attachment to this world

and here is a strange paradoxical tale
though Jesus' breath revives   the beloved's kills

your drunken eyes have wrecked many a home
don't drink any more for you have had enough

as the aging peasant said sagely to his son
light of my eyes   you harvest what you sow

the boy must have given Hafez too large a measure
for the ends of the Master's turban are all awry

Pahlavi: the old Persian language which existed before the Arab invasion

Khosrow: an ancient king of Iran; the name itself came to mean king

62

Two engaging companions
two jugs of mellow wine
time   a book   the corner of some meadow
away from everyone

I would not give up such things
for this world and the next
even if a pack of zealots were on my heels

to trade in this nook of contentment
for all the treasures of the earth
would be like Joseph's brothers selling him off
for a pittance

listen   neither an ascetic such as you
nor an old lecher like me
can change the way the world works

    let us see what the mysterious hand depicts
    in Jamshid's visionary cup
    for no one can recall such times

in the whirlwind of events we can no longer see
if the rose or jasmine survive
and with this sandstorm sweeping through the garden
it is a miracle
that any colors or scents remain

    be steadfast   my heart   for God will surely not
    let Solomon's seal fall into the devil's hands

O Hafez   our world
has been shattered by this catastrophe
where now the counsels of the wise   the judgment of the brahmin

III

THE TAVERN

Open the door   O you who opens doors
for they have closed the taverns again
suddenly and without warning

in this of all seasons

Wine   wine of

The fast is behind us   the feast day come
our hearts rise up

the wine in the cellar is ready   send for it

the merchants of restraint have had their turn
the time for merriment has come

we who are free   and without pretence
who are not concerned with trying to save face
are better than these po-faced hypocrites
as those in the know   know

what harm is there in this
who can find fault with us
what possible consequences could there be
for anyone

as if what we did was likely to cause a riot

we do God's will   do no one ill
we do not contravene the law

in any case   who is without sin

and why should you complain
about the amount we consume
after all

it is not your blood we drink   but the blood of the vine

Last night our master forsook the mosque for the tavern
from now on   friends   what shall we do

how can we   as disciples   turn our faces to the Ka'ba
when our master turns his towards the house of wine

we shall make our home together in this Magian ruin
which has been our destiny since the world began

Ka'ba: the shrine at the heart of Mecca, which pilgrims circumambulate; the
focal point of Islam

Hafez' frequent references to the Magian religion are usually seen as a literary conceit with which to scandalize the orthodox, a kind of in-joke shared with his listeners. Wine was used in some Zoroastrian ceremonies, so the tavern becomes the Magian temple, the tavern-keeper the Elder of the Magi, and the serving-boys his Disciples. But the appeal to Iran's ancient faith goes beyond this. There are several references to the sacred fire and one of Hafez' soubriquets was "kindler of the fire-temple." And on a number of occasions he refers to Ahriman instead of the Muslim Satan, the Zoroastrian Soroush rather than the angel Gabriel. While the picture Hafez presents of the old religion is largely a caricature, it is worth remembering that he need not have invoked it in this way.

Boy   set light to the bowl with the radiant wine
let the minstrels sing that things are going our way

O you who know nothing of the pleasures of drinking
know that we have seen our beloved's face in the cup

some willowy ones there were   giving us the eye
until such time as our graceful cypress appeared

he who finds life through love will never die
for in time's register we shall live for ever

    I'm afraid that on the day of resurrection
    the Sheikh's *halal* bread
    will count for no more than our illicit potion

in the eyes of the one who is
the very testament of beauty
drinking is good   so that is why
we give full rein to our inebriation

    O wind if you pass by the garden of my beloved
    remember to ask for me

      why do you try so hard to forget my name
      when with time   it will be lost in oblivion

    Hafez   scatter from your eyes the seeds of your tears
    so that the bird of union may fall into your snare

halāl: lawful to eat according to the holy law

72

the green seas of the heavens
and the boat of the crescent moon
are swamped by the beneficence of Haji Qavām

Haji Qavām: the vizier of Shah Abou Eshāq in the time of Hafez' youth

What's this about giving up wine

I that am usually
a paragon of moderation and reason

who many a night have diverted piety
with harp and tambourine

what is this rumor about me
following the straight and narrow

if the ascetic does not take the road of excess
he has some excuse
for love is a journey that requires a guide
I follow the Elder of the Magi
who has delivered me from ignorance
everything that my Master does
is the essence of saintliness

it was not until recently that I became aware
of the way of the tavern
why else would I have stayed sober for so long

on the one hand we have the puritan
with his devotions and his pride
and on the other me
with my stupor and my need

on which of these two characters
will you look favorably
in the end

last night I did not sleep a wink
because I could not get out of my head
what some learned gentleman said

if Hafez is drunk yet again
somebody should complain

For the pilgrim who knows the road to the tavern
to knock on another door would be profane

and each one who finds his way to that doorway finds
the secret revealed in overflowing wine

fate gives the crown of excess only to those
who know this head-dress to be the highest honor

he who can decipher from the writing on the cup
the mysteries of heaven and earth
can see the future traced in the dust on the path

    ask of us only the devotion of madmen
    for in our Master's eyes   reason is a sin

The harp

the lute   or its equivalent

the melody

the mode

the tambour

the viol   or its equivalent

As long as there is a word for wine
and a sign outside the tavern
our heads will be dust on the road to our Magian host
for him to tread on

since before time began
I have had his slave's ring in my ear
thus it has been   and thus it will always be

    when you pass by my grave
    pray for guidance
    for it will be a shrine
    for all the reprobates in the world

and to zealots I say   you
whose piety is all about yourselves
get lost   for from your eyes and mine
the secret of the curtain is hidden and will stay that way

    my murderous Turk
    who slays all his lovers
    today emerges drunk again
    let us see this time   from whose eyes blood will flow

the night when finally
overcome by longing for you
I lay my head down in the tomb
my eyes will keep vigil till the resurrection

    but if fate comes to Hafez' aid   true to form
    his beloved's tresses will fall into others' hands

rend: a key term in Hafez, which he uses in his own idiosyncratic way. Originally meaning a vagabond or rake, a bad type living on the margins of society, it gradually came to be used of anyone who rejected or ignored the prevailing norms. Sometimes rendered (a little old-fashionedly) as libertine, which has the right connotations of freedom from social convention, but does not catch the spiritual overtones which Hafez gives it, of which one gloss might be Blake's "the road of excess leads to the palace of wisdom."

Rise up and pour the joyous wine
into the golden bowl
before they use your skull to sweep up dust

in the end we all come to dwell
in that silent valley
but for now let our voices resound
in the cupola of heaven

O cypress with your verdant top
when I am dead cease swaying to and fro
and cast your constant shadow on my tomb

      friend
      it is not proper to look upon the beloved
      through eyes blurred with tears
      but only with the polished mirror of your heart

my heart was bitten
by the snake of your plait
pray send me to your lips for an antidote

      the wealth of these fields will not last
      with the fire of the cup   set fire to the harvest there

I have washed myself in my tears
as the initiates of the Way require
first purify yourself   then gaze on the one who is pure

    may that self-regarding kill-joy
    find the mirror of his perception
    clouded by the vapour of a sigh

O Hafez   when he breathes on you
tear your garment like the rose discards its petals
and scatter it in the path of that nimble beauty

Last night in my sleep I dreamed that a moon had risen
the brightness of whose face
put an end to the darkness of separation

how to interpret this   what kind of sign

that the one who had been my companion
and who had gone away   was returning again

how I wish
he would walk through that door now

O let me repeat the name of my serving-boy
in whom fortune smiled upon me
and who would always bring me
my cup   my bowl of wine
through that same door

good too if in his dream
he had seen his own country
for then the memory of our company
would lead him back here to me

I want a potent wine
that will knock a strong man out
so that for a while I may forget
the iniquity of these times

bring it for no one is safe
from the trickery of the sky
from the games of Venus the harpist
or Mars the warrior

this world which nurtures the low
has placed no honeyed ease upon my table
O heart cleanse my bitter palate
of greed and avidity

throw away Bahram's lasso
seize the flask of wine instead
for I have searched the desert
and found no sign of him
or the wild ass he pursued

it is not inconsistent with greatness
to look upon the indigent
for even the mighty Solomon
deigned to notice an ant

bring me some pure wine
and I will show you time's secret
as long as you do not divulge this
to those whose hearts are blind

Bahram: a famous mythical hunter

the bow of that brow
could always do Hafez harm
but the beloved is merely amused
by the poet's puny arm

Thanks be to God   the tavern door is open
for longingly   my eyes are turned towards it

unable to contain themselves   the jars cry out
in a ferment of joy
for the wine that is there is real
and not some metaphor

Since in Persian the word for he and she is the same, we cannot usually say if Hafez' beloved was masculine or feminine. Sometimes context helps: for example there are references to "soft down" on the face, or to being veiled. It was considered indecent in court circles to write about women or girls, so that suggests an alternative to the more obvious explanation of the male references. On a few occasions Hafez does use the feminine *mashooqē*, rather than the masculine *mashooq*, but this may simply have been for the meter.

Please God let me not spurn wine
in the season of the rose
I boast of my good sense
how could I do such a thing

summon the minstrels
so that I may donate
the sum of my learning and virtue
to the sound of the *nei* and the lute

my heart has grown sick and tired
of debates in the *madrasē*
I shall devote myself once again
to the service of love and wine

where is the messenger of morning
so to that glad countenance
I may voice my complaints
about the night spent alone

when could we ever rely
on the vagaries of time
fill my drinking bowl to the brim
so that I may tell sad tales
of Jamshīd Kavūs and Kai

madrasē: a secondary or higher religious college

Kavūs, Kai (short for Kaiqubād): ancient historical (Sassanian) kings whose
exploits were recounted in Ferdowsi's 10th century national epic, the shāh-
nāmē

87

I do not fear the black ledger
for on the day of judgment
with the abundance of His grace
I shall settle a hundred debts

Hafez has been lent his life
by the one true Friend we have
one day he will see His face
and return his soul to him

Although wine brings happiness
and the wind the scent of the rose
do not drink to the sound of the harp
for fear of the chief of police

if you have got hold of some wine
and someone to share it with
don't take risks my friend
for these are dangerous times

better to hide the cup
up your ragged sleeve
for nowadays blood flows freely
as from the neck of a flask

let us wash our wine-stained garments
in the water of our tears
for this is the month of the fast
and the season of abstinence

are not the upturned heavens
like some bloody colander
that scatters the remains of kings
Khosrow's head and Parvīz' crown

friends
do not expect the wheeling firmament

Chief of police: mohtaseb, the head of the morality police whose role was to
see that the religious law was being observed

Parvīz: ancient Sassanian king, grandson of Khosrow 1st

to bring you happiness
for the pure wine is mixed with the lees

    Hafez you have charmed
    Fars and Eraq with your lines
    now let it be the turn
    of Baghdad and Tabriz

Let those who are full of themselves
die in themselves

let them not know the *ekstasis* of love

If that serving-boy goes on pouring wine
at such a rate
he will have us *illuminati* permanently drunk

and if he carefully arranges his hair
to cover the grain of his mole
how many wise birds will then fall into his snare

O happy that sot who at the feet of his beloved
does not know
whether he is losing his turban or his head

by day   try to be sober   for drinking then
rusts the polished mirror of the heart

the time for dawn-bright wine is when
night begins to draw
the curtain of evening around the pavilion of the horizon

the immature zealot who disapproves of wine
suddenly grows up
the moment his eyes fall on this year's vintage

      Hafez   do not go boozing with the police-chief
      for he will drink your wine   and repay you with a stone

Last night   half asleep   I went to the tavern door
with my gown soiled   and my prayer-rug stained with wine
the Master's assistant came up to me
scolding and saying
wake up   you dozy old tramp

    clean yourself up before you enter
    the sacred precincts of these Magian ruins
    so that they are not sullied by the likes of you

    in your lust for the lips of young boys
    how long will you go on
    staining the pure jewel of the spirit
    with liquid ruby

    be chaste and pure at this time of life
    and do not blemish the honored garment of age
    by paying court to youth

    those who are initiates of the true path of love
    can immerse themselves in that ocean
    without wetting one hair on their heads

    purify yourself
    climb out of nature's deep well
    for foul water will not make you clean

I replied   O you who mean the world to me
surely it is no sin if in spring-time
the rose-petal is tinted with wine

he said
Hafez your acquaintances have had enough
of these sophistries

O how his gentleness   was mixed with such reproof

Paradoxes, contradictions, inversions: the characteristic discourse of mysticism. Up-ending the conventional wisdom, reversing the usual logic. To be poor is to be rich. To serve is to be free. To abandon is to find. To have nothing is everything.

O come back serving-boy
for it is I who want to serve you
eager to be your slave   I pray for you

and with your bright cup that overflows with joy
lead me out of the shadows of confusion

although I have been immersed a hundred ways
in the ocean of sin
since I have discovered love I have become
one of the forgiven

    O learned colleagues   do not chastise me
    for my licentiousness   my notoriety
    since this was set down long ago
    in the book of fate

drink up   for being a lover
is not something one chooses
a matter of free will
but the gift of nature each of us receives

    I who have not left my homeland
    in my entire life
    for love of you am prepared to go into exile

    exhausted and weak   my journeying
    takes me over mountain and sea

O Khezr my sure-footed guide
assist me in my spiritual quest

a long way though I may seem
from the gateway of your auspicious palace
I am   in my heart of hearts
one of those who never leave your presence

Hafez would lay down his life before your eyes
such is his dream   if only he was spared

Khezr: literally "the green one," a mysterious spiritual guide who in ancient myth prevented Alexander from drinking the Water of Life and who also appears in the Koran as a guide to Moses

97

As long as the treasure of my grief
stays buried in the ruins of my heart
so long shall I sit here in this dereliction

> why do you speak of shame
> when my name is a byword for shame
> and why do you ask about my reputation
> when I care nothing for fame

we drink to get drunk   make eyes at one another
wayward   uninhibited   free
disciples of excess
but who in this town is not

and do not inform on me to the chief of police
for he too is an inveterate pleasure-lover

My dervish cell is a corner of the winehouse
my morning devotions a prayer for my master there

if there is no harp to accompany my first draught
I have my own sorry sighs   so why should I care

thank God   I am untroubled by kings or beggars
for my friend's poorest visitor is sovereign to me

my sole purpose in either mosque or tavern
is to be at one with you
as God is my witness   I think of nothing but this

only the sword of doom shall make me strike my tent
it is not like me to abandon your lucky door

from the instant I laid my face upon your step
its resting-place has been higher than the sun

    Hafez   although we have no choice but to err
    be courteous and say   the fault was mine

As the sun of wine rises in the east of the cup
the cheeks of the serving-boy
bloom like a garden of tulips

the wind bends the ringlets of the hyacinth
over the rose
while the scent of those curls
wafts along the tree-lined paths

     of the terrible experience of the night of separation
     a hundred versions can give only the faintest idea

we cannot expect   from the upturned table of the heavens
one morsel to fall
without choking a hundred times

if like Noah you endure the suffering of the flood
such travails will eventually recede
and the millennium of happiness begin

     one cannot find the precious pearl alone
     it is an illusion to think this can be done
     without another's help

if ever the breeze of union with you
blows over Hafez' grave
from the earth of his corpse   tulips in profusion will grow

In this ruined Magian den
I see the light of the divine
strange   this light   and that I perceive it
here of all places

    O leader of the *hajj*   do not lord it over me
    you see the house   but I behold the master

I would open a pouch of musk
in my beloved's hair
a far-fetched idea
like some illusion of Cathay

burning heart   flowing tears
morning sighs   nights when I cry out
I regard all these as aspects of your kindness

at every moment the image of your face
blocks the road of my imaginings
to whom shall I tell the things
I see in this shadow play

what is the musk of Khotan
or the musk-bags of China
compared to the scent
that the breeze brings me each morning

    friends do not criticize Hafez
    for his roving eye
    for I see he is one of those
    who love you dearly

Hajj: the pilgrimage to Mecca, which is one of the basic religious require-
ments of Muslims, if they can accomplish it

Companion   minstrel   serving-boy
he is all these   and more

the earthly image of water and clay
simply a means   a way

bring me a vessel of wine
so that I may cross the sea
to that undiscovered shore

Hafez   our existence is an enigma
our answers   only fables and spells

When the image of your face
was reflected in the wine
the laughing cup sent the seer wild with desire

    since the very first day
    when you appeared veiled before mankind
    people have perceived only the mirror of illusion

these reflections   and the different images we see
are nothing but the light of the wine-boy's cheek
falling onto the wine

love's sheer intensity
leaves the scholars dumb-struck
for they cannot understand how the mystery of love's grief
comes to be found in the mouths of common folk

if I have gone downhill from mosque to tavern
it was not me but the working out of fate
how can we stop revolving like a compass
we who have fallen into the cycle of days

    let us go forth dancing under his grievous blade
    for whoever becomes his victim achieves their end

my heart hung by your hair
above the well of your chin
but alas on escaping fell into its snare

    O master the time has passed
    when you will see me in the cloister again
    for it has fallen to me to occupy myself
    with the wine-boy's face and the lip of the wine-glass

each moment though Hafez' heart is sore he gets
yet another favor from his benefactor
see how this beggar has fallen on his feet

all the Sufis gather   eyeing one another
but among them Hafez
whose poor heart is burnt out   is infamous

What are we to make of the *sāghi*, the serving-boy? Who is addressed and lauded in poem after poem? To some (and given the prevailing Turkish court culture) he is clearly an object of homoerotic desire. But in Hafez things are rarely so simple. He and the *moghbachē* (the Magian priest's acolyte) form part of a wider, complex symbol system which involves wine, the tavern, intoxication, the circle of drinkers, the master and so on. The *sāghi* may be beautiful but he is primarily an emblem of beauty, a manifestation of the very idea or form of the beautiful. The more we think about it, the further away we get from an actual person, a living human being.

The best thing would be for me to pawn my gown
and chuck my useless notebook into the pitcher

since I have misspent my life
as far as I can see
the best thing would be
to collapse into some corner of the tavern

and since self-preservation is
the last thing on a dervish's mind
the best option is to have
fire in one's breast and tears welling up in one's eyes

I shall not try to explain
how the puritan thinks
since that is best accomplished by the harp and viol

so long as we cannot make
head nor tail of the universe
the best plan is to keep
the serving-boy in mind and wine in hand

I shall not get back my heart from one like you
if I have to suffer   best to suffer your hair

O Hafez you are old   time to get along
the time to indulge your vices is when you are young

Bring me a drink

and hurry boy
the wheeling firmament does not delay

the sun of wine has risen in the east of the cup
if you want your pleasures   it is time to get up

we are no puritans   forever going on
about our sins
and other such rubbish

and when eventually the heavens
make jars out of our clay
be sure to fill the bowl of my skull again

     Hafez   it is only right and proper
     to worship wine

     arise and devote your life to piety

God save us from
this self-regarding puritanical
theocracy

for in closing the tavern doors
they open the door to hypocrisy

Friends   the daughter of the vine
has renounced her veil
she went to the Chief of the Morality Police
and managed somehow
to get his permission

revealed now   she makes her entrance
let us wipe away the sweat of her ferment
so that she can explain to colleagues
why she kept her distance

let us embrace her and bind her to ourselves
this merry girl who was all covered up

O my heart   reward those
who brought the good news
for once more the troubadours of love
have found the right key
to cure our hangovers

      no wonder that the flower of my gift
      opens in his breeze
      for the nightingale rejoices in the rose

not seven washes   nor a hundred boilings
will lift the wine-stain from the puritan's gown

O Hafez   do not lose your humility
unlike that jealous swollen-headed rival
who has given up
his honor   his assets   his heart   and his religion

Come let us scatter petals   fill the cup
shatter heaven's vault   and then rebuild anew

if sorrow raises an army to spill lovers' blood
together the boy and I will lay them low

we shall add rose-water to the purple wine
and throw some sugar on the burning aloes
to sweetly perfume the air

O minstrel since you have a melodious lute to hand
play us a fine tune
so that waving our hands and stamping our feet
we may sing out a heady ghazal

O wind carry my dust to that high porch
so that I may catch a glimpse of that sovereign beauty

    one person boasts of his intellect
    another weaves fantasies
    we shall take our case to He who is judge of all

if you want to return to Eden   come to the tavern
and be tipped from the wine-vat into the heavenly pool

    in Shiraz it seems
    no one values eloquence or verse
    come Hafez
    take yourself and us to some other place

If you are drinking pour some wine in the dust
what harm is there in slaking another's thirst

consume what you have rather than being consumed by regret
for time wields death's blade without a second thought

I implore you by the dust of your feet
    O my eye-catching cypress
do not turn your footsteps away on my decease

for angels or men   in heaven or in hell
in every religion abstinence leads us astray

that great artificer of the skies
has closed each of the six exits
from this worldly monastery
leaving us no way out of this deadly pit

reason's progress has been diverted by the wiles
of the Daughter of the Vine
may its trellis stand firm until the resurrection

O happy Hafez   from the inn you depart
this world
may your pure heart be accompanied
by the heartfelt prayers of the people of the heart

IV

THE LOVER

The pupil of my eye   sees only your face
my bewildered heart   repeats only your name

my tears clothe me in my pilgrim's attire
        as I circle round you
though not for one moment do they remain
        undefiled by my heart's blood

        if the angel of heaven does not fly off in search of you
        let it be caged as one cages a wild bird

if the impoverished lover scatters before you
the false coin of his heart
do not chide him   for he has no other money

        in the end he who possesses vision
        will be able to reach the tip of that tall cypress

I will not breathe a word in front of you
of Jesus' life-giving breath
for truly he does not have the skill of your lips

I who am aflame with desire for you
who   as everyone must testify
does not emit even one sigh
in the midst of immolation

and who
on the very first day he saw the tips of your hair
said
there is no limit to this chain of confusion

my heart is not the only one to seek conjunction
for who in himself does not want to be joined to you

The road
the path
the journey
the way

the halt
the resting-place
the destination

You are like the morning
and I like the candle burning
alone   in my room   before dawn

bathe me in the light of your smile
and see how I extinguish my soul

my heart has so many black marks
left there by the brands of your hair
that when I expire
my grave will become a bed of violets

I have opened the doors of my eyes
upon the threshold of hope
that you who have banished me from your sight
will throw me a quick look

    how can I express my thanks to you
    O legion of sorrows
    for that day when all others abandon me
    you will not leave my side

I am indentured to the pupils of my eyes
whose thousand tears at your black-heartedness
enumerate the agonies of my being

such beauty is manifest in every look
but it is only I who catch those sidelong glances

    if when Hafez is gone
    you pass over his grave like the wind
    within the confines of that narrow place
    he will rend his shroud with passion

Apart from losing my faith
and forgetting all I had learned
tell me what I have gained from loving you

although the harvest of my life
has been scattered to the winds
in my anguish for you
by the dirt on your precious feet
I swear I have remained true

and although I am as insignificant
as a speck of dust
see how love's good fortune
and the hope of seeing your face
have raised me to join the sun

bring me wine   for never in my entire existence
have I   for my own good
closeted myself from risk
and not indulged my sensuality

    if you are one of the sober-minded
    who give wise counsel
    don't waste your breath
    scattering your words on the ground
    for they are lost on me   drunk as I am

how can I raise my head before you
for shame at my own inadequacy

Hafez is consumed with fire and yet
never once did his sweet beloved say

    I wounded his heart
    and will send him some balm to soothe it

If I become dust on your road
you shake your hem free of me
if I ask you to turn your heart towards me
you turn your face away

like the brightly-hued rose
you show your face everywhere
but if I tell you to cover it
you cover it from me

I told my eyes to take
a lingering look at you
they replied   do you want us
to shed streams of crimson tears

though you thirst for my blood
I thirst for your lips too
how long will it be before I get
my wish   or you your due

if I gutter out before you like a candle
you laugh like the morning sun
but your heart is so sensitive that
if I suffer   it suffers too

and if like Farhād my soul expires
from bitterness   so what
many bitter-sweet stories
will continue to be told of me

I have relinquished my life
out of longing for your mouth

and yet you still withhold
such a tiny thing as that

Hafez   sufficient
for if this is the lesson of passion
love will recount your story
in every lover's retreat

O you whose bright cheeks
gladden the garden of our lives
come back
for without the rose-bloom of your face
we shall come to the end
of the spring-time of being

if my tears fall like rain   it is only right
for because of the grief you cause me
my existence is nothing but a flash of lightning

one or two glimpses is all I may have of you
O answer my need   for who knows where life leads

how much longer will we enjoy
the early cup and the sweet sleep of morning
come to your senses now   for the chance will go

yesterday you passed by   and did not look my way
O miserable heart that never comes alive

    the one whose whole life turns
    on the point of your mouth
    gives no thought to the encircling doom

I am ambushed on every side
as if by tribes of horsemen
like a rider shorn of his reins

I exist rather than live
but why should you be surprised
for being without you cannot be counted as life

Hafez set down your lines
for on the folio of the world
the trace of your pen will be your epitaph

In the "Rosegarden of Mystery" written just before Hafez' time, Shabestari provides a complete system of equivalences, a code if you like, for interpreting Persian erotic or bacchic poems in mystical terms. Thus the face represents the divine essence, the mole divine unity, the eyes divine sufficiency, the lips divine breath, and so on. Similarly, wine refers to mystical ecstasy and the tavern is the place where all phenomenal realities disappear. Clearly, Hafez' poetry can be read this way. The question is: was it written that way?

O happy morning breeze
carrying the message you know
go to the appointed street
at the appointed time you know

my eyes will follow you
as you carry my secret there
out of simple human kindness
not because I tell you
hasten in the way you know

     and say   my languishing soul
     has almost abandoned me
     O God   may your ruby lips
     revive me in the way they know

     I have penned these few words
     which no one else understands
     but that you may deign to interpret
     in the way you know

     the blade of your sword imagines me
     like a thirsty man water
     O you who have taken me captive
     slay me in the way you know

     how could I not attach my hopes
     to your belt braided with gold
     with something so small so fine
     within it   as you know

Hafez   whether we trade
in Turkish or Arabic
explain the lore of love
in the language that you know

Tell them to leave the candles
they will not be needed in this gathering
for tonight my moon is at the full

and do not sprinkle perfume either
for we have more than enough
with the fragrance of your hair

and do not speak of candy or sugar-cane
for my palate is satisfied
by the sweetness of your lips

my eyes search only for those red rubies
and the circling bowl
and my ears hear nothing
but the sound of the lute and the viol

O heart you do not take the road of love
you have gathered your things together
yet you do not go

it is as if
you have the polo-stick in your grasp
but do not strike the ball
and even with such a falcon on your wrist
you do not go hunting

the cup is fine
and full of strong wine
yet you pour it on the ground
without thought for the welcome calamity
of a hangover

a hundred pouches of musk
are hidden in the ample sleeves of your desire
yet you do not empty one
as a libation to the curls of the beloved

this blood that courses through your veins
you do not use to blush a lovely cheek
and the breath of your being is not fragrant
for unlike the wind you have not acquainted yourself
with the dirt of the beloved's road

I fear that from this bed of roses
you will not gather any
for you cannot bear the idea of the thorn

go Hafez   for even though everyone else
submits to service at the beloved's court

still you do not

All I wish

is to tell you how my heart is
to hear back from your heart

to sweep the road in front of you
with the tips of my eyelashes
to honor you

and vainly to try
to hide from my rivals
what everyone knows

to sleep one night with you
one transcendent night
tender yet exalted
and in the darkness to pierce that pearl

and when morning comes
with the dawn wind's grace

to open like a flower opens

Like the flames in one room
can spread through a whole house
my breast caught fire from my ardent heart
in its fervor for you

from head to toe I melt down
as a consequence of your absence
and my soul is consumed with longing for your cheek

whoever sees the chains of your hair
around your sylph-like features
his lovesick heart burns
for I who have gone insane

  like a moth the candle itself last night
  died in the inferno of my tears

it is no wonder that friends' hearts catch light
out of sympathy for me
for even those of strangers are kindled
when they see me out of my mind

the liquid dispensed in the tavern
carried away my ascetic's gown
and the house of my reason burned down
in the cellar's conflagration

when I decided to repent
my heart cracked like a bowl
now without wine or anything to serve it in
my liver is branded black
like the cup of the tulip

forget our quarrel   return
let us be reconciled
for the pupils of my eyes
having done their penance of tears
burn bright with gratitude again

     Hafez   enough of these conceits
     have some more wine
     for we have not slept a wink all night
     and the candle has burned down in vain

Hafez' ghazals start in a variety of ways. Many begin with a conventional invocation or exhortation, but quite a few start with "if" or "although" or some other conjunction, initiating a chain of reasoning that is then developed in the course of the poem. While readers coming to the Divan for the first time may initially be struck by the style of writing—the metaphors, the epithets, the soaring hyperbole—it is important to recognize the inherent structure, the careful construction of the argument, the simple strength of the syntax.

The heart is love's pavilion
the eyes the mirror-holder to its face

I who do not bow down to this world or the next
bend my neck under the weight
of my obligation to you

some dream of the trees of paradise
whereas I dream of your form

people's imaginations are limited by
the poverty of their aspiration

if my gown is stained   so what
the whole world acknowledges your purity

who am I to enter this sanctuary
when the morning wind patrols
the boundaries of your inviolability

> Majnūn had his turn   now I have mine
> everyone has their day

the kingdom of love   the affluence of joy
all that I possess   comes from your good offices

and do not be misled by my apparent poverty
for Hafez' breast is filled
with the treasure of his love for you

Majnūn: the lover (who went mad) of Leila in the epic recounted by poets both before and after Hafez: Nezāmī, Amīr Khosrow and Jāmī

People said you are the second Joseph
but when I looked closely
in truth you are better than he

your sweet smile is sweeter than if I said
   O Khosrow of beauty
   you are the Shirin of our times

I cannot compare your mouth to a rosebud
for no rosebud is as tight as this

a hundred times you swore
this mouth would satisfy me
why then like the lily are you all tongue

you said you would grant my wishes but take my life
but I fear you will deny me and still take my life

your eyes with their small arrows hard as white poplar
pierce the shield of my soul
O how can one who is so weak with languor
have so strong a bow

   and he whom you banish from your sight
   for even one moment
   in the eyes of men is brushed off like a tear

Each point I made   in respect of your qualities
the audience would say   how masterful his thesis

at first it seemed easy enough
to follow love and excess   but in the end
my life was consumed   trying to attain those heights

I asked
when you would have mercy on my feeble soul
you replied
when that soul no longer stands in the way

    on the gallows Hallaj made this clear
    one does not consult the lawyers on such matters

I have given my heart to you   my playful companion
who are graceful   good-natured   and of good character too

in the depths of my meditations
you distract my gaze
so that now like a drunk I bow before you

the tears of my eyes are like a hundred Floods
but never once
has your image washed off the tablet of my breast

    O my beloved
    Hafez' hand wards off the evil eye

    like the strap upon your shoulder   may it rest

al-Hallaj: a Sufi mystic who was executed in the 10th century for heresy

Traditional Persian houses were built with a high surrounding wall which enclosed both the house and courtyard or garden. This ensured complete privacy and security. Access was usually by a single large wooden door or gate, manned by a doorman or gatekeeper. Getting in was thus not easy, and strictly controlled, and visitors might have to wait outside, perhaps for some time, until permission was eventually given, if indeed it was. Hafez' regular references to porches, thresholds, steps or doors need to be understood in this light.

If I could only make my way
to the place where you live
the good fortune of being with you
would justify all the outlay of my journey

      your hyacinth-curls have robbed me of my composure
      your narcissus-eyes have taken away my calm

since love for you polishes my heart like a diamond
surely it will stay free from the marks of time

      I who am broken in spirit will find life only
      at the moment I am slain by the blade of grief

O my heart and soul
what crime have I committed in your presence
that I whose heart is not my own
can make no obeisance acceptable to you

I who wait at your gate without provisions
debilitated   poor   unable to go on
who find no way out nor in

what should I do next   where should I go
what hope is there for me
since I am weary with grief and the burden of days

my longing for you
could not have found a more desolate place
than my poor heart in which to build its dwelling

      Hafez   be silent   and endure your pain
      and do not divulge the mysteries of love
      to those who know only reason

You have only to look at me
and my pain intensifies
I have only to look at you
and my longing grows and grows

you do not inquire about me
I wonder what is in your mind
you do not try to cure me
perhaps you do not understand

this is no way to behave
to abandon me in the dirt of the road
pass by and ask again so that I
may become the dust you tread

I shall not let go your skirt
until I have turned to dust
but if you come where I lie
that dust will reach out to you

I suffocate with grief
O when will you breathe on me
you who consigned me to hell
but deny responsibility

one night in the dark
when I searched for my heart in your hair
I beheld you face to face
and drank from that crescent bowl

suddenly I drew you to me
and enfolded in the waves of your curls

I put my lips to your lips
and knew a kind of death

    let Hafez bring you happiness
    dismiss his enemies
    for while he enjoys your warmth
    why should he fear their cold breath

Do not give your hair to the wind   or I shall be blown away
do not curl your tresses   or I shall be bound by them

do not raise your head   or I shall raise my cry
do not add lustre to that shining countenance
or I shall be overcome

do not stand on pride   or I shall have nothing to stand on
do not shine like a candle   or it is I who will burn

do not drink with the crowd   or I shall drink my own blood
do not become the talk of the town   or I shall head for the hills

do not behave like Shirin   or I shall turn into Farhād
do not befriend strangers   for fear I become estranged

do not console others   and in doing so make me sad
do not hasten like the heavens   lest Hafez meet his end

O breeze bring me a scent   from the street of my one
I am sick with longing   bring me salve for my soul

give my futile heart the elixir it craves
what I mean is
bring me a trace of the dust from my loved one's door

ambushed by glances   I skirmish with my heart
from that eyebrow and eye   bring me an arrow and bow

I have grown old in exile and estrangement
let some young hand bring me a pitcher of wine

let those who say tut tut   taste two or three cups
and if they refuse   bring it forthwith to me

O boy
do not put back today's pleasures till tomorrow
or else bring me a written guarantee from fate

     last night my heart was overcome when Hafez said
     O breeze   bring me a sweet breath from that street

In Persian culture, the garden is both an actual and a symbolic place. In a dry country, the presence of water, trees, shade, vegetation or grass is something quite special, which contrasts with the often arid landscape all around. Even now, nothing pleases Iranians more than to find such a spot, lay down some rugs and picnic there, especially at the spring-time New Year. But the garden is more than this. It is the very site of paradise (itself an ancient Persian word), the locus of the greatest imaginable happiness, the supreme, the ultimate reward.

My calm my patience and my good sense
have all been stripped away
by this sweet-lipped silvery-lobed young god

this quick and graceful beauty   like a sylph
moonlike being   artful   elusive
this Turk in a tight tunic

with the flames of desire I bubble continually
like a pot placed on the fire

my mind would be at rest
were I to be your shirt
or like your close-fitting bodice
wrap you in my embrace

even if my bones turn eventually to dust
my soul will not forget its love for you

I have been carried away   heart and faith
by your breast   your shoulders
your shoulders   your breast

my medicine your sweet lips
your sweet lips my remedy

If he put me to the sword   I would not stop him
if he pierced me with a dart   I would be obliged

tell him whose eyebrow is shaped like a bow
to loose his arrow at me
so that I may perish by his hand   his arm

the travails of this world cause me to stumble
what can I hold onto but the cup

rise   O sun of the dawn of expectation
for I am imprisoned in separation's night

answer my cries
O Master of the house of ill-repute
make me young again with a drink   for I am old

last night I vowed by the ringlets of your hair
I would not raise my bowed head from your hem

    Hafez   burn these pious robes of yours
    for if you catch fire   it will not be from them

Yesterday I said
I shall dismiss from my mind
my obsession with your cheek

you responded
bring me some chains
so that I can restrain this madman

I compared your height to a cypress
and you took umbrage
friends what can I do
when my beloved cannot bear to hear the truth

I made some forward remark   pray forgive me
dally with me a little   so that I may learn
to weigh my words more carefully

my face grows wan
faced with that delicate faultless nature
boy bring me a jug of wine so that
I may restore some color to it again

O wind   you who pass by the house of Salmā
how long must I search this empty campsite
and wash away the remains
with the Oxus of my tears

Salmā: the traditional beloved of Arabic poetry

Oxus: the river forming much of the northern border of Afghanistan

146

if I manage to find my way
to the treasure of that infinite loveliness
I will turn a hundred beggars like myself
into a Qārūn

O auspicious moon
remember your slave Hafez
so that he may offer his prayers
for that beauty which never wanes

Qārūn: a fabulously wealthy person in Arab literature

147

I vacated my heart   but to no avail
I gave up all thought of self
but you did not take its place

my life passes in such fantasies and yet
to the bane of your long hair there is no end

so mortal is my longing for the dust at your door
that I cannot even see the water of life
in front of me

many heart-felt tales could I tell the dawn breeze
but with my fate no morning ends this night

only the sweet face of my beloved counts
without that   nothing can be achieved

alas
I have not yet sacrificed everything for you
love's labors mean I still have much to do

so fugitive has my sorrowing heart become
that it no longer dares
to venture beyond the ringlets of your hair

noktē: an impression made with the tip of the finger or the end of a stick; a subtle point; a nice distinction

Like the wind I plan to go to the end of your street
and perfume my breath there with your musky scent

I shall scatter before you in the dust of the road
all the honor I have gained from study and observance

     life without wine or love is misspent
      enough of this   from today I get down to work

where is the breeze so that I may sacrifice
to the fragrance of your hair
my soul that is as bloodied as the rose

like the candle at dawn I have been enlightened
understanding now what is my life's great project

as a monument to your eyes I shall demolish myself
and rebuild again the ancient covenant

hypocrisy and false abstinence
have no place in the pure of heart

I shall take the way of the lover and the *rend*

Since you own what I own
and possess all I possess

what need is there to plunder then

My heart has been stolen
by this wandering street-dancer with a painted face
who stirs things up

untrustworthy   fickle   murderous   dangerous

    for the torn shirts of those
    whose visages are as lovely as the moon
    let us sacrifice a thousand pious garments
    and habits of abstinence

since angels know nothing of love
bring me a serving-bowl
that I may sprinkle rose-water on Adam's clay

    I am a slave of incendiary language
    not that which douses the flames
    with cold water

destitute   broken   I come to your court for mercy
for apart from you   I have nothing myself
no hold on life other than your affection

and do not tie yourself in knots
with your own clever play   for in chess it is said
that His Royal Highness the King
has a thousand moves at his disposal

    last night the hidden voice in the tavern
    said to me   accept your lot
    do not try to escape your fate

O tie a cup to my shroud
so that on the day of resurrection
with wine I may dispel the fear of judgment

     nothing can come between lover and beloved
     Hafez   remove the veil from yourself   yourself

What did I do last night   O my sweet Turk
to make you leave me
what misunderstanding
has sent you off   in a huff   on the road to Cathay

no one knows what a visionary light
my eyes have lost
since you quit my sight

     last night the candle burning down
     was as nothing to my own burning

at every breath   without your face
tears well up in the spring of my eyes
and the storm of affliction breaks

I collapsed from the agony of separation
now I will die in pain
for my only medication has gone

my heart tells me
that it will be united with you again
through prayer
but my life has passed in a lifetime of prayer

and how can I gird myself to pray
when I no longer know which direction
why should I even try
when the Ka'ba is bereft of purity

     yesterday when a doctor saw me
     he said regretfully

your case goes beyond
the canons of medicine

friend
call by and ask about Hafez
before they tell you he has gone forever
from this nothing world

The pupils of my eyes are dear to me
for by my soul
they are the very replica
of your Indian mole

if you want to embellish the world
for all eternity
ask the wind for just one moment
to lift your veil

and if you want to do away with
the custom of transience
shake out the strands of your ringlets
so that thousands may go free

I and the morning breeze
are like a pair of vagabonds
I   drunk on the charms of your gaze
it   on the scent of your hair

How long shall our hearts grieve
at the passage of time

imagine   how it would be
if there were no heart   and no such thing as time

I shall not abandon my quest   till I am satisfied
either my body is united with you
who are my soul
or my soul will abandon it

    after my death   open my grave and see
    from the fire in my bowels
    smoke rising from my shroud

O show your face   amaze the populace
open your mouth   let everyone cry out

my heart is filled with regret   and my soul ready to leave
because it has never known   the pleasure your lips could give

I live in much straitened circumstances
because of my longing for that mouth
O when will it meet the needs of the poverty-stricken

    in the hope of catching a glimpse   of the luster of your face
    the wind turns and turns in the garden

these words of Hafez mean   that people will invoke his name
wherever the company of lovers   assemble to play love's games

For all that his poetry seems to circle around a few basic themes (and his vocabulary is not particularly extensive either) Hafez' range of references is wide and includes commerce, law, medicine, farming, mining, hunting, falconry, chess, polo, alchemy, astronomy, astrology, music, dance, art and scholarship.

If I touch the ends of your hair you twist in anger
if I say I am sorry then you tell me off

like the new moon you attract the helpless watcher
with the tip of an eyebrow   then pass behind a veil

you leave me exhausted with your all-night drinking
and if by day I complain then you doze off

the path of love is full of accidents
he who makes haste is heading for a fall

when the gust of pride touches the top of the bubble
the crown of conceit collapses into the wine

do not trade your place   begging at the loved one's gate
for a sultan's domain
one does not abandon shade for the sun's heat

heart do not advertize your charms when you grow old
for such business surely belongs to the realm of youth

when the inky copybook of your dark hair
is finished
wherever one searches   only blank pages remain

Hafez   you cloud your own vision like a veil
remove your self

happy the person who sees to part the curtain

Late in life
young love befell my old head
and the secret I had kept hidden in my heart
came out

much taken by what it saw
the bird of my heart took off
observe O eyes   into whose net it has fallen

sad that so much of my blood
has flowed from heart to gut
for that musky dark-eyed deer

and like musk
all the fragrance that the dawn breeze exudes
it picked up from the dust of your alleyway

    since your eyelashes unsheathed
    their conquering blades
    the beating hearts of victims have piled up

we have been put repeatedly to the test
in this penitentiary
but whoever objects to heavy drinking fails

    a black stone will never
    metamorphose into a ruby
    even if it yields up its soul
    for it cannot overcome its humble origins

Hafez   who hitherto
was strung along by the tips of idols' hair
has fallen for this strange and rare companion

The image of your face accompanies me everywhere
the scent of your tresses leads on my wakened soul

and despite those litigants
who raise objections in the court of love
the loveliness of your countenance settles the argument

listen to what your apple-dimple says
a thousand Josephs have fallen into my pit

if I have not held out my hands
to stroke the lengths of your hair
it is because of my limited reach and wayward fate

say to the keeper of your royal apartments
that some poor recluse sits in the dust of your porch

if Hafez knocks at your door for a year   open it
since for years he has been
overcome with longing for your moon-bright face

    although it seems you are always veiled from us
    you are visible   always   to the tranquil heart

Hafez you have strung together
the pearls of your ghazals
with lines such as these

sing them well

for the heavens have bedecked your verse
with the necklace of the Pleiades

V

THE AGE

God be praised for the justice of the Sultan
Ahmad   son of Sheikh Ovais   son of Hassan Ilkhani

khan   son of a khan   emperor   offspring of an emperor
he whom it is fitting to call   Soul of the World

even without seeing you
my eyes believe in your coming
blessed are you who merit the grace of God

if the moon rises without you   let it be cleft in twain
for you are a miracle of heaven   providence itself

the splendor of your good fortune
captures the hearts of king and beggar alike
may the evil eye spare you
who are both lover and beloved

sport your fine Turkish forelock
for you have in your horoscope
the magnanimity of Qā'ān
the force of Genghis Khān
although far removed from you
we raise a toast to you
for the spirit knows no stopping on such a journey

in the soil of Fars alas I have not blossomed
O for the Tigris of Baghdad
and some aromatic wine

Qā'ān: a son of Genghis Khān

how can the head of he
who is not dirt at his beloved's gate
still the turmoil of his mind

O wind bring me some dust from the door
of he whom I revere
so that I may illumine my heart with it

In her study of ancient Greek thought, Martha Nussbaum contrasts the ideas of *tuche* (chance, fate) and *techne* (means, skills). The latter represents our imperfect attempts to control the former. The ghazals contain a number of words which can be roughly translated as fate, the most important of which is *doulat* (providence) which occurs 78 times in all. Fortune is even personified sometimes, as waking or slumbering. There is a background sense of contingency, uncertainty, vulnerability, which given those troubled times is hardly surprising.

O happy Shiraz   unique among cities
Lord preserve it from decline

may God never allow
the stream of Ruknabad to run dry
of its limpid life-giving waters

between Jafarabad and Mosalla
the north wind comes down from the hills
bearing the faint scent of ambergris

come to Shiraz and seek
from those who have perfected themselves
the abundance of the holy spirit

Good news   for peace
has alighted on the mimosa tree
and come home to its own country
praise be

where is the happy messenger
who brought tidings of this victory
so that I may scatter my soul
like gold and silver
under his feet

with the safe return of the king
to this peerless mansion
the plans of his enemies are consigned
to the pavilion of oblivion

those who break treaties will themselves be broken
for wise men hold such pledges to be inviolable

    he looked for mercy from the clouds of hope
    but all his eyes could make out
    was the dew of his own tears

    he fell into the Nile of despair
    and mockingly the heavens cried
    now you repent   but repentance gains you naught

since the serving boy has a moonlike face
and is one of those who can keep a secret

let Hafez drink   like the sheikh   and his chief justice

A sophisticated city
with beauties on every side
friend   love calls
if you will answer it

the eyes of the world will surely never behold
a fresher youth than this
into no one's hands could fall a better sweetheart

who ever saw such a body
created of the spirit
God forbid that we earthly creatures
should sully the hem of his coat

why do you drive away
one of life's casualties
since all I want from you is a kiss
or at most an embrace

the wine is unmixed   pure
hurry   live life now
for who dares dream of another spring
or count on another new year

in the garden   love's companions
like the tulip and the rose
raise their cups to toast
the image of their beloved's face

how can I undo this knot
how can I show this wound
my pain is a sharp pain
my task an impossible one

with every hair on Hafez' head
tied to a capricious tress
it is difficult for even a moment
to sit still in this place

We know little of Hafez' life and his poetry gives few clues. Apart from one or two brief sojourns in the central Iranian city of Yazd, and perhaps a visit to Isfahan, it seems he spent all his years in his native Shiraz. The idea that he made a sea voyage at some point is probably based on nothing more than some conventional metaphors of waves and whirlpools, though he did receive invitations to foreign courts which he consistently turned down with flowery regrets. Of his personal life we know almost nothing, although one poem may refer to the death of a son.

O Lord bring back that musk-deer to Khotan
bring back the graceful cypress to the meadow

let the morning breeze caress my troubled heart
returning my soul to the body it abandoned

since at your command sun and moon
go to their stations
send me back here my shining companion

my eyes are bloodshot
from searching for that ruby from Yemen
O Lord return that luminous star
to where it can again be seen

      go   auspicious bird   symbol of good fortune
      take these poor croakings to the majestic 'anqā
      say this   that I cannot live without you
      carry this message to him and bring me an answer

O Lord
let he whose native country was my sight
be brought back from exile to his own homeland

Khotan: a region of north-west China

'anqā: a mythical bird of power and good fortune

Yemen was regarded as a remote but beautiful country and the source of cool
winds

The standard of the prince of flowers
has been raised at the edge of the field
O Lord may his arrival
bring blessings to cypress and jasmine

happy this royal coming into his own
for everyone now knows his proper station

> spread the good news that Jamshid's royal seal
> has   in you
> finally and happily prevailed
> for the Name of the Highest inscribed on it
> has stayed the Devil's hand

> may your house prosper for ever
> for in the dust at your door
> at every breath comes a wind from Yemen
> bearing the fragrance of mercy

glory to this son of Pashang
and his world-conquering sword
for he takes his rightful place
in every telling of the *Shāhnāmē*

> like a polo-pony under your saddle
> you have tamed the twists and turns of fate
> O you who are the pick of horsemen
> make your entry on the field
> and strike the ball with your stick

> may the shining streams of your sword's blade
> water the channels of your realm
> plant the tree of justice   uproot wickedness

no wonder if with the breeze of your sweet nature
the Chinese musk-deer thrives here on the torrid plains

even hermits   gather to see you
push up your cap   reveal your face to us

     I consulted reason and it said   Hafez imbibe
     boy   do as my trusted counsellor says

     and wind go tell the servants at our prince's feast
     to grant me a drink from that gilded cup of his

Peace and tranquillity
in this world and the next
come down to an understanding
of these two maxims

show loyalty to your friends
restraint towards your enemies

Good news   my heart   for the west wind has returned
and that harbinger come back from a distant land

O dawn-bird raise your voice   like David's psalms
for thanks to the breeze
that rose like Solomon is here once more

in the morning air
the tulip scents the bouquet of wine
its heart scarred   it too has come back
hoping to salve its wound

where is the wise man who understands
the tongue of the lily
so that we might know why you left   why you returned

God-given fate has been generous to me
for that stony-hearted idol
has taken the path of fidelity again

my eyes searched constantly for that caravan
till the sound of its bells reached the ear of my heart

    although Hafez broke his promise and caused you pain
    to his door in peace and kindness now you return

At dawn the mysterious voice
whispered the good news in my ear

Shah Shoja's time has come   drink without fear

the time has gone when men of vision
were sidelined
men who despite having much to say
kept their lips buttoned up

let us tell those tales that we have been bursting to tell
and to the sound of the harp
let us toast each other openly and drink
what previously we consumed behind closed doors
for fear of the regime

last night I saw them coming from the tavern
carrying on their shoulders
the Imam who leads Friday prayers
with his prayer rug slung over his shoulders

    O heart let me direct you
    on the right road to salvation
    do not flaunt your license   or your abstinence

we see signs of divine illumination
in the king's clear-sighted judgments
if you want to be part of his inner circle
ensure that your reasons are pure

and may your heart's orisons
be only to his glory
for his heart is the confidant of the angel Soroush

kings know the secret
of what is best for their kingdom

Hafez
a beggar in the corner should not raise his voice

I am astonished that the king of kings
having listened to such fresh sweet verse
does not cover Hafez in gold from head to toe

From friends we expect friendship
but that it seems is naïve

who knows when the tree of loyalty
will bear fruit
for the time being I have gone and planted a seed

dervishes are men of few words
if not I would have something to say to you

your deceitful eyes were full of plans for war
I thought they were irenic   I was wrong

it was not the burning bush of your beauty
that set fire to my heart
but the breath of my own desire

some telling points were made
but no one objected
I acted with due respect
but this was the response I got

    Hafez it was you yourself
    who gave me your heart

    I did not have to send the bailiff in

The sun merely holds the mirror to your beauty
black musk does not have the darkness of your mole

I washed the palace courtyard of my eyes
but it was no use
for the army of your images
could not be billeted in so small a space

your charm and grace
have reached their zenith
O my orb of loveliness
Lord let them not set before the final day

no official has ever signed an imperial document
in a hand more elegant than the shape of your brow

O my sad heart   how are you surviving
in the loops of that hair
for the wind   distraught
told me of your predicament

the rose gives out its perfume
O enter through the gate of peace
for your auspicious face
is to us like a New Year

let the attraction of your eyebrows
outdo the crescent moon
so that we may number the heavens among our bondsmen

in the garden of vision   my dark pupils
have become pinpoints   reflecting the light of your mole

and so that I may once more applaud my fate
let me have news of the festival of union

    how should I frame my case   in my lord's presence
    in terms of my penury   or his impatience

    Hafez   many heads have been caught in that lasso
    do not cherish false hopes   for it is not your place

While you are on the surface of this earth
make good use of the power you possess
for time has reduced
the many who lie beneath to powerlessness

I have tried my luck in this town
now I must collect my things
and haul myself out of this abyss

biting my nails
I am consumed with remorse
as if my sighs had set me on fire
or my body been dismembered like a flower

> but yesterday evening what joy it was
> to hear the nightingale sing
> as on the rose-bush the rose
> opened wide to listen

> saying   O heart   rejoice
> even though that quick-tempered friend of yours
> complains vociferously about his misfortune

> for even if the tsunami of events
> inundates the heavens
> neither the mystic nor his chattels will get wet

if you want to be spared
the hard lessons and soft betrayals of this world
refrain from your own weak promises   harsh words

> Hafez   if it was always possible
> to get what you want
> Jamshid would not remain so distant from his throne

As in Europe at that time, the situation of a court poet in Iran was somewhat precarious. There were inevitably rivals and sometimes enemies who would not be above insinuating disloyalty or, worse, impiety. The ruler and his officials had to be kept sweet, though there does seem to have been a reciprocal obligation to reward merit and acknowledge support. And in some cases it is clear that a genuine attachment developed between the two, transcending the difference in status.

Remember when I dwelt at the end of your street
and from the dust at your door my eyes garnered their light

and when because of our closeness
    I like the open lily   you the rose
my tongue voiced all that was in your heart

and when the heart used the language of ancient wisdom
it was love that explained what the meaning was

my heart had resolved
never to be without that friend
but what can we do   my heart and I
now that all our efforts have proved vain

last night remembering my companions   I went to the tavern
but the wine-jar was filled with blood   its neck on the ground

I inquired everywhere about the pain of loss
but the Mufti of reason had no reason to offer on this

it is true that the turquoise signet of Abū Eshāq
shone brightly and hopefully   but not for long

    Hafez
    you heard the laughter of that strutting partridge
    oblivious to the falcon's fateful claws

Mufti: a senior religious figure who applies the law

Abū Eshāq: a ruler of the time and one of Hafez' patrons

Although I am a servant of the king
when I say my morning prayers
I am monarch of the kingdom of dawn

with treasures up my sleeve   though an empty purse
I am the visionary cup that reveals the world
and the dust of the true path

    sober in that presence   yet drunk with pride
    afloat in the ocean of faith   yet drowned in sin

when my handsome fate looks kindly down on me
I mirror his face which so resembles the moon

each night as the blessed king sleeps
I keep watch over his head and crown

should he not appreciate this
that while he slumbers I stand guard for him

and he knows that however lofty my vocation
I sew a bloody shroud for his enemies
and a mantle of triumph for his victorious friends

in me there are no false colors
I am black as the viper   red as the tawny lion

    O Shah Mansūr   pray tell your treasurer
    to give Hafez what he is owed
    for you yourself   in our presence
    agreed that it was his due

O east wind   take this message from me
to the inhabitants of the city of Yazd

may your polo balls be the skulls of those
who know nothing of gratitude

Yazd: a central Iranian city to which Hafez went for a while

At the time of the evening prayer   when far from home
the tears of strangers come
sadly I begin to recount the tale of exile

at the thought of my beloved and my own land
I weep so bitterly that I plead with the world
to give up the whole idea of travelling

I belong to the country of my loved one
not the province of strangers
O You who protect me   return me to my friends

with your guidance   O God   I shall find the right road again
so that I may plant my ensign in front of the tavern

apart from the north and the east winds
no one knows me in this town
stranger that I am
I have no other confidant but the wind

to me   the air of my beloved's house
is the water of life itself

O send me a breeze from the good earth of Shiraz

If that bird of paradise came through my door again
for all my gray hairs   my life would come back again

though my tears fall like rain   I live in the hope that
fate's lightning-flash will light up my eyes again

he who crowned me with the dust of the soles of his feet
I beseech God to send back quickly to me

I shall set off after him   and if I do not return
to my dear companions   word will come back of me

if I do not throw down my soul before he whom I honor
what value has this jewel   what use will it be

if it were not for the birds' serenade   and the sweet sleep of
morning
he would have heard my sighs and turned back again

from the rooftop of happiness   I shall beat the drum
of good fortune regained
if I see my journeying moon appear once more

    Hafez
    we yearn for that king of the shining countenance
    use your best endeavors
    so that he may return in safety to this door

On the word of an enemy
you turned away from your friend

no one becomes an enemy to a friend

Winter clouds have lifted
March winds usher in the New Year
I need my stipend for music and wine   tell me it is here

beauty is on parade
but my purse is cause for shame
love and poverty are hard to combine   but it seems it must be done

there is a dearth of munificence
so to preserve my honor
I shall trade in my patched gown   in exchange for flowers and wine

perhaps my luck will turn
and give me another chance
for I saw while still praying last night   the breaking of the new dawn

with a hundred thousand smiles
the rose returns to the garden
as if it had sensed the presence there   of some generous soul

no matter if we rip open our clothes
in a state of ecstasy
one has also to cut one's cloth   to the constraints of a good name

who was it but I who spoke
so tastefully of your lips
who was it but I who suffered   the tyranny of your hair

I don't know who fired the arrow
into the poet's heart
I know only that his blood   drips from every fresh line

if it does not please the king
to give justice to love's wronged
those who languish in the corner   must give up all hope of ease

One of Hafez' last poems—we know this from the ruler to whom it is addressed—is a panegyric to a new king who had just displaced the existing royal family with which Hafez had been strongly identified. What price loyalty? But this was an age of regional conflict, shifting alliances, fratricidal quarrels and relatively frequent changes of regime to which all concerned, not just court poets, had to accommodate themselves.

Happy the day when he whom I love comes back
dispelling the grief of the grief-stricken

I led out the piebald steed of my eyes
hoping that they might see
the regal image of that royal cavalier

my heart   like prey   flies expecting his arrow
imagining that ready to hunt he will return

I laid myself down like dust at the end of his roadway
hoping that by this route he would arrive

if my head is not scooped up by his polo-stick
what shall I say of it   what use can it have

and do not imagine that a heart
that has entered into a pact with the braids of his hair
is one to which tranquillity will return

my tears will not   like waves   beat on the shoreline
if once again I find
he with his narrow waist seated by my side

        what suffering have the nightingales endured
        all winter
        in the hope that spring would once more be renewed

Hafez there is hope
that the great artist of fate will return that figure
lovely as a cypress   to your fond embrace

May you never need the ministrations of physicians
may your delicate form never come to any harm

in your health lies the peace of every horizon
may your body never suffer any pain

when the plundering wind of autumn comes to the meadow
may it bypass the tall cypress standing there

in this world's market-place
where you are on show to all
may there be no place for those who wish you ill

both form and substance depend on your well-being
may you know no inner grief nor outward hurt

and whoever casts a malevolent glance at you
may his eye burn up like wild rue in your fire

    do not ask for candy or rose-water to soothe you
    for you have the sweet confection of Hafez' words

Though there are many who would want me dead
with you as my friend   I fear no enemy

hope of re-joining you keeps me alive
otherwise
each moment of absence would be for me perdition

if I do not scent your perfume on each breeze
out of grief
I shall tear my collar like the windblown rose

do my eyes succumb to sleep   letting go your image
never
will my heart ever become used to separation
never

your wound is better than another's ointment
your poison better than their antidote

the blow of your sword brings me eternal life
for my soul delights in being your sacrifice

do not rein back your horse   for if you strike
I shall make of my head a shield
and not let go of your saddle-strap

how can eyes see you as you truly are
everyone understands in proportion to their vision

Hafez will be cherished by the populace
only when
in the dust at your door he lays his wretched face

It is important to learn to keep your promises
to be sincere

otherwise those who are around you
will learn all about
the exercise of arbitrary power

No friendship to be seen
what has become of friends
when did loyalty come to an end
what happened to the famous bond

the rose has lost its blush
and where is the spring breeze
no one allows that friends have rights
where is gratitude now

this used to be the city of friendship
the good earth of goodwill and trust
but where have our leaders gone
who sets an example to us

for many long years now
not one precious stone
has come out of the mine of integrity
O where has our honor gone

it is as if the ball
of magnanimity
had been tossed into the field of play
and no rider contested it

O where is the brightness of the sun
the labor of wind and rain
no longer does anyone want to drink
where have my companions gone

a thousand roses have bloomed
but no bird raises its cry

what has become of the nightingales
and their countless melodies

no longer does Venus sing
as if her lyre were destroyed
the water of life is dark
O where is my sure-footed guide

Hafez be silent now
for nobody understands
who is there left to explain
the whirligig of time

Power, or lack of it, is a pervasive theme in the ghazals. There is the power of the ruler and his officials to which a court poet was directly subject. The beloved exercises absolute power, according to convention, over the lover. Even the tavern boy has the power to serve or delay serving the wine. And ultimately there is the power of the heavens: destiny, fate, time.

I am the falcon on the wrist of the king
Lord how could they have forgotten
my fondness for my perch there

alas that a nightingale like me
with such a sweet voice
should now be caged
my tongue silent as a lily

the climate of Fars is perfect
for cultivating the low
let me find a companion for the road
so that I may strike my tent and go

but as to the blessed Tūrānshāh
who in his munificence
showers me with such favors

my indebtedness hangs like a necklace round my neck

Tūrānshāh: chief minister of Shah Shoja and a great protector of Hafez

How simple his going
how difficult for I who remain

my face is caked with dust
and my eyes cannot stop their tears
but the turquoise sky
requires this kind of mortar
to build its edifice of joy

    camel-driver   see   my load has fallen
    God help me it was in the hope
    that I would be blessed
    that I followed the camel-litter

was it because of the jealousy of the moon
that my own moon with his arched eyebrows
made his home there in the tomb

I shall play no more chess
for all my moves have failed
what can I do   for fate itself
has taken me unawares

I have decided to put an end to my woes
if I get the opportunity

    the theater of the heart
    has no room for adversaries
    when the devil leaves   the angel makes its entry

to spend time in the company
of those in authority
is like the longest of long nights

pray for the light of the sun
that it may rise again

waiting for the masters of the universe
who do not deserve the epithet human
how long must one sit wondering
when will my lord appear

    do not stop begging in the street
    for you will find your true reward
    in the glance of some passing stranger

good and bad
each one sets out his stall
we shall see who catches the eye
whose wares are accepted in the end

O you   my amorous nightingale
pray for longevity   for eventually
the garden will turn green again
and the rose-tree bloom in spring

Hafez' disdain for this worldly pavilion
comes as no great surprise
for everyone knows that those who frequent the tavern
become oblivious to everything

The world shows no interest in art
and I have nothing else

how can I trade in these unwanted goods

Wine   poetry
are the only true friends I have left
in these times

do not burden yourself
with the things of this world
travel lightly
for the path to salvation is narrow

and take your pleasures as they come
for we cannot trade in this precious life for another

it is not just my own impotence
that weighs me down
the learned scholars too
deal only in abstractions

I see nothing
that could be regarded as stability
in this turbulent world
nothing of real value

my heart had overflowed with hope
of seeing your countenance again
but doom like a highwayman
has cut the road

play with the strands of your beloved's hair
and do not repeat the old *canard*
that it is all down to the influence of the stars
Venus or Saturn

at no hour of the day
will you find him in his right mind
for this Hafez of ours
is drunk on the wine of eternity

Having recently captured Shiraz (the story goes) Tamburlaine summoned the aged Hafez to explain why he had not paid his dues. Not long before Tamburlaine had massacred over 100,000 Isfahanis who had unwisely murdered some of his tax collectors. You, said the all-conquering Mongol, who say you would give away Samarkand and Bohkara (two of the finest cities of his empire) for your beloved, why can you not find the money to pay your taxes? Sire, replied Hafez, it is precisely because of such profligacy that I am penniless. He was let off.

Master of all   defender of the faith
perfect king
Yahya   son of Mozaffar
just ruler of the world

your court provides a sanctuary for Islam
opening to us on earth
a door for the heart   a window for the soul

spirit and reason alike pay homage to you
as they should
for your benevolence extends
to all men everywhere

O king
the heavens whirl like dervishes
at your festivities
do not withdraw your felicitous hand
from the garment of this chant

drink
and bestow the world on us
for with the lasso of your curls
the necks of the malevolent
are placed in chains

from now
the heavens will revolve in the direction of justice
let us celebrate
for the tyrant will no longer reach our gates

Hafez   the pen of the sovereign
dispenses our daily bread
no need to be concerned
about your livelihood

Plant the tree of friendship
so that it may bear the fruit
of your heart's desire

uproot the sapling of enmity
for it will produce
nothing but suffering

Good news my heart
someone will come endowed with Jesus' breath
in those sweet breaths   I scent the scent of you

do not complain about the sorrows of absence
for last night
I read my fortune and it said a savior would come

I am not the only one to rejoice
at the fire in the sacred valley
Moses also came in search of a flaming brand

there is no one in your street
who has no reason to be there
everyone follows the path of his own instincts

no one knows where the beloved tarries
all that reaches us is the sound of the camel bells

    if he thinks to inquire
    about one who is sick with grief
    say there is still some breath left in him

    and ask about the nightingale in the garden
    for I can hear cries coming from that cage

O friends
the beloved has it in mind to torment Hafez
a royal falcon whose quarry is a fly

Each bird comes to the rose-garden of the king
with its own contribution

the nightingale to sing its song
Hafez to offer his blessings

Do not agonize
about the nature of being
for all that is perfect
comes to nothing

the splendor of Asaf
whose horse was the wind
and who understood
the language of birds

has gone with the wind
and wherever we search
we find nothing of him
or his entourage

Asaf: known as Solomon's minister in Persian literature, but here confused
with Solomon himself, who had these attributes.

The language of love is easier to translate than that of friendship. Loving; the lover; the beloved: these words find their equivalent in every culture. But in English at least, "friend" does not carry the weight that it does in the Divan, and our "companion" has lost most of the medieval, heraldic strength it once had. By comparison, in Hafez' time friendship could be a matter of life and death, the confidant would be privy to important secrets and the companion might accompany one on a hazardous journey. And in a predominantly male culture, the emotional bonding between men could be intense.

Remember the time
when we friends were all together
remember   remember those days

my palate is as bitter with sorrow
as if it had ingested poison
remembering when we cried out
drink up   long life   enjoy

if I have slipped from the minds of my friends
they still people my thoughts
I think back to their fidelity
beset as I am by this calamity

and though tears stream down from my eyes
continually   like a river
I remember the river in Isfahan
and the gardens of Kārān

after this   sad to say   Hafez' secrets
will have to remain unknown
for all those who shared them
and kept them   have gone

Isfahān: a city in central Iran, with gardens along the river Zāyandērood

Why should I not resolve
to go back to my own country
why should I not become dust once more
in my friend's alleyway

since I cannot endure
exile and estrangement here
I shall return to my own city
and be a person of importance there

I shall become one of those
allowed to enter the inner sanctum of union
and be one of the servants of my lord

 since we do not know where life is headed
 at least let me be with the one I cherish
 on Judgment Day

if I complain about fate's long sleep
and my own destitution
let me do it secretly

 my calling has always been as a lover
 who scandalized the town
 with his profligacy
 let me follow my vocation

may the grace without end or beginning
see Hafez on his way
if not
may he be ashamed of himself eternally

Last night the messenger breeze brought me the news
that the days of trial and affliction would be cut short

let us give new costumes to the morning minstrels
so that they may sing
these tidings that the dawn wind has brought

we shall set off for Shiraz
watched over by our companion

blessed be that friend
who blesses me with his company on the way

    see   O maiden   how the keeper of heaven
    leads you down into this world for the heart of a slave

    strive to mend my broken spirit
    for this felt bonnet has broken many a crown

how many cries have risen from my heart
to the pavilion of the haloed moon
when it remembers the shining down-fringed cheek
of he who is the moon of that pavilion

    Hafez has raised the standard of Mansur to the skies
    for his refuge is the threshold of the king of kings

This stooped body
may seem harmless to you

but from this bow
I can still loose arrows
at the eyes of my enemies

I have no refuge in this world   other than your threshold
nowhere to lay my head   except at your door

if my enemy drew his sword   I would throw down my shield
since I have no arrows but my plaintive sighs

why should I turn away from the ruin of the tavern
since I know no other habit   no better way

and if fate should set fire to the harvest of my life
I would say burn   for it is nothing but straw

I am slave to those cheating eyes   that natural poise
but drunk on self-regard   you look at nobody

    do what you will   but do no harm to others
    there is no other sin   according to our *sharia*

O king of this great land   rein back your horse
for the roads are filled with those who clamor for justice

    now that I am ensnared at every turn
    I find safety only in the strands of your hair

do not barter the treasures of Hafez' heart
for dark moles   dark tresses

for no black slave could demonstrate such art

sharia: the religious law

That brigand of time has not fallen asleep
do not drop your guard

if he has not succeeded today   he will tomorrow

At dawn in the tulip-field I asked the wind
who are these martyrs in their bloody shrouds

it said   Hafez   neither you nor I
are party to the mystery
sing ruby wine and the sweetness of sweet mouths

cling to your friend   forswear the enemy
be a man of God   and safe from Ahriman

Ahriman: the Zoroastrian devil, or strictly speaking, principle of evil

They say that Shah Mansur
has forgotten Hafez

O Lord may he remember
to cherish his poor dervish

The good news has come
that the bad times will pass
since one thing does not last   neither will the other

although in the eyes of my beloved
I am no better than dirt
likewise my rival will not always be preferred

and since the chamberlain slays each new arrival
with his sword
no one can take up residence in the sanctum

why do we allocate praise or blame
to good and evil in the scheme of things
since on the page of being no writing will remain

they say that in Jamshid's court the cry was
bring wine   for even Jamshid is not immortal

let the rich man take his impoverished heart in hand
for he will not hold onto his gold and silver forever

O candle   you must see
consummation with the moth as a blessing
for none of this business will last beyond morning

on the emerald vault above it is written in gold
that apart from magnanimity nothing endures

Hafez
do not despair of your beloved's kindness
for this spectacle of tyranny and cruelty
will pass

VI

THE BELOVED

No sherbet from his ruby lips did we enjoy
and he's gone

we did not have our fill
of gazing at his moonlike face
and now he's gone

it is as if he tired of our company
he packed his bags   we could not stop him
and he's gone

however much we prayed the prescribed prayers
and recited the Koran
he's gone

he tricked us into thinking we would never
have cause to reproach him
see how in the end we bought into his lies

he paraded himself along the elegant paths
but never once did we stroll with him
in the garden of union

like Hafez we wail and cry   all night through
complaining
we did not even bid farewell to him
and he's gone

You said

did you go out to gaze at the new moon
instead of the curved moon of my eyebrow

shame on you

for a lifetime now your heart has been slave to my hair
do not forget your loyalty to your friends

and do not try to exchange sweet reason
for the scent of my Indian-dark tresses
for compared to it   even musk is worth next to nothing

in these age-old fields the seed of constant devotion
will come to fruition at harvest-time

boy   bring wine   and I shall explain the secrets
of the course of the ancient stars and the new moon

see   at the start of each month   in that crescent shape
the sign of Zow's helmet and Siāmak's crown

Hafez
the Magi's porch is the refuge of the faithful
sing to him of what you have learned from love
and listen to what he says

Zow, Siāmak: legendary Iranian kings

Older, archaic words sometimes come into my head as I work on Hafez: "plaint" as a response to some perceived amorous injustice (or real courtly one); "argument" not as a disagreement but a series of reasoned steps; "devotion" as an expression of love or commitment (including religious commitment); "tale" as an unfolding story. It makes me think: if some medieval or even Elizabethan poet had somehow got hold of Hafez, would he have made a better job of it?

Every sight of you is pleasing
every place you are is good
your ruby lips' sweet nothings
bring gladness to my heart

like a fresh rose-petal
your existence is delicate
like a cypress of paradise
your deportment exquisite

sweet your airs and graces
comely your mole and down
beautiful your eyes your brow
your stature and bearing fine

the garden of my imagination
is filled with your images
and my heart scents the fragrance
of your jasmine-scented hair

on love's road there is no avoiding
the flood that sweeps all away
but I have found reassurance
in my supplications to you

allow me to die before you
for in my sad condition
my suffering is made pleasurable
by the beauty that I see

in the desert of the quest
there are dangers everywhere
but Hafez   minus his heart
journeys under your protection

My pleasure in my beloved   knows no bounds
all my labors have been rewarded   thanks be to heaven

O fickle fate   hold tight in your embrace
those lovely ruby lips   that golden chalice

   the elders who know nothing
   the sheikhs who have lost their way
   tell all sorts of stories
   about our goings-on

may God forgive any piety we show
we who have renounced the ascetic's rule

how can I describe   absence from you
a hundred tears in one eye   sighs from one soul

may the infidel never know the sense of despair
of the cypress at your height   the moon at your face

   predilection for your lips   has made Hafez forget
   his nightly reading and his morning prayer

Though hidden from me
      yet to God I entrust you
you have seared my soul
      yet my soul adores you

I have kept back the streams of my eyes
      to water your fields
so that in your heart might grow
      the seeds I sow there

O my faithless physician
      let me die before you
inquire after your patient
      for he waits for you to come

until I lie shrouded
      in the dusty ground
believe me I shall never
      let go of your hem

and if I must go to Babylon to find you
      deep in some evil well
I will use all my powers of sorcery
      to bring you back

show me the *mehrāb* of your eyebrows
      so that some day at dawn
when I hold out my hands to pray
      I may rest them upon your neck

mehrāb: the prayer-niche in a mosque which is orientated towards Mecca

236

God grant that my friend return safely
and deliver me from the bonds of castigation

O wind bring me the dust of the road
that my dear friend has traveled
that I may fill my eyes with it   and give it lodging

bring me help
for my way is blocked in every direction
by that hair   that face   that mole   that cheek and down

today when I am in your hands   show me some mercy
for tomorrow when I am dust   what use will remorse be

to those who discourse on love
I have nothing to say
except peace be upon you   go

O my poor dervish   you that have nothing
do not expect to be spared this sword
for love's tribe exacts tribute even from the dead

throw your ascetic's gown onto the flames
for the arch of the wine-boy's eyebrows
has replaced the *mehrāb* of the *imām*

God forbid that I should lament your injustice
for the cruelty of the lovely is kindness itself

but Hafez will not cut short his account of your hair
for its chains shall bind him till the resurrection

imām: religious leader, here of a mosque

I   all helplessness and despairing need
the other   all haughtiness
and drunk overweening pride

    the secret I have not shared
    and will share with no one
    I shall confide in that friend who will keep it
    and he alone

to describe properly your hair
fold upon fold
cannot be done briefly
for that is a long story

recalling Majnūn's heavy heart
and the flowing tresses of Leili
the face of Mahmud of Ghazni
and the soles of Ayāz's feet

    I have seeled up my eyes
    like a young falcon
    so that when they open
    they may see only your face

whoever comes to the Ka'ba of your street
to the *qibla* of your eyebrows
finds himself in the very eye of prayer

Ayāz: a young slave boy who served King Mahmud so well that one only ever
saw the soles of his feet as he abased himself before him, so much so that the
king fell in love with him

Qibla: the direction of prayer towards Mecca

friends

if you want to understand
how Hafez' heart burns
inquire now of the candle
before it melts down

The language of love in Persian poetry seems to have originated in oral, popular love poems. However with the growth of court poetry and in particular the ghazal, it gradually became transposed and used in three other ways. The first was in relation to the prince, whom it became de rigueur to describe in amatory terms, extolling not only his power, justice and generosity but his beauty. The second was the sāghī who, as the dispenser of wine, became the object of erotic hyperbole. The third area was the mystical relationship with God, which came to be expressed in terms of passion, separation and union. Love, or rather the language of love, is not only at the heart of Hafez; it is at the heart of the problem of understanding him.

O that a breath of wind
would bring me the scented dust
from the road of my friend

would blow away the sorrows from my heart
and bring me news of the one who possesses it
relay those uplifting words
that come from the mouth of my beloved
and bring me tidings from the secret world

and so that I might perfume my senses
with the gentleness of your breeze
bring me a waft of my beloved's breath

O wind   out of fidelity
carry the dust from the path of my dearest one
unpolluted by others
and unseen by the watchful guardian
bring me the dirt beneath those feet
to soothe my bloodshot eyes

there is no place
for innocence or immaturity
in those who risk all
bring me some message from my artful lover

I give thanks   O meadow-bird   that you are free
to enjoy life's pleasures
for then you can bring news of the rose-bower
to those who are caged

my palate has turned bitter in your absence
let me have some blandishment
from that sweet mouth

how long it is since I saw that longed-for face
boy
bring me the cup that serves as a looking-glass

Hafez' pious robes mean nothing   stain them with wine
and carry him legless from the market-place

Where do you bide   in what dwelling   where
O candle that lights my heart   consumes my soul
to whom do you belong

you who have almost destroyed
the edifice of my heart and my religion
whose lodging do you share
in whose arms do you lie

whose spirit is gratified by your lips
lips that should be close to mine
to whom do you give promise of wine

Lord I ask again
whose leave I must obtain
to enjoy the bounty of that company
and see with my eyes those joyful rays
like the moth sees the flame

each one murmurs his incantation
but nobody knows as yet
which spell will capture that tender heart

whose jewel is this   whose priceless pearl
whose radiance   whose countenance
whose Venus   whose Moon

    I sigh for poor Hafez
    whose heart has been driven insane
    by your absence

but the question comes back
and with the hint of a smile

mad about whom   for whom

That night when the object of my desire
rises like the moon over the horizon

perchance a beam of light   will fall upon my roof

West wind if you chance to pass
through the country of my friend
bring me the sweet scent of his hair

upon his soul I swear
I would forfeit my own soul
willingly   if you brought back
a message from his presence there

and if they do not let you in
bring me the dust outside his door
for my two eyes

                              since being poor
my only hope of seeing him
lies in his image in my mind

my heart that was as steady as
the tallest fir has now become
a willow weeping by a stream
and all for pining for that form

although I know he would not give
one cent for me   I would not trade
one hair of his for all the world

        what would it matter if his heart
        were set free from the bonds of grief
        O sweet-voiced Hafez   always a slave
        always subservient to his love

Do not abandon me   you who are the light of my eyes
beloved of my soul   confidant of my wild heart

lovers will never relinquish the hem of your skirt
though you have torn up the garment of their patience

may the eye of good fortune protect you from all harm
for you have brought seduction to perfection

     you deny me this love   O Mufti of our times
     but you have an excuse
     for you have never beheld   one such as this

jelvē: presenting a bride to her husband for the first time unveiled; beauty; the appearance of; the manifestation of; appearance; manifestation

I swear by your life   that if my life were my own
it would be the least of the gifts
I would offer your servants

if my heart had not been attached
to the strands of your hair
how could I not have fallen
into this dark pit

like the sun in the sky
your face has no peer in any direction
a pity then that your heart
lacks one particle of affection

if my dear life were eternal
I could perhaps meet the price
of the dirt beneath your feet

if only you would appear at my door
like a ray of light
so that my two eyes might be placed under your orders

the cypress would doubtless acknowledge
the superiority of your stature
if only it had ten tongues like the lily

    this complaint of Hafez
    might never have become known
    had he not been part of the dawn chorus

You said that my head
would be tied to your saddle strap
like game from the hunt

fine by me   so long as
you are not inconvenienced by the burden

I begin with this striking point

on that moon-like visage see the beauty spot
and then observe how the chains of those curls
bind both mind and soul

> I scolded my heart saying
> do not wander in the desert
> like some wild animal
> it said
> have you seen those lion-taming eyes
> the grace of that gazelle

your ringlets are a puppet theater
for the gentle morning wind
a hundred disciples of the heart
dangle from every strand

> those who worship the sun
> ignore the beloved's face
> O you who would censure us
> do not gaze at that face but this

those heart-stealing curls
act like a halter on the wind
and with those Indian wiles
seduce the pilgrims of the way

> I have abandoned my self
> in the search for that one
> whom nobody has seen
> nor will ever see the like of
> wherever they might turn

251

if Hafez is found weeping
in the corner of the *mehrab*
it is obvious why
and to those who criticize me I say
look at the curvature of that brow

    O fate   do not desert
    the campaigns of Shah Mansur
    see the keenness of his sword
    observe the strength of his arm

Hitherto you were more considerate to lovers
your reputation for kindness spread to the ends of the earth

    at the king's door   a beggar once observed
    whoever lays on the feast   it is God who provides

remember the night-time sessions
where with those sweet-lipped ones
we talked of love's secrets and of lovers' trysts

and although both heart and faith were borne away
by the star of that gathering
we discussed the nature of virtue and of grace

from the dawn of time until eternity's evening
love and friendship are bound by one covenant

before that green roof and enamelled vault
were raised to the sky   my eyes
were fixed on the vault of my beloved's eyebrow

if the shadow of the loved one fell upon us lovers
what does it matter
for we wanted him and he was filled with desire

if the thread of my prayer-beads has snapped   forgive me
for my hand was laid on the arm of the silver-limbed boy

and if on the Night of Power
I consumed my morning draught
do not complain

for my beloved turned up drunk
and there on the ledge of the prayer-niche
was a jug of wine

    in the time of Adam   in the garden of Eden
    Hafez' lines
    illustrated the pages of the book of flowers

That friend who made of our house an enchanted place
was   like a *peri*   faultless from tip to toe

the heart said to itself
I shall stay in this town
in the hope of seeing him
unaware   poor thing   that he had gone away

that one whom I longed to gaze at
was like a moon   and in his wisdom
combined perfect manners with great intuition

some baleful star has snatched him from my grasp
what can I do
it is all down to the orbits of the heavens

you must understand   my heart   that you are poor
while he was a crowned head in the kingdom of beauty

not only did he unveil the secrets of my heart
but since time began
his skill has lain in stripping away illusion

my happiest times were those spent with my friend
as for the rest   it was pointless   meaningless

how pleasant it was to be there
with the flowing water   flowers   the verdant grass
alas that such transient riches had to pass

peri: a beautiful fairy

255

at the sight of the rose showing off to the morning breeze
the jealous nightingale will kill itself

    all the treasure of happiness
    that Hafez has received from God
    comes from his morning studies   his nightly prayer

You who are life to me
I want you   and I know that you know
for you see the unseen and read what is unwritten

  what do the censorious understand
  of what passes between lover and lover
  for of all people the blind are least able
  to see what is kept hidden

shake loose your hair   set the Sufi's feet tapping
so that at each step in the dance
from every patch on his gown
false idols may fall on the floor

all lovers look for liberation
in those eyebrows that bind the heart
for God's sake stop for a moment
unknot your brow

the angel kneeling before Adam
was in its own mind
kissing the ground beneath your feet
for in your beauty it found
something better than mankind

the lamp of our eyes is lit
by the breeze of our beauties' hair
O Lord may this gathering
be spared the scattering wind

alas that the pleasures of the night
end in the slumber of morning

O heart you do not value time
until you can no longer use it

those pilgrims on the caravan should not
become angry with their fellow-travellers
put up with the hardships of each stage
and think of the comforts in store

    Hafez you have been beguiled
    by the vision of those curls
    I fear you knock at the impossible door

A friend looks at some of my translations and says: these are poems about themselves. About words. About language. About being what they are.

May your loveliness illuminate each vision
may the beauty of your face surpass beauty itself
your hair is like the plumage of the *homā*
may the hearts of kings shelter under its wing

may the person who is not attached to your curls
be twisted this way and that like they are
may he who does not worship your countenance
forever drown in the blood of his own entrails

O my idol when your eyes loose small arrows
may my wounded heart be broken like a shield
and if your red lips grant me a honeyed kiss
may my soul's palate be sated with its sweetness

every breath I draw my longing for you grows
at every hour let your beauty be renewed
Hafez' soul is in thrall to the vision of your face
look this once upon your lover's throes

homā: a mythical bird which offers protection to rulers

260

Last night the road to sleep
was flooded by my tears
remembering the line of your down
I traced a pattern on the water

with my gown consigned to the flames
and your eyebrow in mind
I raised a wine-cup to that place of prayer

my beloved appeared to me   and from a distance
I placed a kiss upon that moonlike face

gazing at the serving-boy
and listening to the message of the harp
in these two ways
eye and ear told me of my destiny

each bird of thought
that took off from the branches of words
I caught again in the fine net of your curls

and till dawn
I drew the image of your face
working in the attic of my sleepless eyes

hearing this ghazal   the boy brought me a cup
I spoke these lines and drank in that pure wine

Hafez is filled with happiness
and I have had favorable auguries
regarding the long life and prosperity of his friends

261

The moon has not the brightness of your face
beside you
the rose does not even possess the luster of grass

my soul lodges in the nook of your eyebrow
the king has not a better retreat than this

I looked   but the eye of that black-hearted one
did not turn to see if any friends were there

boy   bring me a large measure to toast
that sheikh who has no prayer-house anywhere

how long will my heart smoulder because of your cheek
have you ever seen a mirror not clouded with sighs

suffer in silence   for surely your tender heart
cannot bear to hear the victims' pleading cries

there are many who suffer the arrogance of your tresses
and who is there not marked by love's black brand

observe the impudence of the narcissus
that opens in front of you
an insolent eye observes no etiquette

say to him who cannot find his way to your doorway
go   wash your sleeves in the blood that courses within

if Hafez prostrates himself before you
do not chastise him
for love's infidel   O my idol   commits no sin

sabr: patience; resilience; endurance; but more than that, the capacity to hide or contain one's private grief, anger or frustration, to continue behaving within the accepted norms of life, which may be sorely tested sometimes; also, the bitter taste of aloe

I laid my head upon his path
but he did not come near me
I looked for a hundred kindnesses
on his part
but he did not even see me

the floods of my tears did not wash out
the contempt from his heart
rain-drops simply run off granite
leaving no mark

O Lord protect this brave young warrior
for he has not bothered to protect himself
from the arrows of this melancholic's sighs

neither fish nor fowl slept all night
with my wailing
but that young rogue never lifted his head

I wanted to die burning for him like a candle
but he did not come to me as the dawn breeze does

O soul of my soul
what thick-skinned thick-headed person
would not shield himself with his life
against the wounds of your blade

Hafez' pen   which is the tongue of our gathering
told no one this secret   till someone had pared its head

If that line of perfumed down
had written me a line
the heavens would not have written off
another page of my life

even if separation
in the end bears fruit in union
I would wish that the world's landlord
had not planted such a seed

      only he who has companions like *houris*
      and a palace like paradise   can afford to forgive

I am not the only one
to have made of the Ka'ba of the heart
a temple of idols
at every step one comes across
a monk's cell or a synagogue

love's hostelry is not luxurious
since we do not have golden pillows
let us make do with bricks

do not   for the gardens of Iram
or all the pomp of Shaddad
forfeit one glass of wine   one taste of the lip
one meadow's edge

Shaddad: a tyrant who created the beautiful gardens of Iram

O knowing heart   how long will you have to know
the pain of this mean existence
how sad that the fair should come to love the foul

the Sufi's stained robe
brings ruin upon this world
where shall I find a true wayfarer
by nature pure   a citizen of the heart

why did Hafez relinquish the tips of your hair
such is fate
was it within his power   not to let go

How many times have I asked that you befriend me
that you give my restless heart what it searches for

that you become a lamp to those eyes
that do not close all night
that you share my innermost desires

that among all those graceful lords who parade their slaves
you agree to become my master

and that if I complain about those carnelian lips
which set my heart pounding
you will tell no one

that on those tree-lined paths
where lovers walk   holding one another's hands
that if it were in your hands
you would take mine

even the gazelle of the sun would be meager prey
compared to you who resemble the musk-deer
if I managed to hunt you down

three kisses from two lips are surely my due
if you do not pay up   you are in debt to me

I shall know if my wishes have come true
when in the middle of the night
in place of my flowing tears
I find you beside me

although as a *hafez* I am well-known
to all and sundry in this town
I am not worth one barley-corn
unless out of loving-kindness
you consent to be mine

hāfez: a person who has learned ("preserved") the Koran by heart and whose
role is to recite parts of it on religious and public occasions

Thanks to him   no thanks to him
who plays upon my heart
if you are a connoisseur of love
listen closely to what I say

for each service I rendered I got
neither praise nor pay
may the Lord protect us from tight-fisted masters

nobody offers a cup   to the parched lips of the *rend*
as if all those who understood true fellowship
had left the country

but however much you humiliate me
I shall not turn from your door   for I prefer
the despotic lover to the fawning pretender

O heart do not become caught up
in the lassos of those curls
for there you will come upon
the severed heads of the innocent

with a single glance
your eyes drink up my blood
and yet you allow it   O my beloved
it is not lawful to shelter murderers

in this dark night I cannot see
where I am going
let the Pole Star come out of hiding
and point me the way

lost in the wilderness
at every turn my apprehension grows
beware the desert and its winding trails

how can one even think of the destination
when so many stages loom ahead at the start

but love will answer your call
if like Hafez you are one of those
who knows the Koran by heart
in each of its fourteen recensions

Prince or serving-boy? Companion or lover? Male or female? Human or divine? Such ambiguities and uncertainties to do with the objects of Hafez' emotions can trouble us. But the emotions themselves are clear: need, longing, despair, hope, joy. It is perhaps these that make him a poet who still speaks so directly to us, in such different circumstances and all these centuries later.

Crowned heads are enslaved by your potent eyes
and the sober are incapacitated
by the wine of your ruby lips

    the west wind betrays you   and my tears me
    if not   lover and beloved would be a secret

when your face appears between your two plaits
people lose their footing left and right

pass like the wind over the beds of violets   and see
how they are chagrined by the trespass of your hair

    our lot is paradise   away theologians
    for it is sinners who deserve the greatest indulgence

it is not just I who laud those rosy cheeks
a thousand nightingales do so on every side

    Khezr   my sure-footed guide   give me a hand
    for I go on foot while others mount their steeds

come to the tavern and drink
till your cheeks are as purple as the Judas-tree
but avoid the cloister   where all is dark deeds

    may Hafez never escape those tangled curls
    for it is their lasso that strangely makes him free

Since my wandering heart
embarked on the waves of your hair

from that long voyage   it no longer plans to return

The vision of your beauty is at the full
as is my love
rejoice   because such beauty will never wane

and the great labor of your virtue
has been brought to perfection
as has my love
rejoice   for such virtue will never suffer decline

it is impossible to imagine reason
configuring a better example than this

life's joy would be fulfilled
if for just one day
my daily allowance was to be with you

with you   one year would go by like a day
without you   one moment seems like a whole year

how can I see your image in my sleep
since of sleep itself I have only an image

take pity on my heart   for from love of your face
my feeble body has dwindled like the new moon

Hafez   do not complain
for if you hope to be united with your friend
you will have to learn to cope with separation
better than this

There are no words to describe love, says Hafez in one ghazal. This might be taken as the kind of conventional statement often made by poets about the limitations of their medium but with Hafez I think it is something more. The fact that his poetry is repetitive (without actually being repetitious) suggests to me a struggle to try to grasp or express something that is perhaps ineffable: rather like an artist who endlessly, obsessively paints and repaints a still life.

As soon as the ends of your hair
fell into the hands of the wind
my melancholy heart was split in two with sorrow

your dark eyes are the very primer of magic
pity that all I have is a corrupt copy

see   that black spot surrounded by your curls
is like the small dot on the letter j

and those musky strands falling on your paradisal cheeks
adorn them like a peacock landed in Eden

O solace of my soul
my heart in its desire for your fragrance
has turned to road-dust   left there by the wind

but this dusty body cannot rise like the dust does
at the end of your street   so utterly has it collapsed

since like a cypress your shadow falls on my tombstone
like the breath of Jesus   revive my mouldering bones

I see that he
who had no station other than the Ka'ba
at the thought of your lips
has taken up residence at the tavern door

    though lost
    Hafez is partnered by his grief for you
    for this has been the pact since the beginning

On the slate of my heart there is only the straight *alef*
of the figure of my beloved

what can I do
since my master taught me to write no other letter

alef: the first letter of the alphabet

There is no light
outside the radiance of your countenance
and all my days have turned
into a dark moonless night

patience was my remedy
for separation from you
but how can I be patient
when it lies beyond my powers

at the time of our parting
I wept so bitterly
that deprived of your face
no light was left in my eyes

even my image of you
quit them   saying
how sad this little corner is
where nothing grows

being with you
postponed my doom
but now with your fateful absence
I sense my time has come

and it cannot be long surely
before your guardian informs you
that somewhere   a long way from your door
this poor wretch has expired

and then what use would it be
if my friend came to see me

for all that would remain in that body
would be my parting breath

if my eyes are empty of tears
there is still my blood to shed
nothing of me escapes
no part of me is spared

Show your face
and obliterate any sense I have
of my own existence

let the wind carry off
the scorched earth of my love

since I have given my heart   even my eyes
to this calamitous storm
let the torrents of grief come
and sweep my dwelling away

alas   who will now smell
the fresh amber of your hair
O foolish heart   dismiss the very idea

let the sighs of my breast
extinguish the great fire-temple of Fars
let my tears inundate the Tigris in Baghdad

last night you said
I shall kill you with my long eyelashes

O Lord remove unjust thoughts from his mind

    but Hafez   do not forget
    how sensitive   how delicate he is
    banish this wailing and crying from his court

I do not know
who this person is within me
I who am heartsore

for when I am quiet   he is in uproar

THE FAITH

O heart   take care to live in such a way
that if your foot stumble
the angel will catch your hands held out in prayer

Come Sufi
divest yourself of hypocrisy
strike out these false accounts

we shall use the pious donations to purchase wine
and wash the charlatans' robes
in the liquor of the tavern

drunk we shall rip the veil
from the face of the mystery

we shall jump out at the Sufis' festival
purloining their wine
and making off with their partners

we shall pleasure ourselves
and if not be racked with guilt
the day we pack life's belongings for the next world

    where can I find those graceful eyebrows
    curved like the new moon
    so that I may catch in the hook
    of my golden polo-stick
    that celestial sphere

tomorrow if we are not allowed
to enter the gardens of heaven
we shall expel the young men from the chamber
and the maidens from the garden

    Hafez you go too far with these insults
    do not poke your feet out
    from under the quilt

These preachers who make great show
in the *mehrab* and the pulpit
when they are in private
get up to other things

    I have a problem
    about which I would like to consult
    the most erudite member of our gathering

why do those who command us to repent
repent so rarely themselves

one might almost conclude
that they did not really believe in the day of judgment
the way they come before the great judge of all
with their false claims   their bending of the rules

    I   on the other hand   serve the Master of the Ruin
    whose carefree customers   owning nothing
    pour scorn on affluence

O Lord   reinstate these upstarts on their asses
who so pride themselves on their Turkish slaves   and their mules

Although we may think of Sufis and Dervishes as much the same, Hafez is consistently critical of the first while identifying with the second. This may be because already by his time the Sufis were established religious orders with all the potential for organizational arrogance and hypocrisy that goes with that. Whereas *darvīshī* was a condition or a state of mind characterized by utter humility, having or being nothing, which reflected the original ordinary sense of the term: poverty, indigence, destitution.

O sober puritan
do not presume to criticise the *rend*
for the sins of others will not be ascribed to you

do not be concerned
with whether I am virtuous or sinful
be mindful of your own salvation
for everyone reaps what they sow in the end

drunk or sober   everybody seeks that friend
in the mosque or the synagogue
everywhere is the house of love

as for me
I worship the very bricks of the tavern
if my critics cannot comprehend this
tell them they are blockheads

do not deny my hope of eternal salvation
what do you know anyway
of what lies behind the curtain   good or ill

I am not the only one to have fallen from grace
abandoning solitary piety
my father Adam relinquished the garden of Eden

    if this is how you behave   well and good
    if this is what you are   so much the better

Hafez   if you raise a cup on Judgment Day
you will walk straight from the tavern into heaven

The threshold
the porch
the doorway
the door

the precincts
the chamber
the inner sanctum

The Sufi's coin is not always pure
unalloyed

how many fake vestments
should be consigned to the flames

our Sufi who is high on his morning prayers
avoid him in the evening when he is drunk

it would be good if there were some kind of test
or assay
whereby the faces of liars all turned black

I have said many times and say it again
that I who have gone astray
do not follow this path of my own volition

I am like a parrot placed behind a mirror
what the eternal Master tells me to say   I say

whether I am a rose or a thorn
is a matter for the gardener
he plants me and I grow

friends do not deprecate
my lost heart   my confusion
I have a jewel   and search only for the one
who can see it

although red wine blemishes a patchwork gown
do not blame me
for with it I wash away
the tint of hypocrisy

nights I exult and mornings I despair
the laughter and tears of lovers come from elsewhere

  Hafez has told us not to breathe in
  the dust at the tavern door
  but how can he blame us
  for we smell the sweet musk of Khotan

The trees are heavy-laden
with their attachments

O happy cypress   free of the burden of grief

I confided in the wind   all my fond hopes
trust in God's grace   the wind replied

the evening supplication   the morning prayer
are the keys to the treasure you are searching for

go forth this way   and the road will lead you
to the one who is keeper of your heart

no pen can give tongue to the mystery of love
no person express the nature of that longing

this courtly old world   is pitiless
so why remain attached to it

why should a great bird   scavenge for bones
its shadow fall   on the undeserving

no one profits   from the market of life
except the dervish   who wants nothing

O God   enrich me with poverty
and make me content with humility

Once   in another country   a wayfarer
spoke the following riddles to a companion

O Sufi   wine does not mature
until it has been in the cask for forty days

what properties does the seal on Solomon's ring
have   if it is not upon his finger

God tires of the robes of piety
if there are idols hidden up the sleeve

it has grown dark within
perhaps from the hidden world
someone will come and light a lamp

those who aspire to true spirituality
expect nothing
no sense of exaltation
no solace for the heart
no burning faith

show me the way to the tavern
so that I may inquire of some seer
about my own destiny

Hafez no longer applies himself to his studies
with others or on his own
for the scholars know nothing really

Although Hafez is generally scathing about Sufis, and distances himself from them, there are seemingly traces of Sufi (and behind that Gnostic and Neo-Platonist) thought in his work, in particular the idea that the world is a divine emanation rather than creation (the image of rays of light). This means that divine beauty may manifest itself, although in a less pure or clear form, in human beauty.

In all these ruined Temples
there is no one as foolish as me
who has pawned his gown one place
and his notebook somewhere else

    my heart   which is the mirror of my king
    has become cloudy now
    I beseech God to send me a companion
    who will help me to see things clearly

I took the hands of the adorable wine-seller
in an oath of repentance
swearing never to drink again
except in the presence of a made-up face

    I have dammed up the stream of my eyes
    with the hem of my garment
    so that   who knows   some graceful cypress
    might sprout up at my side

O send me the ship of wine
for without the visage of my beloved
in the corner of each eye
my tears have created a sea

    let the candle explain these subtleties
    with the tongue of its wick
    for the moth is unable to speak

O do not be distressed if the narcissus
imitates the sorcery of your eyes
for the wise do not follow the blind

and do not talk to me about anyone else
I who worship love
for apart from my sweetheart and my cup
I care about nothing

yesterday at the tavern door
I was gratified to hear a Christian say
to the accompaniment of drum and *nei*

if what Hafez has   is truly Muslim
alas   if after today   Tomorrow comes

Do you hear what the harp and the lute are saying
hide your wine   for it has been outlawed

    they tell us not to speak of love's mystery
    or listen to tales of it

what a hard line they take

    they reject the very principle of love
    the glory of lovers
    they trammel the young and denigrate the old

    they intrude upon the Elder of the Magi
    at the very climax of ecstasy
    see what these so-called disciples do

pour out the wine   because
    the *sheikh*
       the *hafez*
          the *mufti*
            and the *mohtaseb*

if you observe them closely   all are frauds

sheikh: sufi leader

hafez: reciter of the Koran

mufti: senior religious judge

mohtaseb: chief of morality police

The metal of Jamshid's cup
comes from a mine in the other world

yet you expect it to be made of potter's clay

At one point, according to some sources, Hafez faced the capital charge of heresy, avoiding this only because the regime was then overthrown. Even at this distance, he still induces a sharp intake of breath because of the seemingly sacrilegious way he treats some of the cherished symbols of his religion (although he is always reverential towards the Koran itself). How did he get away with it? And why did he do it? The usual explanation is that he subscribed to the radical Sufi notion of *malāmatī* (literally, attracting reproach, scandal or blame) which systematically subverted all formal religious symbols and practices in order to undermine spiritual attachment to anything but the One.

Let us spirit away the Sufi's robes to the tavern
and bring to the marketplace of unreason
ecstatic outpourings   ravings   speaking in tongues

from our spiritual journey let us bring back
as a gift for the *qalandars*
Bestami's cloak and carpets of mystic prayer
and so that the hermits
can gather for their morning drink
let us send a harp to the leader of their devotions

   O You with whom we sealed that convenant
   in the valley of faith
   let us bring it like Moses to the appointed place
   saying   show your face

we shall beat the drum of your glory
from the pinnacle of heaven
and carry the banner of your love to the roof of the skies
we shall cover our heads with the dust of your street
proclaiming your glory on the field of resurrection
and if the ascetic tries to bar our path
with prickly objections
we shall remove him from his garden to prison

O let us be ashamed of our own stained robes
if we speak of any miracle comparable to these

qalandar: a branch of wandering Sufis, known for their outrageous behavior

Bestami: a 9th century Sufi mystic

if our hearts do not grasp the value of each moment
when the time comes
we shall be distraught at how we have wasted it

from these vaulted ceilings above   temptation falls
quick   let us take refuge in the house of wine

how long must we wander in the wilderness of desire
ask the way
so that we may understand what is necessary

Hafez do not concern yourself
with the mean-spirited
make your case before He who is judge of all

I follow the Elder of the Magi

O Sheikh   do not be upset

why

because what you talk about

he brings about

The ignorant are bewildered
by the looks we give one another
winks   glances
the games we play

let them think what they want
I am what I seem to be

　　reason would suggest
　　that we are the pivot of the compass
　　but love knows we are spinning round

God has indentured us
to those with sweet lips
we are their slaves   and they our noble lords

　　we are poverty-stricken
　　but yearn for wine and song
　　a pity we cannot pawn our pashmina gowns

to boast about love
and then complain about the behavior of the beloved
is the sign of a charlatan
love's dilettantes deserve to be spurned

　　my eyes are not the only place
　　where your face appears
　　sun and moon act as its mirror also

bats   being blind   cannot describe the sun
for even visionaries are dazzled by that reflection

if the pious do not understand Hafez the *rend*
who cares

the devil flees from those who know the Koran

The problem with the codes used to interpret Hafez is that they are self-contained: they are not falsifiable. Moreover, they are reversible. So just as the apparently worldly poems can be read in a spiritual way, so the apparently mystical ghazals can be decoded as court poems. However, it is much more difficult to interpret the small number of homiletic ghazals, which give spiritual advice or guidance, other than in terms of what they actually say. This suggests that at some point, and in some way, Hafez had some kind of formal spiritual role.

It is only through endeavor
that the novice becomes a master
if you do not follow the path yourself
how can you become a guide

under love's tuition in the school of Truth
be diligent my son so that you in your turn
may become a father

wash your hands of the base metal of existence
so that like the people of the Way
you may practise love's alchemy
and transmute it into gold

    eating and sleeping merely distance you
    from your proper station
    only when you do without them
    will you find your true self

if the light of God's love
illuminates your heart and soul
you will outblazon the sun
and if you immerse yourself   even for a moment
in the great sea of God
believe me the seven oceans
will not wet one hair on your head

from head to foot you will become
the light of God
and on the path of glory lose all sense of either
and if God's face becomes your only vision
you will see everything

when the foundations of your being
have been overturned
know in your heart
things will never be the same again

    Hafez if yearning for oneness fills your mind
    you must become like dust
    at the door of those who truly understand

Come   heart
let us seek God's protection
from those with short sleeves and long arms
the Sufi who plays tricks
and engages in sleight of hand
as if he could outsmart the conjuring heavens

let Fate crack an egg in his hat
since he tried to deceive
those who are party to the mystery

O do not engage in artifice
for those who are not pure in heart
will find that love
has slammed the door of meaning in their face

that day when the portal of Truth
is revealed to us
will put to shame all those wayfarers
who mistook illusion for reality

O graceful partridge where are you going
do not be taken in by the posturing

of the devout cat

Hafez your only duty is to pray

do not be concerned
whether He has heard you or not

No one has seen your face
yet you have a thousand minders

you are still only a rosebud
yet you are serenaded
by a hundred nightingales

however far away I am
which no one should have to be
I hope to be united with you soon

and if I came to your street
it would not be so strange
for already there are a thousand strangers
thronging that place

was there ever a lover
whose beloved did not even look to see
how he was
O master I feel no pain   but even if I did
there is a physician

in love there is no distinction
between monastery and tavern
for the rays of the beloved light up
everywhere that is

there where the Sufi practises
there also one finds the monk's rule
and the name of the Cross

when all is said and done   Hafez' effusions
are not meaningless

but make for strange tales   and memorable lines

Hafez refers mainly to the face and head; there is relatively little reference to the rest of the body, apart from stature and poise. And even with the head it is selective: the hair above all; the eyes, eyebrows and eyelashes; the mouth; the cheek; the dimple on the chin. The reason is that each of these means something: the hair connotes confusion, the eyelashes are like darts, the dimple is a well; and so on. It is a poetry not of description or observation but signification.

Joseph   abandoned   returns in the end to Canaan
do not despair

Jacob quits his hut of sorrow for a garden of joy
do not despair

your broken heart will one day surely be mended
your unresting mind will find a place to rest

and if for a while the heavens seem set against us
remember fate does not always take the same turn

if the springtime of life comes back to the beds of flowers
the songbird will be shaded by the parasol of the rose

if the tide of nothingness sweeps away the ground of your being
since Noah is your Master   do not despair at this

and if you do not know what lies behind the curtain
remember there are things of which we are not aware

if your yearning for the Ka'ba takes you through a desert
strewn with sharp thorns   do not complain

if the halt is dangerous   but the road even more so
no journey is endless   do not   do not despair

if you are loveless   and blocked at every turn
God knows all   alters all   offer up your prayer

alone and destitute in the profundity of the darkness
Hafez pray   read your Koran   do not despair

315

VIII

THE MYSTIC

You   parrot   who speak
of the mysterious   the esoteric
please God may your beak be never deprived of sugar

may your head remain green
and your heart stay blithe forever
for the elegant way you have depicted
the down of our companion

so far you have spoken in riddles
to those colleagues assembled here
for God's sake now unveil the mystery

    come boy
    throw rose-water from the bowl onto our faces
    though fortune wakes   we are drowsy still with sleep

what melody was it that the minstrel played
in our private gathering
that had drunk and sober dancing together

and with the opium the servant put in the wine
our partners have lost their turbans and their minds

    Alexander was denied the water of life
    for it cannot be obtained
    through either fear or favor

come and listen to those who suffer pain
for they say a lot in a few words

319

that Mongol idol is the foe of the true faith
and of the heart
God preserve my heart and my religion

and do not reveal the secrets of inebriation
to those who are stone cold sober
or expect a mere drawing on the wall
to tell the story of the soul

through the great good fortune of Mansur our king
Hafez has become expert in the art of verse
to his servants he acts like a lord
may the Lord of all protect him from distress

feiz: being plentiful, copious (water, etc.); being brimful or overflowing; generosity, abundance; what cannot be contained

O royal falcon
you who see far and wide
perched high on the *sedre* tree
your true nesting-place does not lie
here in these confines of adversity

I do not understand what has befallen you
in this place of snares

do you not hear the falconer's command
from the high turrets of heaven
calling you home

sedre: a heavenly tree mentioned in the Koran, beyond the reach of angels

I am slave to he
whose spiritual vocation
is untainted by any lingering attachments
under these wheeling heavens
the velvet blue of the night-sky

    bring wine   for see
    the entire edifice of our hopes
    is baseless
    as if our lives rested upon the wind

accept what is given to you
and do not knit your brow
for the portal of free will
does not open to us

do not allow events to trouble you
and remember well what I tell you
for I learned love's mysteries
from a traveller on the road

and do not expect this treacherous world
to honor its word
for it is like an old crone
who has taken a thousand men to her marriage bed

Like a compass   the heart spun in every direction
even at its center   it turned upon itself

Dawn   in the tavern   and the mysterious voice
that acts as my guide   said

come back again   you that for so long
have frequented this place
and like Jamshid drink from that visionary cup
whose rays disclose the secrets of heaven and earth

       at the tavern door the wandering *qalandars*
       pass round the imperial diadem

a brick under your head   feet on the Pleiades
see the reach of your power   the office of your glory
for we lie propped up
at the entrance to the tavern
whose roof is higher than heaven
even though its walls are low

do not venture this far without Khezr your guide
for fear of losing your way in the dark

O heart if you are granted
the suzerainty of poverty
the smallest of your provinces will extend
from the moon to the earth's foundations

       but my Lord
       what do you know of poverty
       do not give up the privileges you enjoy
       at the court of Tūrānshāh

Hafez
have you no shame at this display of greed
what have you done
to ask for this and the next world as reward

More accustomed perhaps to poetic understatement, the English-speaking reader may initially find Hafez' hyperbole way over the top; although it is curious, in my experience, how soon it comes to seem normal, natural, even necessary. Such hyperbole was already a well-established literary device long before Hafez' time. It may also reflect court life: the more exalted the personage, the more extravagant the compliment. But I wonder if it also stems from something else, difficult to put one's finger on: a need or capacity for the ideal perhaps: the call of the perfect.

When my love lifts the cup in his hand
the market in idols collapses

trembling I fell at his feet
so that he might raise me up

like a fish I slipped into the sea
so that his hook might catch me

everyone who saw the look in his eyes
said   fetch the police to detain him

happy the heart of he who like Hafez
has sampled that primordial wine

Listen to me

and bind the heart to a beloved
whose beauty is not decked out with jewelry

We come to this door not out of vainglory
but as sons of Adam
seeking refuge from his original sin

from the edge of nothingness we have found our way
to the house of love
we have made the long journey to the province of being

we glimpsed the fresh growth on the chin of the beloved
so from the gardens of paradise
we came looking for the tender shoots
of his loving-kindness

and with the treasure that Gabriel revealed
we have come begging to the palace gate

where is the anchor of your infinite pity
the vessel of your grace
for in this sea of mercy we are immersed in sin

gone is our reputation   our honor
O send the rain cloud that will wash us clean
for we stand now at the bench of our own actions

    Hafez throw off your cloak of finest pashmina
    for we join now that caravan
    where the burning fire of our sighs
    consumes everything

And if the Elder of the Magi
were to be my guide
what difference would it make

there is no head
that is not party to God's mystery

I kiss the rim   drink the wine
I have discovered   the water of life

I keep the secret   from everyone
allowing no one   to take my place

but the wine meets Those lips and turns to blood
the rose sees That face and perspires with shame

O bring the bowl   do not think of Jam
for where is Jamshid   and where is Kai

minstrel boy like the moon   play your harp well
pluck at the strings   so that I cry

hold your tongue   Hafez   for a while
and listen to the story of the tongueless *nei*

The dust of my body
　　　veils the face of my soul
blessed be the moment
　　　I remove that veil

this cage is no place
　　　for a songster like me
I shall fly to the rosebeds of heaven
　　　for I am a bird of that garden

why I came into this world
　　　or where I came from
alas I understand nothing
　　　of my own being

how can I range like a bird
　　　in the air of paradise
when my body is trapped in contingency
　　　like a prisoner nailed to a board

do not wonder at the scent of passion
　　　that rises from my heart's blood
for I am a fellow-sufferer
　　　of the musk-deer of Khotan

and do not as others would
　　　compare the gold thread of my tunic
to the candle-wick
　　　for the flame burns deep inside

come　　　relieve Hafez
　　　of his existence

for in your Presence
no one will hear him say

it is me

fanā: utter and complete destruction; annihilation; reduction or reversion to nothingness, either physical or spiritual

If you use the dust of the tavern
as *kohl* to embellish your eyes
you will be able to make out
the secret of Jamshid's cup

    do not forego wine or the sound of minstrels
    for under the great vault of the sky
    their song will drive out the sorrow from your heart

the rose of your desire will unveil itself
if you attend to it like the morning breeze
but you must resolve to take the first step
if you want to profit from love's journey

to experience that divine presence
but also to manage the things of this world
you should rely on the boundless grace
of the visionary

    the beloved's beauty is not veiled or concealed
    let the dust of the road settle   and you will see

but if you are not prepared
to abandon the house of nature
how can you embark on the spiritual way

    begging at the tavern door is an elixir
    engage in this and you will turn dust to gold

kohl: a powder used to darken the eye-lids

O heart   if you can come to know
the illumination of spiritual discipline
like the laughing candle you too can lose your head

but you who desire most of all
the cup of wine and the beloved's lip
do not aspire to any other thing

     Hafez   if you pay heed to this royal counsel
     you will travel the royal highway to the real

Their solitude is nothing less than heaven
true greatness lies in great humility

the treasures and the talismans of glory
lie in the dervishes' compassionate gaze

in the alchemy of their company is
that which transmutes base metal into gold

the sun lays down its lofty crown before them
seeing the glory of their entourage

though the armies of oppression straddle the world
their time is now for all eternity

the only wealth that does not in the end decline
to put it simply
is the wealth of the dervishes' piety

O rich man do not parade your selfishness
for all that you possess
your riches   even your head
lies under the protective wing of their holiness

the countenance which kings seek in their prayers
appears only in the mirror of their face

I am the slave of the Asaf of our times
for his outward nobility   his inner grace

Acquire the gnostic's pearl
so that you may take it with you

it is for others to leave
legacies of silver and of gold

In the time before time began
the rays of your beauty appeared

love was made manifest
and set the whole world on fire

Satan saw it
but did not comprehend

this love which is our lot
this love which falls to man

love that precludes an easy life
filling the heart with longing

love   the mystery
guarded by the invisible hand

love that confounds reason
when it goes to light its lamp

love the jealous lightning
that turns the world upside down

For weeks now I have not slept
looking for that vision
as if I had been drinking night after night
O take me to the tavern

    the walls of my cell are stained
    with my very own blood
    if you washed my body in wine
    your hands would have good reason

it is for this that the Magi
hold me in such high esteem
that in my heart there is
an inextinguishable flame

    what was it the minstrel played yesterday
    for my mind filled with longing
    as my life drained away

last night from the very depths of my being
came such expression of my love for you
that the cavity of my breast   still echoes with my passion

For years
my heart searched everywhere
for Jamshid's cup

not knowing that what it looked for
it had itself

When the weary   pursuing their quest
have come to the end of their strength
it is unchivalrous to ill-treat them

we do not expect   and you would not approve
such behavior unbecoming in a master of the way

    dark the eye not cleansed
    by the water of love's tears
    dark the heart in which
    no flame of kindness burns

seek protection under the wing of the *homāyūn*
for crow and kite dress no plumage of good fortune

if I seek my salvation in the tavern   do not censure me
for our master opines   in the cloister there is none

if there is not the ritual purity
necessary in the presence of the divine
there is no difference between the Ka'ba
and a pagan shrine

that house will not be blessed
which is not pure and chaste

    Hafez   cultivate learning and courtesy
    for in this noble gathering
    those who lack manners
    are unworthy of such company

homāyūn: **a bird of good omen which gives protection**

To be close to the heart   is to be closeted with the beloved
he who does not understand this will be denied

if my heart reveals itself by coming out
from behind the drapes of seclusion
do not upbraid it
thanks be to God it is not veiled with thought

all the Sufis retrieved the gowns they pawned for wine
mine alone remains in hock to the tavern

others got drunk and it was quickly forgotten
but all over the bazaar they still tell my tale

my dervish apparel cloaked a hundred faults
I traded it in for music and for booze
leaving me only with my infidel's belt

every drop poured out for me by that crystal hand
became pearls of tear-drops falling from my eyes

my heart alone has loved from Beginning to End
I know of no one else who has been so faithful

I have heard nothing sweeter than the song of love
which is the only reminder
we have of our lives
beneath this circling cupola of the sky

    the narcissus fell ill because it tried to compete
    with the narcissi of your eyes
    but without your artfulness it did not recover

one day   intending to return
Hafez' heart set out
to view the exhibition of your hair

but now it will be its prisoner for ever

Whatever problems of interpretation we run into, we have to keep reminding ourselves: Hafez knew what he was doing. If a word had a double meaning, he knew. If a line or a phrase was ambiguous, he knew. If a ghazal could be understood at more than one level, he knew.

I shall not forsake love
nor my beloved   nor wine
I have foresworn them a hundred times
but will not do so again

I shall not compare
the dust of my dear one's street
to the gardens of paradise
the shade of the Tuba tree
or the abode of the heavenly maidens

all the teachings of the scholars and the seers
only point the way
I have used one metaphor   and will not repeat it

how shall I know my own mind
until I find myself
in the middle of the tavern again

scolding   the cleric said   wine is forbidden
I replied to his face
I do not listen to every donkey that brays

angrily   the sheikh of the order ordered me
to forego love   .
I have no wish to quarrel with my brother
but I cannot obey

the extent of my piety is evidenced by the fact
that I do not dally with the city's beauties
on the pulpit steps

Hafez
if you reach the entrance to the Magi's house
you are on the very threshold of good fortune

do not cease to kiss the very dust at his door

Last night   before dawn   I knew deliverance
in the darkness I was given the Water of Life

my being was transformed by that manifest radiance
from the chalice of glory I was offered wine

how blessed that morning   and how happy
that night of destiny   when I was set free

for turning my face towards the mirror of beauty
I saw what it was there   that was true

if I exult now   joyful   no wonder
for I was needy and they gave me alms

the heavenly voice that brought me the good tidings
gave me the strength to suffer this world's woe

through faith
and the breath of those who rise to pray at dawn
I have been freed from the grievous bonds of time

'aql: reason; reasoning; rationality; the intellect: consistently portrayed as something limited, to be transcended, in the Divan

With the beginnings of love for you
came the beginning of unknowing

oneness with you would be
the consummation of unknowing

many there are who
plunging into the state of union
ended up in a state of unknowing

neither union itself
nor he who is united
survives knowing unknowing

show me one heart who following the true path
does not display upon his countenance
that dark unfathomable mole

whichever way I turned there came to me
voices raised
confused   amazed   wondering   questioning

because of love
Hafez' entire existence has become
root and branch

like a young tree or sapling
growing   towards unknowing

In that time without beginning
the Sultan of Eternity
gave us the treasure-trove of the sorrows of love
from the moment we turned our faces towards
this empty caravanserai

where we break our journey

I saw the green fields of the heavens
and the new moon like a sickle
my mind turned to my own fields
and the time of harvesting

I said   my star were you sleeping
when the sun rose in the east
it said do not despair
for we have Original Grace

if you ascend like Christ
pure holy and chaste
your light will light up the sun
with a hundred golden rays

and do not place your trust
in that thieving morning star
for it took away Kavous' throne
and the belt from Kai Khosrow's waist

what is the halo of the moon
or the glimmer of the Pleiades
and all the great show above
compared to the light that is love

Two paths   two ways

on the one hand   self-discipline
on the other   self-destruction

on the one   the hermit's vigil
on the other   drunken ruin

on the one   the droning sermon
on the other   the sound of the viol

on the one hand   piety
on the other   the free spirit

on the one hand   sobriety
on the other   the limpid wine

on the one hand   the dead lamp
on the other   the torch of the sun

"The heart has its reasons that the mind knows nothing of." Hafez would surely have approved of Pascal's dictum, for it conceives of the heart not simply as the seat of the emotions but as an intelligent organ, with its own logic, its own rationale, its own ways. And as the source of that movement we call love.

Last night I dreamed that the angels
were beating at the tavern gate
kneading Adam's clay
they made measures out of it

the hidden seraphims
the purest of the pure
sat down and drank with me
who beg from door to door

the angels could not bear
the weight of heaven's trust
so the lot fell to man
and this one who is insane

there is some excuse for
the unending wars of religion
for unable to see reality
people cling to illusion

God be thanked that now
there is peace between Him and me
when the maidens of heaven heard
they danced   draining their cups

fire is not that which we see
in each laugh of the candle's flame
fire is that which burns up
the harvest of the moth's being

since poets first used their pens
to comb the tresses of speech
no one like Hafez has unveiled
the complexion of our minds

356

Vainly my heart sought
among those lost souls who wander by the shore
that precious pearl which exists
outside the shell of this universe

Dawn
hail falls from the winter cloud
bring me my morning drink   and make it good

I have fallen into the ocean of I and we
bring me wine
so that I may be rescued from identity

drink the blood of the cup   for such blood is not forbidden
get down to work   for there is work to be done

boy come quick   before I am ambushed by despair
O minstrel   keep repeating
that same air

bring me my cup
for the harp leant its head on my shoulder saying
listen to this stooped old man
when he counsels you to be happy

bring me wine   so that like the *rend*
who is liberated from everything
you may hear the minstrel sing

he is self-sufficient   he needs nothing

If I listen to the objections of the pious
I shall never master the skills
of drunkenness and excess

one can forgive the moderation of the novice
but why should I
who am infamous throughout the world
think about what is proper

call me king of the headstrong
I who have nothing to my name
for in lack of reason I outdo them all

      mark your brow with the blood of my heart
      so that everyone may know
      that I who would be your sacrifice
      am an infidel

for God's sake let me be and go your way
so that you do not realize
how far I am from being a real dervish
under these clothes

      O wind
      carry to my beloved these bloodstained lines
      for those dark lashes have pierced my jugular

what business is it of any of you
whether I indulge or not

      Hafez   ever mysterious
      spirit of the age

THE MORALIST

We do not speak ill   or want what is not right
we do not sully another's gown   or embellish our own

we do not fill learned books with sophistries
or reduce life's mysteries to a pack of cards

it is wrong to judge people   rich or poor
by what they do or do not have
what matters is to avoid wrong-doing

fate will wreck the barque
of the finest   the best
do not place your trust in that undulating sea

if the king will not drain the dregs with us free spirits
we shall show no reverence for his filtered wine

if a friend is wounded by some jealous gibe
tell him we do not listen to every fool

> Hafez   if your enemy is mistaken   forget it
> but if he speaks the truth   do not reject it

X

THE POET

Again the nightingale

What need have I of society
when I have you

why should I want company
when I can be alone with you

why should I criss-cross the desert
when I know where you dwell

why should I beg when I am in
the very presence of munificence

why should I search the seas
when I have found this pearl

Unlike in my own country, for Hafez rain is always beneficent. It waters the ground and feeds the streams. It keeps the dust down and stops it blowing away so that it becomes lost forever, an idea that seems to have held a peculiar horror for him.

Muslims   once I had a heart
which I consulted when problems arose

whose counsel helped me to regain the shore
when I fell into the whirlpool of sorrows

who shared my pain   was a wise friend to me
and gave support to all the community of the heart
but which I lost in the street of my beloved

      O what a tugging of heart-strings there was then

art brings with it the pain of privation
but what petitioner
was ever more deprived than me

      be kind to this lost soul
      for once it possessed consummate skill

after love had instructed me how to speak
my words were the talking-point of every circle

      but who now can speak of Hafez' artistry
      for it has become clear to all and sundry
      he no longer cares about his poetry

Your musky curls make the violet twist with envy
your enticing smile tears the veil of the rosebud off

O sweet-scented rose   do not drive your nightingale
to burn himself out
for he prays for you faithfully night after night

I who would weary of the speech of angels
put up with the chatter of this world because of you

love of your countenance is my true nature
the dust at your gate my paradise

passion for you is my destiny
in your happiness I find my repose

the beggar's coat may have treasures up its sleeve
but whoever begs from you becomes a king

my eyes are the throne on which your image sits
O liege of mine
I pray that you never leave your rightful place

of the ferment of love's wine
my mind will not be free
till my passionate head is dust at your palace gate

    your cheek my cool meadow   in the springtime of beauty
    the eloquent Hafez   songbird of your house

See how one poem
traverses space and time

how this child of one night
accomplishes a year's journey

For some time now
I have been of service in the tavern
in my humble attire
attending to those more fortunate than myself

I lie in ambush waiting for the chance
to catch some strutting pheasant in my snare

     the public preacher does not have
     even a sniff of the truth
     mark my words
     for I say them to his face   not behind his back

like the wind   fitfully
I make my way towards the street of my companion
asking my fellow-travellers
to help me realize my great endeavor

no longer will the dust of your alleyway
have to put up with my importuning
for you have shown me so many kindnesses
my love
that I will stop whining

     the beloved's hair
     lies like a snare across our path
     and that glance is shot like a bolt of calamity

     remember   O heart   how often I warned you of this

O you who in your mercy   veils our faults
hide from the gaze of those who wish me ill
these audacious thoughts I have when I am alone

in public a divine
a drunkard in our private gatherings

see
my effrontery   observe
the artifice with which I fool the populace

Remember when you stole a glance at me
the impression of your love could be seen on my face

remember when your reproachful looks half-killed me
your sweet words revived me like Jesus' miraculous lips

remember that intimate drinking party at dawn
numbering just you and me   and God with us

remember when your cheeks set light
to the taper of joy
the intrepid moth was this singed heart of mine

remember how in that decorous gathering
the raucous laughter came only from the wine

and when the red wine smiled at us in our cups
what stories passed between your lips and mine

remember when my Moon fastened his helmet
from his stirrup the new moon raced to tell the whole world

remember when I sat sodden in the tavern
what I lack now in the mosque I had then

remember how your corrections permitted Hafez
to string every loose pearl that he possessed

O sovereign beauty   redress my loneliness
without you my heart begins to fail   come back

the garden rose does not stay fresh forever
while you have power   help those who stand in need

last night I complained to the wind about your hair
it said you are wrong   dismiss that somber thought

a hundred elusive breezes
writhe in the chains of those tresses
O foolish heart   see what your friend is like
and do not pretend you are some airy steed

separation from you has so weakened me
that I have little endurance left to draw on

    O Lord to whom might I make the point
    that in this world
    that beauty which is all around   shows its face to none

boy
without your face   the rose-beds lack all color
bring back the grace of the tree-top to the garden

the pain you cause me is my medicine
in my lonely bed
your memory my companion in solitude

    in the compass of fate we stand at the axis of submission
    subject to what you in your wisdom decide

true liberation is liberation from the self
self-regard apostasy in our religion

these blue enamel heavens have seared my soul
bring me wine so that I may
dissolve these troubles in an enamelled bowl

Hafez the night of separation is over
the sweet scent of union here

blessed be your joy   O my demented lover

Hafez' home is now
the court of the emperor

the heart has returned
to he who held it
the soul to the one it longed for

A nightingale was holding in its beak
the petal of a brightly colored rose
but even with this beautiful token
in its possession   was crying its heart out

I asked why   in the very eye of union
it lamented in such a way and it replied

    it is precisely because of this manifestation
    of my beloved that I am distraught

    if my friend would not join me   I cannot complain
    for he is a mighty king and would be ashamed
    to be seen with a beggarman

    neither flirtation nor supplication
    have any effect upon my comely companion
    happy is he who obtains any favors
    from those with such airs and graces

arise and let us dedicate our lives
to the pen of that great artist
who has created all these marvellous images
within the compass of this earthly circle

and if you are a pilgrim on love's road
forget about reputation
for the good Sheikh San'an pawned his robes to a barman

    blessed be that gentle *qalandar* as he goes
    wandering here and there on his journey
    telling the praises of God with an infidel's girdle

under the palace roof
of he who resembles a being from heaven
Hafez' eyes

are fixed on those gardens beneath which rivers flow

For many years now
I have followed the path of freedom
so that as wisdom decrees
I might imprison worldly cupidity

I did not find my own way
to the roost of the fabled *anqa*
but only under the hoopoe's guiding wing

the quest for fulfilment
broke all the rules
thus I found peace in the chaos of that hair

give shade to my wounded heart O you who are
the very treasure of what I desire
for I have reduced my own house to a ruin
through longing for you

I vowed to stop kissing the lips of the serving-boy
now I bite my own for listening to such fools

whether you drink or not is up to you
or me
whatever eternity's sultan said   I did

I hope through grace to get to paradise
though I have often kept the tavern door
and if I have consoled my old head
with the company of some young Joseph
it was the price
of putting up with living in this hole

no hafez under the curving niche of the heavens
has known the joy that I have known
from the blessing of the Koran

and if I sit at the top table
because of the treasures of my verse
it is no wonder
as for years I have served my lord the treasurer well

and indentured myself to past masters of the divan

pardē: a curtain, not covering a window but dividing two spaces, the inner and outer, demarcating the difference between the private, intimate, hidden world and the open, public realm

For a long time I have not heard from my heart's keeper
he has not written a word nor sent a greeting

I sent him a hundred missives
but that king of cavaliers
has dispatched no messenger or message here

no one with the deportment of
a strutting partridge   elegant gazelle
has come my way
I who am feral now   irrational

he knew that the bird of my heart
was about to take flight
but did the chain of his script restrain it   no

   no wonder I cry out
   for that tipsy sweet-lipped boy who fills the cups
   knew I was drinking and did not fill me up

and no matter how much I boasted about
his grace and favor   and my situation
I have heard nothing regarding my own position

   Hafez know your place
   and keep your opinions to yourself

   you have no reason to complain
   kings do not communicate with minions

In the studio of my eyes I drew your face
though I had never seen anyone else like you

and although I shared the reins with the north wind
in hot pursuit
I could not catch even the dust of your graceful movement

it is the fault of your dark eyes
and graceful neck
that like the wild gazelle I flee human company

how many tears have I shed
in the hope of drinking nectar from your fountain

from your wine-dispensing lips
how many imitations have I bought
how many darts have your keen glances
aimed at my wounded heart

worn out
how many loads have I borne to the end of your road

O morning breeze
bring me a speck of dust from that alleyway
because in that earth
my nostrils scent the blood of a wounded heart

by my head passed a swathe of air
and at its sudden fragrance   like a rosebud
I bared my suffering breast

in the night of your hair I abandoned hope of life's day
and dismissed any thought of fulfilling
my longing for the circle of your mouth

by the dust of your feet and the gift of sight I swear
that without your countenance
I have no brightness in the lamps of my eyes

O heart do not let
the taunts of those who are envious
disconcert you

listen to them again
and you might learn something

My sense of impotence weighs me down
the stature of others puts me to shame

I shall lose my mind to love
unless I am taken in hand
and bound by one whose hair has the strength of chains

    ask of my eyes the state of the universe
    for from night to morning I do nothing but count the stars

    but gratefully I kiss the lip of the cup
    for it has revealed the mystery of time to me

I am thankful that my forearm
does not have strength enough to do others harm
and it is no more than gratitude demands
if the wine-sellers are the object of my prayers

with a head as sore as Hafez   still
I trust in the mercy of the Head of all

    but you
    you would not raise me from the dust
    even if I wept pearls   not tears

O Lord under the influence of which star
is that blessed Night of Power which initiates say
falls tonight

so that the hands of the unworthy
should not reach to touch your hair
each heart trapped in its ringlets cries out   Lord
Lord

I lie half-dead
at the bottom of the well of your dimple
while thousands bend their necks before
the elegance of your throat

the moon mirrors the face
of my chevalier
and the crown of the noonday sun
is dust beneath the hooves of his mounted steed

the sun is in a fever every day
longing for the glistening sweat of his cheek

I am not about to abandon
the ruby-red lips of my beloved
nor the cup of wine
understand   my puritan friend   these are my religion

he who fires arrows at my heart
from beneath his drooping lids
still nourishes my soul with his fleeting smile

the Water of Life flows
from the beak of Hafez' eloquence
God what quenching comes
from the black crow of his pen

Happy the day I move on   from this desolate staging-post
in search of my love   and comfort for my soul

and although I know that a stranger
may not find his way
I shall be guided by the scent of that flowing hair

though like the morning breeze
I have a weak body and feeble heart
I shall set off determined to find that graceful cypress

if my heart is seized with terror at Alexander's prison
I shall gather my things and go to Solomon's kingdom

and if like a pen I have to walk on my head
I shall do so with teardrops falling from my eyes

I swear that if ever I am set free
from this travail
I shall head for the tavern door   chanting ghazals

in my longing for you   like a mote dancing
I shall make my way to the edge of that shining sun

 the thieving Arabs show no pity for
 the heavily-laden pilgrim
 O pious Persians come to my aid
 so that I may travel safely and at ease

and if like Hafez   I find no way out of this desert
I shall follow in the train of the Asaf of our days

Let me teach you about
the Alchemy of Felicity

stay out   stay well out of bad company

Although everything I do
has got caught up in the knots of your curls
I hope for some undoing through your kindness

do not attribute the flush on my cheeks to joy
for as in a wine bowl
the blood of my heart is reflected on the surface

the musicians' melodies will transport me
out of my skin
alas if then I am not here to pay court

I am that magical poet
who with his incantations
draws all the sweetness from the reed of his pen

we trudge through the desert filled with a hundred hopes
O guide of lost hearts do not let me down

since I cannot expect   O east wind
to see you as you pass
how then can I ask you to ask my friend

with the yarns he spun me
my good fortune was lulled
where is the happy breeze that will rouse it again

each night all night
I stand guard at the sanctuary of my heart
letting in only my thoughts of you

yesterday you expressed the view
that Hafez was all show
where can I turn to now   but the dust at your gate

Quite a few of Hafez' ghazals lament the passage of time, the loss of youth and onset of old age, often with a valedictory ring. There is of course no guarantee that Hafez wrote these in his declining years; it was a standard literary theme which he may have chosen simply to demonstrate his poetic prowess at one stage or another. However, I do sometimes wonder how he felt towards the end, looking back on a relatively long life, with all that happened in it. And it is then that I realize, with a start, that despite living with him all this time, I hardly know him.

O dawn breeze if you pass
by the banks of the Aras river
pause to kiss the earth of that valley
and perfume your breath

I dispatch a hundred greetings every second
to the beautiful Salma
whose encampment you will find there
filled with the camel-drivers' shouts
and the tinkling of camel-bells

kiss the camel-litter of my beloved   and trembling explain
how I am consumed by absence

    O kind one   come to my rescue   hear my cry

I who treated the lessons of the wise
like the speech of the rebeck
have had my ears boxed by separation
which is lesson enough for me now

    do not be afraid to enjoy
    the pleasures of darkness in this city of love
    for the night-birds and the nightwatchman are friends

love's play is no game   heart give it your head
otherwise love's ball will not be struck
by the polo-stick of desire

rebeck: a bowed, three-stringed instrument

the heart yearns to give up its soul
to the inebriated eyes of the beloved
whereas the sober-minded individual
surrenders his will to no one

      while the parrots profit from being in sugarland
      the wretched fly belabors his head in frustration

all that I ask now is that the name of Hafez
should come to the tongue-tip of His Majesty's pen

And how would it have been
if the sweetheart's heart had been sweet

if it had been   we would not be as we are

if fate had raised my head and cherished me
my seat of honor would be the dust on your steps

since I do not even dream of you
what prospect is there of our being together
deprived of the one   surely I should have the other

and if one was to estimate the total value
of the wind-borne fragrance of your curls
each tip would have to be priced at a thousand souls

    O Lord
    how could the check for my happiness have bounced
    if it had been guaranteed against misfortune

how I wish you might appear from behind the curtain
like a teardrop through a veil   so that
your dictates might flow freely before my eyes

    if the way to the center of love's circle
    had not been barred
    Hafez' spinning head would never move from there

I do not know why the turtledove laments
by the side of the stream

unless like me   it sorrows   night and day

Veil the rose-petal with the hyacinth
that is
cover the blush of your cheeks with your dark curls
and annihilate a world

teasingly
open the narcissi of your sleepy eyes
and consign the narcissus itself to embittered slumber

wipe the perspiration from your brow
filling the garden on every side with rose-water
like the containers of our sight

the season of the rose   like life   hurries on
boy   hurry   circulate the rose-red wine

smell the scent of the violet and caress the hair
of your beloved
note the tulip's hue   and resolve to drink your fill

since it is your custom to slay your admirers
consort with my enemies   repudiate me

open your eyes and look
at the wine-glass surface
and see how our lives are founded on a bubble

    Hafez seeks to be at one with you
    by way of prayer
    Lord grant the wishes of the troubled heart

khosh: pleasing, pleasant, pleasurable; delightful, sweet, good; occurs over 200 times in the ghazals and still a common word in everyday Persian.

If that Turk from Shiraz
would take my heart in hand
I would cede whole cities
    Bokhara   Samarkand
for that Indian beauty spot

     boy   bring the dregs of the wine
     for in paradise you will not see the like
     of the rose-garden of Mosalla
     or the banks of Ruknabad

       alas these sweet teasing gypsies
       have sown confusion in this town
       robbing our hearts of equanimity
       like the Turks devour a spread

what need has my perfect companion
of my imperfect love
what need has such a face of beautification

     come speak of minstrels and wine   and less of fate
     for no wise man has ever unpicked that knot

     or will

now I understand how the love
of the daily-growing beauty of Joseph
drew Zuleikha out from behind her modest veil

you have spoken ill of me   God forgive you
yet I am pleased
harsh answers seem sweet on your lips

O you who are dearer to me
than my own soul
pay heed
for gilded youth values the counsel of elders
more than its own life

      Hafez   you have strung the pearls of your ghazal
      declaim it well
      so that the heavens may scatter upon your verse
      the glittering necklace of the Pleiades

Hafez   the season of the rose
has once again come round

enough of this spirituality

take this world's cash in hand
and do not ask how or why

I drink in your drunken eyes
as drunk you make your entrance
to the temple of wine

in the hoof of your steed
I descry the shape of the new moon

beside you the tall pine stands diminished

if your perfume is sweet it is because
it has been sprinkled upon your hair
and if your black tincture is arched
it is because it has been applied
to the bow of your eyebrow

when you stand up to go
the candles of our hearts melt down
but when you sit down again   a cry goes up
from the assembled company

in the end   how can I speak of you
when I know nothing of myself
but how can I not   when my eyes fall on you there

    come back   so that my life may come back
    even though the spent arrow   does not return

Do not become beholden to others
for their favors

for in this world and the next
the grace of God
and the king's largesse are enough

I see no end to the dolor of time
no remedy for this but purple wine

I shall not stop patronizing the Magian inn
why   because for me that is the best plan

in my parlous state   nobody will give me a drink
see how everyone in this world is heartless

do not take the elevation of the sun in the cup
as a prognostication of a pleasant life
why   because I can see nothing of the sort
in the horoscope

the mark of the people of God is to be a lover
keep that to yourself
for I see no sign of it in the sheikhs of this city

and do not ask me to describe my beloved's waist
fine as a hair   by which I am bound
for it is so small I cannot see myself there

since your tall form left
the river bank of my gaze
in place of the cypress I see only flowing water

and pity my bedazzled eyes
that these two mirrors do not show your face

    I shall not abandon the ship of Hafez' art
    for in this ocean I can see
    no other freight of words that transports the heart

I know nothing of Alexander
Darius

their story

ask me only to speak of love and fidelity

May the peace of God   so long as night succeeds night
and the lute strings resonate

be upon the valley of Arak and those who live there
and that house in Lawa high above the dunes

I voice a prayer for all who are travelers
strangers in this world
I pray assiduously   constantly

    do not weep   O heart   for in the chains of that hair
    to be confused is yet to be composed

I die of longing and want only to know
when that joyful herald will bring me news of meeting

    O God   with your boundless grace
    watch over him at each stage in his journey

my devotion to you consoles me
every moment of the day
and the thought of you accompanies me everywhere

the line of down on your cheek
adds a hundredfold to your beauty
may you live for a hundred glorious sunlit years

let the small mote
at the center of my heart
be filled with passion till the resurrection

and let us praise the masterful painter
who delineates that crescent shape around the moon

where could I find a king like you to serve
I who am reckless   infamous   a *rend*

as long as you are what you are
who cares about wealth or status

    God knows Hafez' mind
    he need not answer thus to anyone else

I have come, without realizing it, to think of Hafez more and more as a dramatist rather than a poet, in the sense that he stands somewhere behind his work, deploying his tropes and themes, elusive (but commanding) to the end.

All that is produced
by the immense workshop of the universe
amounts to nothing

break out the wine
for all the trappings of this world mean nothing

the heart's only desire
is for true communion
without that   heart and soul are nothing

do not lead your life in the hope of finding shade
under the trees of heaven   for if you look closely
O flowing cypress of mine
it is nothing

and you my puritan friend
do not imagine that you are safe
from the machinations of fate
for the distance between cloister and tavern
is as nothing

salvation comes
without blood sweat and tears
a paradise gained through work and striving
is nothing

all we have is a few days' grace
in this stopping-place
enjoy your time here   for time itself is nothing

boy   seize your chance
as we wait on the shores of the sea of oblivion
for the space between shore and sea
is nothing

    Hafez has become a celebrity
    but for the true *rend*   success and failure mean nothing

Even if like the lily
Hafez had ten tongues

like the rosebud   in your presence
his lips would be sealed

A bloody business   these musky curls
the faintest scent of which
sets hearts racing

    boy   bring me some wine
    so that I may console myself
    about love's travails
    and if my Master tells me to
    pour it over my prayer-carpet
    for he knows what love's wayfarer should do

what respite do we have
here in this stopping place   this halt
what tenure of pleasure

    nothing lasts   the caravan moves on
    nothing remains

and what is more
because of my self-indulgence
my reputation has gone
and my secrets will soon be out
for I have become
the talking-point of every gathering

    how can those who stand carefree on the shore
    comprehend
    the dark   the waves   the terrors of the sea

Hafez stay
do not absent yourself   even for a moment
if you wish to be received   into that presence

and when in the end you find what you desire
forget the world   for that is everything

I am a Sufi
but of the Order of the next world

for now
I bide my time in the Magian hostelry

The musk-laden morning wind will come again
the old world will become young again

the Judas tree will offer its purple cup
to the jasmine
and the narcissus' gaze fall on the anemone

after the long tyranny of absence
the nightingale
will fly clamoring to the court of the rose

    if I quit the mosque for the tavern do not reproach me
    for the sermon is tedious and time is short
    if you put back today's pleasures until tomorrow
    who will stand surety for your bet

    and do not hand in your cup in the month of Shaban
    for you will not see the sun of wine again
    till the end of Ramadan

the rose is precious   treasure its company
it came to us one way and will leave another

O minstrel play something new   sing a ghazal
entertain our intimate gathering with your art

for how much longer will you speak to us
of what has passed   and what is still to come

    it was for you   Hafez entered this world
    step forward to bid him farewell   for he must depart

**shaban: the eighth month of the Islamic calendar which precedes the month
of Ramadan when Muslims fast between sunrise and sunset**

Most of us will have brought some expectations, some preconceptions to a reading of the ghazals, preconceptions perhaps of which we are barely aware and that surface only in and through our encounter with the text. So a good question might be: what is it in Hafez that surprises us? And why?

The flaming torch of the sun
that rises in the eastern sky
is lit from the hidden fire inside my breast

When shall I be one with you   so that finally I may arise
soaring clear of the world's snares   like a bird of paradise

if you give me leave   I will give you my oath
that if you were to take me as your slave
I would give up lordship over the earth

O God from your guiding clouds   send rain down
before I turn to dust and cannot be found

O love come sit with music and wine by my grave
so that at your scent
dancing I may rise out of the ground

rise up before us   you who move sweetly
so that moving and circling   we may abandon ourselves

though I am old   hold me one night in your arms
so that young again   I may rise at dawn from your side

    and in the end
    let Hafez have one final glimpse of you
    so that he may arise and leave this world behind

NOTES

BIBLIOGRAPHY

ACKNOWLEDGMENTS

I am an Irish poet who happens to know Persian. In 1964, a year after leaving Cambridge, I took up a three-year job as a lecturer in English Literature at the Faculty of Letters in Isfahan. I knew almost nothing about Iran, having gone there mainly from a desire to see the world: well, half of it anyway, since the Iranians have an expression *esfahān nesfe jahān* (Isfahan is half the world) which dates from its heyday as the capital in the seventeenth century; and it remains a remarkably beautiful city. Once there, however, I quickly became immersed in this fascinating country with its proud, passionate people and ancient, complex culture.

I set about learning the language and in due course, with the help of local writers, began translating some of the "new poetry" (*she'r-e no*) of the 20th century. In my third year, however, I turned to the classics, and made some translations which were published soon after and much later anthologized (Squires, 1968; Washburn and Major, 1998). After I returned to Europe things took a different turn, and Iran and its poetry receded though never wholly disappeared from my life.

To cut a long story short, I took early retirement from my academic career (in a quite different field) ten years ago and decided to return to this unfinished business, and to Hafez who presents perhaps the ultimate challenge for the translator in this field. The paradox is that while there is an extensive literature in English about his work, the work itself has proved difficult (some would say impossible) to translate, despite attempts going back to the 18th century. There exist literal, and faithful translations of the ghazals, but inevitably these do not bring across much of their poetic quality. It is hard therefore for those who do not know Persian to understand why Hafez is held in such high regard in his own country.

I discovered, along the way, that I was not the first Irishman in the field. In 1848, James Clarence Mangan, one of the best-known 19th century Irish poets, published an Ode of Hafiz, probably derived from German translations which he had come across. Soon after, he was accosted by a scholar who said: Mangan, this is not Hafez, this is you; to which Mangan replied: well, it's half-his. I have tried to be much more faithful to the original, but my over-riding aim as a poet has been to do justice to the poetry of the ghazals. The notes that follow set out my general approach, discuss some of the problems involved, and provide detailed cross-references to the text.

Hafez is perhaps the best-loved but also most problematic of all the great Persian poets. It is said that if an Iranian household had only two books, they would be the Koran and the Divan; and the latter is even used for divination, by letting a page fall open at random, and interpreting what is found there. Moreover, Hafez is revered by all manner of people: he appeals to young and old, conservative and liberal; he is part of what it is to be Iranian, at home or in exile. In the view of one writer, his work has been raised to the status of a "national scripture" (Ferdowsi, 2008). He has had his critics, both in his own and recent times, but they have been few and far between.

While Zarrinkub (1349) among others has attempted to reconstruct a biography of Hafez, the general though not universal view is that our knowledge of his life is "extremely sketchy" (Khorramshahi and Yarshater, 2002 updated 2012). Even the dates of his birth (1315/17?) and death (1389/90?) are uncertain. Although his family were probably originally from Isfahan, he grew up, lived and died in his beloved city of Shiraz, capital of the south-central province of Fars or Pars, from which we get the words Farsi and Persia (p and f were close in the language). Although he lived in the century between the two major Mongol invasions, there were frequent local wars and changes of regime. Despite these, Shiraz had a vibrant cultural life. The name Hafez is in fact a title, given to those who know the Koran by heart and can thus recite it on public occasions, so he would probably have had a formal religious role. From the dedications in many of his poems, we know that he was part of the court circle and close to some of the rulers, but he may have associated with other social and religious groups also. He left Shiraz for central Iran on at least one occasion, probably because he fell temporarily from favor, but although he was invited to foreign courts in Baghdad and India when his fame spread, he never went. That is about all we know for certain, although there are numerous other stories about his life.

Hafez came near the end of what is sometimes described as the golden age of Persian poetry, and one finds many echoes in his work of previous poets such as Nezāmi, Sanā'i, Attār and Sa'di (Khorramshāhi (1387) cross-references these thoroughly). He wrote almost all his poetry in the *ghazal* form. Although *ghazal* is an Arabic word meaning a short love lyric, the form developed most fully in Persian poetry, where it diversified to encompass a range of themes and tones.

The ghazal may have evolved out of part of the older multi-part *qasidē* (ode); the other main poetic forms were the *rubāī* (plural *rubāiyāt*, quatrain) and the *masnavī*, the narrative or epic. The ghazal can vary in length but in the Divan consists typically of about seven couplets. These follow a number of strict metrical patterns and are linked by a monorhyme of the end syllables of each couplet which runs right through the poem. (There is an internal rhyme within the first couplet, creating the AABA form found also in the quatrain, familiar to us from Fitzgerald's *Khayyām*). The couplet is never broken down and is always self-contained, without enjambment. This makes it difficult to know if someone else inserted one later. The final couplet (*maqta'*) refers to the poet by name (*takhalos*) as if by a third person or the audience, and acts as a kind of *envoi*. Hafez' work was not fully collected until well after his death and although there are now several well-established editions, textual variants and problems are legion: one estimate is that 80% of the ghazals have at least five variants in terms of the number or order of lines, let alone words (Farzad, 1978). Farzad also estimates that of the 839 ghazals usually attributed to Hafez only 491 are authentic. That figure is also disputed, although it is close to the 486 in the Khānlari edition I have used. Within the Divan (which means selected or collected poems) the poems are ordered alphabetically by the end of the first line.

Why is Hafez loved and revered by Persian-speakers all over the world? To try to answer this question, it is useful to distinguish between what a poem says and what it does (Squires, 2010). The distinction is not clear-cut, but where the first relates to the meaning or interpretation of the text, the second points towards the poem as an event or experience. Hafez' popularity stems partly from what his poems say, although here again there is a paradox. It is difficult to paraphrase or summarize his ideas and in purely intellectual terms his writing is not particularly striking or original. What he has to say about, for example, free will and predestination or spirituality and hypocrisy was not unusual for his times; moreover he is not always consistent and one comes across apparently contradictory views or stances in different ghazals. There is a thread, as in most Persian poets, of moral guidance and wisdom, which Iranians still refer to and value. But what the poems "say" lies at a deeper, less explicable level, in the expression of the fundamental experiences of longing, separation, happiness, fulfilment or despair, and above all our basic human need for transcendence, for something beyond the self. To use Hafez' own terms, the poems relate not so much to the mind as to the heart; not the Romantic heart as the seat of the emotions, but Pascal's heart which has its own kind of knowing.

This in turn relates to what the poems do, what kind of linguistic event they constitute, how we experience them, and involves analyzing how they move, their pace, dynamics and momentum, patterns and variations, twists and turns, flow and counter-flow, tension and resolution. Both the Persian and foreign literature on Hafez is largely concerned with the exegesis of meanings, and is thin on this kind of aesthetic or prosodic analysis, often contenting itself with ritual references to the beauty or skill of his writing, but one has only to hear Iranians declaiming or singing Hafez to know just how important it is in the experience of the poems. It is of course impossible for the non-Persian speaker to grasp this fully, but perhaps some sense of it may be gained by taking just one couplet at the beginning of a well-known ghazal (KH93) with a literal English translation beneath:

> *Zān*   *yār-e*   *del navāzam*   *shokrīst*
>   *bā*   *shekāyat*
> About that   friend/beloved   who caresses my heart   there is thanks
>   with   complaint

The line is kick-started by the preposition, which with its *z* consonant and long *ā* sound creates an immediate aural momentum. The long *ā* (the longest of all Persian vowels, although the long *ū* is also resonant in words like *dūsh*, meaning last night) recurs and links the first three main words, with the phrase closed neatly by the enclitic pronoun *am* (my). We might expect the line to continue with this uncomplicated praise of the beloved but no: with the alliteration and symmetry of *shokrīst bā shekāyat* we are immediately confronted with paradox, irony, contradiction. Much of the pleasure of Hafez' poetry lies in such sudden twists and turns, such reversals; the world is not simple; one can rarely drop one's intellectual guard. Also, the last word sets up the expectation, which comes from the opening lines of Rumi's famous *Masnavi*, of a rhyme with *hekāyat* in the next line, which duly arrives:

> *gar*   *nokte dān-e*   *'eshqī*   *khosh*   *beshno*   *īn*   *hekāyat*
> if   you are an expert   in love   carefully   listen to   this   tale

Nokte-dān (literally knowing the finer points) is a phrase typically used in scholarly argument, but here it is applied to love, and not just the Koranic *hub* but the full-blooded emotional commitment of *'eshq,* which is closer to the Greek *eros.* This is another characteristic of Hafez' verse: the mixing of registers, here of the cognitive-analytic and emotional-affective. Are we thinking or feeling? Hafez' language engages both. The if/then structure of this line, which is common in the ghazals, exemplifies the syntactic strength of the writing; another common pattern involves the first line in a couplet ending with "but" *(valī)* which then leads on to the complementary second line; other patterns involve question and answer, or command and response. This line again falls naturally into two parts, allowing a particular emphasis at the beginning of the second half on *khosh,* which is a common adverb meaning "well." The two "o" vowel sounds link the adverb and verb here, and *hekāyat* at the end whets our appetite for what follows.

There are other interesting aspects of Hafez' prosody. Arabic words are formed by permutating a basic root (usually of three consonants) and Hafez plays on these permutations often within the same couplet, creating both aural and semantic similarity and difference. (This was a common feature of Persian poetry. Meskoob [1371: 171] quotes a line of Manoochehri which goes: *tō ma'shooq-e mamshooq mā 'āsheqāni.*) English has nothing like this, but like English, Persian has two main sources, and Hafez exploits both older Persian words and their Arabic equivalents to give linguistic variety. Rather like the contrast between concrete Anglo-Saxon and abstract Latinate words, Hafez sometimes juxtaposes the shorter, concrete Persian with the often longer, abstract Arabic, although some of the key terms in his poems come from the former, and he uses some words which reach right back to the very origins of Iranian culture. He will happily play on the double meanings of other words. Frequently he creates aural trails in his poems which run through the lines and across the couplet breaks. Since in Persian the verb comes at the end of the sentence, the rhymes are often verbs, and since (like English) Persian has a lot of compound verbs this gives a great deal of flexibility. In sum, it is Hafez' control and use of language which gives his poetry its special aural quality and makes it so memorable. Such language goes deep in us, and we are often hard put to explain why it resonates in the way it does.

There is also a historical, cultural aspect to Hafez' language. Persian, although it contains many Arabic words, is quite different from Arabic (or Turkish), and in a country with historically shifting borders language has long been a defining element of national identity (Meskoob, 1992). Persian/Farsi has

427

changed remarkably little over time, so that the modern Iranian can read this text written around the time of Chaucer almost without pause, though the accretion of meanings over so many centuries makes the translator's job even more difficult. Hafez' use of the language is exemplary: simple yet powerful and graceful. Khorramshahi notes the strength and ease of his syntax, his use of conversational phrases, his musicality (Khorramshahi, 1387: 32–33). Hafez does not employ a particularly large vocabulary, nor is he unusually convoluted: his work belongs to the simpler "Khorasani" style rather than the later, more ornate "Indian" one. Indeed the fascination of it lies partly in the way such linguistic discipline can be so generative semantically. It is not surprising that many of his lines have entered popular memory, and are quoted on a daily basis. When once I asked an Iranian friend why Hafez has such a special place in their hearts, she replied simply: because he is one of us. While the academic literature is largely concerned with the interpretation of meanings, for many ordinary Iranians it is perhaps his style that speaks so directly and personally to them.

"Style" here is not some decorative adjunct but part and parcel of what the poetry is, and needs to be seen in the broader context of Persian culture. There has always been a powerful aesthetic impulse in that culture which seems to have survived the many historical changes it has undergone. This is perhaps most obvious in Persian art and architecture, but it is evident also in the music, which is less well known in the west. It finds expression in dress and manners too. And of course in the long tradition of Persian poetry, of which Hafez is one of the supreme exponents.

That said, he remains a deeply problematic poet. Since there is no definitive edition of his work there are, as noted above, many textual difficulties, above all in the differing order of couplets in different editions. However, the main problem lies in the interpretation of his poetry, which leads to sharp differences between scholars. The writing on Hafez is all too often dogmatic and based on limited samples; indeed one would not guess from some commentators that a different perspective was possible at all. Some scholars see him as a worldly, by turns lyrical, didactic or ironic, court poet. Others see him as an otherworldly symbolist, who belongs to the already well-established Persian tradition of mystical writing. Some interpret his work primarily in moral or ethical terms, while some, in particular Soviet scholars, view him as a radical even revolutionary thinker, a fearless critic of hypocrisy, conformity and the other ills of his times.

Some read him as a straightforward advocate of the joys of love and wine. Others again see him as a celebrant of the continuity of Iranian identity: more than any other poet except Ferdowsi he evokes the ancient or legendary past. One even comes across claims that he was a closet Zoroastrian. Western readers should not be lulled by the stylized, hyperbolic or seemingly precious nature of the writing. There is nothing anodyne about Hafez. He is controversial, provocative and dangerously free like the figure of the *rend* he invokes.

While the other great Persian poets are all complex in their own ways, we know roughly where we are with them. However, with Hafez there is a fundamental ambiguity and elusiveness, and I have seen it as my job to reproduce this rather than try to impose a single, unified interpretation. A translator has to respect the surface of the text, as well as being aware of its depths, and the Hafez that appears in my translation is a multi-faceted, varied, even inconsistent one. It may be that he wrote differently at different stages in a creative life of perhaps 50 years, or that he responded as a professional poet to the varied requirements of different audiences. One can only arrive at a singular interpretation of his work by decoding the poems consistently either in terms of spiritual meanings or court allusions, and down-playing or ignoring the other aspects of his writing that don't fit the paradigm.

This in turn relates to the paradox of his popularity. If Hafez were simply a 14th century court poet it is unlikely that he would still appeal to so many people in the way he does: how many European court poets are read today? Likewise, if he was essentially a mystical poet, his popularity might be great but the reasons for it would be clear, as is the case with Rumi. Hafez' popularity is and has always been widespread, going well beyond Iran: one of his main commentators was a Bosnian Ottoman (Sūdi, died c.1597) and when the great Urdu poet Iqbal published a poem in 1915 attacking him ("Beware of Hafiz the drinker/His cup is full of the poison of death" [Ernst, 1997: 201]) it created such a storm in the Indian sub-continent that he subsequently had to withdraw it.

However it is not just the extent but the nature of Hafez' appeal which is hard to explain. True, his poetry is much more varied than selections of 30 or 50 ghazals would suggest; not only do we have the core themes of love and wine, but poems (or more usually parts of poems) about friendship, exile, rivalry, hypocrisy, authority, freedom, old age and the passing of time. We have panegyrics praising the ruler and vilifying his enemies, poems about morality, poems offering spiritual guidance, poems of ecstasy and spiritual awakening. Perhaps because of the range of his work, he seems to be all things to all people; his pull does not appear to diminish with time; he inspires contemporary poets and artists in other fields; and older Iranians often seem drawn back to him towards the end of their lives. It is possible that people now read things into him and get things from him which he never intended. However, I suspect Hafez was well aware of what he was doing.

TRANSLATING HAFEZ

If his work is difficult to interpret, it is doubly difficult to translate. There are various problems. To begin with, the Divan is simply a collection of poems, arranged in alphabetical order. We can only date a minority of these, and there are very few biographical pegs to hang them on; in any case he is not a personal, autobiographical poet. There is thus no obvious structure for presenting his work. This would not matter in a small sample, but there is a real danger that in any larger collection the reader will simply get lost.

Initially I translated a set of about 60 ghazals, but while some people thought they read well enough in English, I sensed that they did not bring out the various facets of Hafez that I was beginning to recognize. Gradually, and pragmatically, I began to arrange them in sections. It must be emphasized that the ten sections I have finally arrived at are not watertight. Hafez does not compartmentalize like that, and many of the key themes and images run right through the Divan.

A second problem has to do with the apparent lack of internal coherence or "organic unity" in the ghazals. Western readers who come across them for the first time may be put off by the disjointedness of the poems, the jumps between one couplet and the next, or sudden changes of course in the middle of a ghazal. Losensky (1998b: 167) argues that "Hafez's poetic argument proceeds by the paratactic juxtaposition of different voices and points of view." By contrast, one of Hafez' severest Iranian critics, Kasravi (2006), put the incoherence down simply to the search for rhyme. Ever since one early translator in the 18th century (Sir William Jones) characterized the ghazals as "orient pearls at random strung" this has been a major issue in the critical literature (see in particular Bausani [1958], Hillmann [1976] and Meisami [2003]) with some commentators arguing that the ghazal is constructed on a "molecular" basis of free-standing couplets, and others arguing that there is in fact an underlying logic and progression, if one knows what to look for. While some western writers have made a strong case for a "unified" reading, it is worth pointing out that one of the first modern Iranian books on Hafez broke the ghazals down completely into single or small groups of couplets (Hoozhīr, 1307/1928) which exemplified specific themes. Lāhūri's extensive commentary (Lāhūri, 1384) is indexed only by couplet, not by poem. And Khorramshahi (1387: 34) argues that Hafez revolutionized the ghazal partly by giving "independence" to each couplet. While this may sometimes create problems of "coherence," prosodically it means that the poems are continually re-launched, giving them a powerful dynamic and momentum: they do not stall or sag.

My view now is that this discussion is over-generalized and over-polarized. As my translations show, there are some ghazals which are manifestly "coherent" in our terms. There are many more which, though not linear, are nevertheless unified in terms of the relation or parallelism between their parts. That said, one sometimes finds one or two couplets (*beyt*, pl. *abyāt*) which seem to have little or nothing to do with the rest, and the final couplet (the *maqta'*) is quite often unrelated to the body of the poem; indeed one modern edition (Neisāri) leaves many of them out. But beyond that there are many ghazals which appear as loosely structured collections of couplets—characterized in de Fouchécour's French edition as *assemblages*—unified by the rhyme-scheme and little else.

I developed a method of "triage" as a means of addressing this problem. I would posit a dominant theme for a ghazal and list all the couplets which exemplified that in the first column (+). I would assign any couplets which might or might not be related to it to the second column (?) and any couplets which appeared to be unrelated to the third (-). This provides an initial "take" on the poem, but such raw data have to be interpreted with caution. Given the ambiguity of Hafez, the middle column is often problematic. Even the "unrelated" couplets may in fact form a parallel to the main theme, the analogy of an analogy. And if one posits a different dominant theme or rationale, as one sometimes can, a quite different distribution may result. One can end up with several "triages" of the same poem, which point towards different readings. In some cases, this relativized or under-determined interpretation seems to me to come closer to the reality of the poem.

We also have to be careful not to impose Western expectations about form on the ghazal, and the best analogy for it may lie not in European poetry but music. Hafez' poems often read like variations on a few basic themes. Such themes would have been well-known to his audience, so the circular or iterative movement of the poems would not have been perceived as a problem. Moreover, since the poems were often performed to music, with instrumental passages weaving in and out of the words and between couplets, the continuity that we expect on the page was less important. It is also possible that the editorial collation of different versions has led over time to more inflated, less coherent texts.

The unity or lack of unity of the ghazal can also be seen in other perspectives. Much Islamic art is also characterized by iterative, non-linear patterns. Western modernist poetry can also be non-linear: Broms (1968) refers here to Rimbaud and Mallarmé and one thinks for example of the collage construction of *The Waste Land* or the *Cantos* and the striking juxtapositions of imagism. There is a kind of circling around the ineffable in some kinds of spiritual writing, western and eastern. One might even contrast the Aristotelian *telos* with the Platonic form. A good deal thus depends on the templates we bring to a reading of the poems.

I have tried to deal with the "coherence" problem in several ways. Normally, I have attempted to translate the entire ghazal, though often varying the left-hand margin to mark internal shifts and breaks. Where the structure has seemed less unified, I have sometimes translated part of the poem, or divided it into several pieces, or used single couplets which seem viable on their own. (I think the resulting variation in the length of the pieces also helps with the overall dynamics of my text.) I have deliberately started with a number of shorter, simpler pieces, which form a kind of overture, since I think the modern western reader can only gradually take on board the full complexity of the ghazal, and I have left some of the most disjunctive poems till near the end. In some cases, I have had to abandon any attempt at translation since I simply could not make the poem work in English, and I still have over 30 unused literal translations.

At the level of my text as a whole there are both linear and non-linear elements. I am conscious of it having a beginning and end, although the final section is reflexive rather than conclusive. In sequencing the poems in each section I have taken some account of progression, usually dramatic rather than logical. However, I do not think the Divan can or should be presented as a kind of narrative, and my interpolations are deliberately non-linear. In other words, I have tried to mirror the ambiguous or polysemic structures of the individual ghazal at the level of the collection as a whole.

The third major problem in translating Hafez is the sheer cultural distance between him and the modern western reader. This manifests itself in both obvious and subtle ways. His poetry is full of references to Iranian history and legends which are unfamiliar to us. It assumes a detailed knowledge of Islam that most western readers will not have. It reflects the society and culture of 14th century Iran. There are uncertainties about gender which stem from the fact that in Persian the word for "he" and "she" is the same. But there are more subtle differences also. We may think of poetry as the expression of an authentic, individual self, and believe that the work will lead us back to the author, to the "real" Hafez. However, Hafez was working to a different aesthetic. The poetry is highly stylized. It presents a persona rather than a person. Except for occasional flashes, it is not biographical. It has only an oblique relationship with sense perception, direct experience or the empirical world. This last point represents a real problem since one of the great strengths of English lyric poetry is its very concreteness, its grounding in the specifics of the senses. In translating, I have thus had to guard against an unconscious tendency to "empiricize" the original by bringing it closer to direct observation or perception. This might make it more comfortable for the anglophone reader, but it would falsify the original. Hafez is already at one remove from perception; what he describes has already been processed; we are always in a world of meanings.

A second difference relates to our notion of originality, which we tend to value highly. However, as is clear from the debate about art in Orhan Pamuk's book *My Name is Red* (2001), such a notion was alien to older artistic traditions in that part of the world; the artist or poet belonged to a tradition, and the art lay in deploying, not overturning its conventions. A third difference relates to the audience. We know that Hafez' audience often comprised the local ruler (his patron) and his court, although in the lively culture of Shiraz described by Limbert (2004) he may well have had other audiences as well. What is difficult to reconstruct is the nature of his relationship with those who listened to or read him; but it is likely that different couplets were sometimes addressed to different people.

The distance between us and Hafez is I think more one of time than place and perhaps for that reason some writers have argued that he should be seen as a medieval poet, comparable if at all with European poets of that period, rather than (implicitly) the 19th century romantics in whose time he first became widely known in the West, especially through the work of Goethe. While there may be some affinities with the conventions of courtly love, such comparisons are hazardous and historically sloppy. To begin with, *media aevum* (middle ages) belongs to a European historical schema, and Iranians, rightly I think, dislike it being applied to their own past. There were also major differences between the Iran and Europe of those centuries, not least in the existence of the socio-economic institution of the bazaar (which features regularly in Hafez' poems) and the existence of mystical orders as distinct from individuals (which again make regular if usually negative appearances). Islamic science had already by Hafez' time developed well beyond its European counterparts, and although there must have been cultured discussion going on in many a European court, there was nothing quite like the *majles*, a cross between a salon and a forum.

Such difficulties led me, over time, to add a layer of annotation to the text itself, in the form of short prose notes (in bold type). These act variously as commentary, explanation, foil, dialogue, reflection. They typically open up questions rather than imposing a view. They are intended to form a bridge between him and us; or to use another image a scaffolding which, like all scaffolding, can be dismantled or dispensed with when there is no longer any need for it. This kind of "hybrid text" is common in modernist poetry; I have simply applied it to the process of translation. (Goethe's *West-östlicher Divan* could be regarded as a different kind of "hybrid": a collection of his own poems inspired by Hafez. Goethe also added a detailed prose commentary—the *Noten und Abhandlungen*—to the final edition; see Tafazoli 2012.) In addition, my prose interpolations, which are sometimes simply lists or definitions, serve to punctuate the poetry and cut its sweetness, which otherwise would be like drinking glass after glass of Sauternes, and would cloy.

The risks of this approach must be set against what many see as the long history of failure to translate, not single ghazals, but the *oeuvre* of Hafez as a whole. There are various reasons for this. Although Hafez is regarded as a complex poet in the original, Iranians have much of the cultural capital needed to appreciate him. They have this because, as noted above, Farsi has changed remarkably little over the centuries and because there is still a powerful oral tradition. Not for nothing has one writer labelled Iran an "empire of the mind" (Axworthy, 2008). But it is precisely such cultural capital that the western reader lacks. Bahrami (2012) using a typology developed in a different context by Leppihalme (1997) analyzes various ways in which key allusions in a text can be translated, but the problem goes well beyond these, to our general understanding of what Hafez is doing. Indeed, as Davis (2004) cogently argues in "On not translating Hafez" (2004), it involves our very conception of what constitutes poetry.

There are other problems for the translator. The writing in the original is very condensed. This is partly a matter of syntax: verbs may be omitted, words used simply in apposition, for example in the formula "I and this, you and that." However, it is mainly a matter of semantics. Hafez worked within a living and highly sophisticated poetic tradition which by his time had built up a rich store of tropes and themes. Rather like the modern jazz musician, he delighted in "quoting" others, as others would echo him afterwards. So although his vocabulary is relatively straightforward, the words are freighted with allusions and resonances which his audience would have recognized and appreciated. To unpack all these in translation would completely destroy the flow of the text. (The ghazal sometimes strikes me as a short poem doing the job of a longer one, such is its density.) It is, in my view, pretty well impossible to make an adequate translation of any single ghazal, but I think I have captured most aspects of the original somewhere in this long text which covers over half the poems.

There is also a wide range of tones in the original. Hafez is usually described as a lyric poet, but a wider knowledge of the Divan introduces us to a number of different voices: panegyric, ironic, acerbic, homiletic, elegiac, ecstatic. It is easy enough to present a single, unified Hafez by selecting a subset of his poems, but the whole is much more varied. I have tried to capture this range, sometimes through the use of varying verse forms. I have also tried to be generally faithful to both the sense and tone of the Divan. The vast majority of my translations are therefore close, though by no means always literal. Persian is a strongly idiomatic language, and sometimes the only solution is to find an equivalent, rather than literally exact, expression. With some ghazals, however, I have had to create a more oblique version rather than direct translation, indicated in the notes by a "v."

Because of the syntactic and other differences between Persian and English, there could be no question of reproducing the metrics of the original. However,

I have tried to reflect the style of the Divan in three ways. First, I have made considerable use of assonance and internal rhyme to echo the aurality of Hafez. I have used end rhymes on occasion, usually near or at the end of the poems, but more sparingly, since I think they can sound too obvious. Secondly, I have arrived at a degree of regularity in the rhythms and patterns of many of the poems, though some are freer. I have also used the contrast between long and short lines to create some of the momentum I find in the original. Thirdly, I have erred towards the formal rather than colloquial in terms of diction, and employed a small number of archaisms in order to distance the writing a little from the present. It goes almost without saying that other translators could adopt, and have adopted, different stylistic approaches.

Social scientists are sometimes enjoined to "listen to the data" and likewise translators should listen to the text rather than impose historical or religious templates on it. Such close reading alerts one to the slight inflections of voice and tone or shifts in linguistic register which help to place the lexical meanings within a wider field of sense and audience. Certainly, in the case of the Divan, it has led me to read some poems as primarily courtly or convivial (there can be differences between these two) and other poems as didactic or spiritual (and again there are differences). However the social science advice implies a kind of innocent empiricism, as if the text was simply there to be heard. With Hafez, it is not. Indeed, much of the travail lies in trying to establish what meanings he was presenting in the first place.

As noted in the Preface, the French *traduire c'est trahir* neatly expresses the impossibility of producing a truly faithful, authentic translation, if only because one is using a different language, with all the baggage that entails. Beyond this, any further intervention, such as a translator's preface or accompanying notes, risks intruding on the reader's own response, although the literary notion of "response" is by no means simple and implies, I would argue, some acquaintance with the relevant tradition. Beyond that again, translation risks not merely intrusion but imposition. The translator may bring to bear assumptions and preconceptions, perhaps unconscious, that reflect his or her own time, place, ideas or values. I suspect this is why translations often date quickly and come to seem in retrospect a product of their own age.

In the case of Middle Eastern literature, there is the added problem of the legacy of "Orientalism": the imposition of cultural stereotypes which, according to Said (2003) facilitated 19th and 20th century European colonial domination. These included images of mystery, sensuality or effeminacy, timeless serenity, fatalism and despotism, but most of all a disabling passivity which led to "backwardness." I have addressed some of these images where relevant in these notes; most simply do not apply. I should also stress in passing that there is nothing passive about Hafez. He may write about languor but there is nothing languorous about his writing; indeed it is hard to think of a poet who is more in command of what he is doing, who exhibits such positive energy and verve, line after line, poem after poem.

Said's thesis has been subject to various criticisms, chiefly that he focuses on external factors in the modern history of the Middle East, and largely ignores internal ones. His work thus needs to be complemented by reference to authors such as Lambton (1991) and Kuran (2011) who deal with internal issues such as land tenure, inheritance rights, the role of the *vaqf* (trust), capital formation, legal processes, social structures and religious norms, all of which arguably impeded the development of the region in the 19th century, in addition to European (including Russian) colonialism.

Given the risks of intrusion and imposition, why have I framed Hafez' work in the ways that I have? The difficulty of Hafez lies at three levels: (1) the ambiguity of his words, (2) the (lack of) structure of his poems and (3) the unknown chronology of his work. I know of no other poet, Iranian or western, in which these three levels of problem come together in quite the same way (although there is a debate to be had about Sana'i here). Together they constitute the peculiar *problematique* of Hafez and explain why some Iranians regard him as impossible to understand and many foreigners as untranslatable anyway.

TEXT AND CONTEXT

To end with an anecdote: some of Shakespeare's sonnets were on the degree course in Isfahan when I was teaching there. We worked through several, and then I asked the class what they made of them. Why, they said, pleased, these are just like our own mystical love poems. I objected that they were not usually read in this way, but they persisted and the interesting thing was that whatever I pointed to in the text they could find a spiritual interpretation for it. It was a sharp lesson for me in what I call the textual fallacy: the notion that one can abstract text from context. Every text forms part of a linguistic system, a literary tradition, a cultural ethos and a historical and social setting. Translation thus becomes a matter of finding an equivalent for one text-context in a different text-context, and that has been my guiding principle.

The main purpose of my thematic divisons, interstitial prose pieces and these notes has been precisely to bring context into text, to enable an English-speaking audience to read the poetry in the light of some ambient knowledge, to anchor it more firmly in its time and place. Some of the other prose pieces are more personal, to do with the translation process itself, thus creating a reflexive "triangle" of translator, text, context. The danger, as noted above, is that in trying to make the work more accessible in these ways, I shall be seen as imposing my own "take" on the original. However, the longer I have worked on these translations (eight years) the more I have come to appreciate Hafez' power as a writer, and so I have every confidence that he will see me off.

NOTE ON TRANSCRIPTION

There is no generally accepted convention for transcribing Farsi and short of using a completely phonetic system (IPA) which is itself a kind of code, it is difficult to see how one could be agreed, since the sounds do not always correspond to those of English. As will become clear from the notes and bibliography, existing practice varies a good deal, and readers need to allow for this. I have tried therefore to keep things as simple as possible. Following Lambton (1953: xxi) and my own ear I have transcribed the *kasre* as a short e not i, hence Hāfez not Hāfiz. The latter stems from the system for transcribing Arabic which is still extended to Persian in some universities. I have transcribed the *zamme* as a short o, not short u, hence *gol* not *gul*, although the sound is somewhere in between. There have been vowel shifts since Hāfez' time, but since no "long" vowel has become a "short" one and vice versa, these do not affect the meaning, and I have used the modern transcriptions throughout.

Where a familiar English version of a word exists I have used it, e.g. Darius, Isfahan, Koran. (Although qur'ān is more correct, the initial Arabic consonant does not exist in English.) In a few cases I have felt it important to retain the original Persian word rather than translate it, e.g. *nei* (wooden flute).

I have indicated long vowels in Persian thus: ā, ē, ī, the first time they are used, and then because of their cumbersome nature usually dropped the length marks in the text, reinstating them in the bibliography. Sometimes one finds y used instead of i. Short vowels are not normally written down in Farsi, and that also can lead to variations, for example between -ad and -ed. The letter *vāv* is a particular problem. As a consonant, it corresponds to our "v" but as a vowel it varies between "o" and "oo" or even "ow," and I have transcribed it as these, although I have also used the long "ū" where it has become established, as in "Sufi." I have omitted the silent *vav* as in *kh(v)ājē*. Following the usual convention, I have transcribed *ghain* as gh and *ghaf* as q (although these were different sounds in Hafez' time they are now similar in modern Tehrani Persian) and indicated *ain*, a rather variable glottal stop, by normal English speech marks rather than some special symbol. This leaves unspecified the differences between the various letters sounding h, s, t and z, but should give enough detail for readers of Persian to work things out. Although the *ezāfe*, which forms a syntactic link, is unwritten in Persian, I have transcribed it as *e* or *ye*.

Since the Iranian new year begins at the spring equinox there is no exact correspondence with the western calendar and more than a 20% chance of getting it wrong. I have therefore given the Iranian dates where relevant; as a rule of thumb add 621. Finally, I have used the ancient and modern name Iran for the country and its people, and Persian for the language and literature, the latter simply because it is more familiar to us.

NOTE ON SOURCES

My primary source has been the edition of Khānlarī, P.N. (ed.) (1362) *dīvān-e hāfez: khāje shams-oddīn mohammad* (2nd revised ed.) Tehrān: khārazmī (2 vols, text and appendices). I have also referred regularly to Qazvīnī, M. and Ghanī, Q. (eds) (1320, third printing 1381) *dīvān-e khāje shams-oddīn mohammad hāfez-e shīrāzī*. Tehrān: nashr-e mohammad; and on occasion to the older edition of Abdul-rahim Khalkhālī, of the same title, first published in 1306 (third printing 1366) Tehrān: ketābforoosh-e hāfez. Since Ordoubadian (2006) had already made a translation of most of one of the other main editions, that of Khorramshāhī (1387), I decided not to use it as a basis for translation but have referred extensively to the latter's notes and commentaries. I have consulted and cross-checked with a number of existing translations, noted in the bibliography, but primarily with the literal French translation of Fouchécour (2006) whose work in terms of both the text and notes has been invaluable.

While the vast majority of poems in the Divan are ghazals, some other forms of poems are usually included at the end. These constitute 10% of the whole (465 couplets out of 4640 in the Qazvini and Ghani edition) and as Meisami (2012) notes, are typically regarded as marginal and have received much less attention (although one *masnavi*, The Wild Deer, is a fine poem). However the ghazals are commonly if imprecisely referred to as "the Divan" and I have followed this usage. There are two concordances of the Khanlari text of the ghazals by Meneghini Correale (1988) and Seddīqīān (1366, reprinted 1383). Except where otherwise stated, the figures I give are from the first. I have also consulted the various line by line Persian commentaries by Sūdi (1341–7), Heravi (1378) and others, though the references are too numerous to annotate.

My main Persian-English dictionary has been F. Steingass (1892, reprinted 1970) *A Comprehensive Persian-English Dictionary*, Beirut: Librairie du Liban but I have cross-checked with other sources, especially the detailed annotations of Fouchécour (2006). Dehkhoda's Persian-Persian dictionary came online as I was working (Dehkhodā, A. (1372) *loghat nāmē*. Tehrān: enteshārāt-e dāneshgāh-e tehrān). I also consulted M. Mo'īn's *farhang-e fārsī*, tehrān: amīr kabīr, 1342. The most recent Persian-Persian dictionary I have used is Anvari, H. (1385)

farhang-e feshurde-ye sokhan (chāp-e dovvum) Tehrān: sokhan. For a translation of the Koran I have primarily used *The Qur'an: a new translation by Tarif Khalidi*, London: Penguin, 2008.

I have drawn on a range of valuable articles in the on-going *Encyclopaedia Iranica* (of which the online version is accessible at www.iranica.com) some of which are cited in the bibliography below. I also gained a great deal from the papers and discussions by Iranian and foreign scholars at the conference on *Hafiz and the School of Love in Classical Persian Poetry*, University of Exeter/Iran Heritage Foundation, 2007. I have included some of these in the bibliography; for the published conference proceedings see Lewisohn (2010) the title of which amends "school of love" to "religion of love."

NOTES ON THE TEXT

The text is based on 248 of the 486 ghazals (i.e. just over half), 16 of which are divided into two or more parts.

The first number in each case is the page number. The second KH number refers to the ghazal in Khānlari (2nd edn). KH indicates a complete or almost complete translation of a ghazal. (KH) in brackets indicates an extract of any length from a ghazal, and "v" a freer version rather than translation. B = *beyt* (distich/couplet) and hemistich/line 1 or 2 (*mesrā*). I have used the more familiar terms couplet/line, since rhyme is not essential to the definition of a couplet.

All Hafez translations are in normal type; all the interstitial prose pieces in bold.

I. LOVE

I have deliberately begun with short extracts from a number of ghazals which are intended to act as a kind of overture, introducing some of the main themes of the Divan. This may surprise the Persian speaker, but I do not think one can plunge the modern western reader immediately into the full complexity of the poems. As the text goes on, the proportion of complete ghazals, with all their subtle internal movements and shifts, increases. As noted above, I am trying to create not simply a collection of ghazals, but a text that forms a whole.

3 KH(1). The opening lines of the opening ghazal; some of the rest follows on p.7. Both Hillmann (1976) and Meisami (2003) provide interesting analyses of this poem, which is often regarded as a *shāhghazal* (king ghazal) but appears at first sight rather disjointed. Golāndām, Hafez' first editor and friend, placed this ghazal at the beginning rather than in its alphabetical place (12th). It starts not with a religious invocation but with a call (the Arabic phrase *alāyāihā*) to the wine-boy to come. It may be that Golandam wanted to begin with this symbolic cry, or that he placed this ghazal first because, couplet by couplet, it announces the key tropes and themes of the Divan, rather like the overture to an opera. Given the complexity and pivotal nature of the poem, I return to it with a complete version in Part X.

4 See Meisami (1991). As noted above, the translations are interspersed with other pieces which both punctuate and act as a commentary on the original, and this is the first. For a previous example of this approach see the playful but serious *After Lorca* (Spicer 1974.)

5 KH(2)

6 KH(3)

7 KH(1). Another extract from the first ghazal, order changed. B2: as well as meaning "scent" *be būyē* has the sense of hope or expectation here (Khorramshahi 1387: 93) which I have tried to express in my first line. "Hearts fill" is a compression of *che khoon oftād dar delhā*, literally "what blood falls in hearts." As Khorramshahi also notes, blood is something of a cliché in the Divan, suggesting variously passion, suffering, sacrifice or cruelty; here there may also be an allusion to the blood involved in the formation of musk by the musk-deer. For a lucid analysis of this complex couplet see Meisami (2003: 419–20). B3: I have preferred Khorramshahi's first interpretation of *sālek* here (p.99). B4: although in modern Persian *manzel* means "house" in Hafez it has more the sense of a staging-post on a journey. As with many words in the Divan, it will bear a spiritual interpretation. Lāhūri has *amn o 'eish* rather than *amn-e 'eish*; the metrical equivalence of the *ezāfē (e)* usually meaning "of" and *o*, meaning "and," is a basic source of ambiguity. *'eish* itself can be read in various ways, ranging from comfort through to love-making (see Avery 2007:18) but here I have gone for the somewhat ambiguous "pleasures" in the light of the preceding couplet. B5: "Master" here translates the *pīr-e moghān*, the Magian old man or spiritual leader, the first occasion on which we meet this key figure. I have translated *rāh o rasm manzelhā* as "customs of the way" since I think the dominant sense is of a journey (with stages). KH1 is a particularly complex ghazal and the length of this early note exemplifies the kinds of problems facing the translator.

8 KH(3)v. In Persian poetry, the mole (*khāl*) is considered a beauty spot and the hyperbole lies in the fact that something so small can evoke such great love. (A small mouth—see the next poem—and small waist were also conventionally beautiful; indeed there is a hyperbole of the diminutive to the point of invisibility.) However, the mystics also regarded the mole as dark and mysterious, a symbol of the ultimate, unknowable singularity or ipseity. A full version of this well-known but complex poem comes in the final section, but even this brief initial extract hints at the range of cultural reference one finds in the Divan. Because of its geographical position, Iran has always been exposed to influences from various directions, and indeed has historically shown a capacity to absorb and domesticate these. In addition to the expected references to the Arab, Muslim world, there are references, as here, to India, and to China (Iran was on the silk route). "Turks" refers to the Mongol-Turcomans, who came down from what we now label central Asia. There are implicit influences of the neo-Platonists and one explicit reference to Plato himself. And Alexander of Macedon remained (and still remains) a traumatic memory.

9 KH(58)v. Order changed.

10 KH(355). B2/1: the syntax is ambiguous and I have read *ān khoshtar ze hosn* as if it were in speech marks; Fouchécour (2006: 902) translates differently. Hafez sometimes uses "that" to symbolize the ineffable or unknowable, and it is tempting to capitalize it, though Persian does not have capital letters.

12 KH4. B1: it may be useful at this early stage to analyze the first couplet of this poem in some detail, since it exemplifies many of the problems and pleasures of translating Hafez. The first problem comes with the adverbial positioning of *belotf*. This surely means "kindly say" rather than "say kindly": the kindness relates to the act of intercession, not its content, since the breeze is simply a messenger, not a speaker. As often, however, the existing translations vary: Avery has "please say" while Fouchécour opts for the latter ("dis avec délicatesse") and Gray has "gently say." However *belotf* might be an abbreviation of the full Arabic invocation *belotfi' llahi ta'alala* which roughly translates as "for God's sake." The word *lotf* itself has various resonances and the commentaries by Sudi and Heravi qualify it here as *narm* or *molāyem*, soft or gentle. But we must also listen to the poetry, and the repetition of the little "*be*" sound gives the opening a quiet, pleading feel. There is also a strong symmetry in the repeated pattern of short and long a's in *ghazāl-e ra'nā-rā*. While Hafez refers several times in the Divan to *āhoo* (deer) and there is a longer *masnavi* poem about the *āhoo vahshi* (wild deer) this is a rare, perhaps unique use of *ghazāl*, although he does refer to *ghazālē* (little gazelle) in KH448/6. Sudi glosses *ghazāl* as *āhoochē* (little deer) and the sense I get is of lightness, delicacy, even vulnerability. The dictionary gives the adjective *ra'nā* as graceful, although Sudi relates it to red or yellow colored flowers, which may be where Avery gets his "dappled" from. However the English also makes its own demands. I would like the first line to have the smoothness of the original, and the vocalic assonance of "O dawn wind kindly" makes a good beginning. It also allows the mid-hexameter stress to fall on the important verb "say" while "nimble gazelle" reflects the aural patterning of the original, though this time with consonants rather than vowels. However, the translation of *ra'nā* depends partly on the next line, in which *kooh* picks up the sound of *begoo* in the first. Whereas *sar gardan* is to wander, *sar dādan* (here) is a transitive verb, to cause to wander or lead astray. I have therefore combined the slightly ironic "nimble" with the idiom "lead a merry dance" to retain the light-footedness and visual sense of the gazelle. But not too visual: an Iranian colleague suggested "prancing" but I find that too choreographed; as noted earlier Hafez' work is not grounded in concrete perception like much English lyric poetry. Some have translated *biābān* as desert but it literally means "place without water"—the arid plains of the Iranian plateau—and I have kept to that as closer to the original (the obvious words for desert are *dasht* or *sahrā*) and also because I need a longer third line to exemplify the runaround the lover is having, instead of being, as he should, in the town and probably at court. (Iran was already quite an urbanised country in Hafez' time, and anywhere outside was seen as empty and often threatening.) However, I have had to lose the slight echo of (ironic) reward that comes with the word *dādē'i* separated from *sar* on its own and, to a Persian audience, the implicit parallel with the wanderings of the lovelorn Farhād of legend. I have also lost any sense of the orthography of the Persian, and the way that the vertical strokes of *ghazāl-e ra'nā-rā* might be said to represent visually the leaping gazelle, a point that might seem strange to us, but not in a culture where calligraphy is so important. But I have achieved the half rhyme of "gazelle" and "hills" which, to me, helps to bind together this opening couplet and get the poem off to a tidy start. B4: as Khorramshāhi notes, *nazar* (seeing, sight, vision) is one of the most complex words in the Divan, especially in view of its various compounds: the knowledge/science of sight, masters of sight, and here the people of sight. Others have translated this as "insight" but I find that too internalized. The word can also have particular theological or mystical connotations, and Sufis emphasize the contrast between *nazar* and *khabar*, vision and mere information; for a discussion see the various references in Lewisohn (1995). B5: *bād peimoodan* is an idiom that means to attempt something absurd or impossible, but of course the word *bād* is close to *bādē*, meaning wine. B8: I have added "storeyed" to indicate that both Christ and Venus only ascended to the fourth or third of the seven heavens in Muslim

446

theology; and have added "himself" since "*masīhā*" (the Messiah) is the final, emphatic word in the poem.

13 KH(91). The first line reminds me of a striking comment that to Iranians Hafez is the closest yet most distant of their poets (Meskoob 1371: 6). Meskoob actually set out to write a quite different book but was ineluctably drawn back to Hafez, whom he describes as "impossible." He calls his book a *safarnāmē*, a travel journal, and it forms an intense meditation on the imagery of the Divan. The style is idiosyncratic and difficult and I am not convinced that the sustained abstraction of the writing always gets a purchase on the poetry. However, it surely demonstrates that far from being mere literary devices, metaphors and symbols are fundamental to the way we construct and construe the world: we do not and cannot think otherwise. Tellingly, he ends by quoting KH431/3 on the inability of language truly to capture the mystery of love (see p.294 below).

On a more mundane level, personal pronouns are a problem for the translator of Hafez. He uses both *man* (I) and *mā* (we). The latter may refer to "I and my heart" (as psychologically distinct entities) or to an implied group (a circle of companions or a gathering). However it also functions as a more humble form of "I" (Fouchécour, 2006: 97). Even now, Persian has highly graduated forms of address implying deference/authority. I have therefore translated it variously according to context. The person-object in the poems is sometimes referred to as *to* (you, singular, intimate) and sometimes as the third person singular ū (*oo*) which can mean he or she. (For an interesting discussion of the shifts between second and third person within poems see Losensky 1998a.) Where the context strongly suggests a gender, I have translated accordingly, but in all other cases I have standardized the person-object as the gender-neutral "you," which is not ideal but I think preferable to writing he/she, (s)he or imposing an English gender.

14 KH(10)v. Order changed. The first line is one of many references to "reason" which in the Divan is always negative and opposed to "love." In line 4, "Verse" is capitalized because of the allusion to the Koran although the word (*āye*) can also mean a sign or manifestation. The last line is my gloss on the beautiful word *shabgīr*. It is appropriate to comment here at an early stage on Hafez' language. Three general points should be made. First, it was a public not private language, part of a well-established, shared poetic discourse. Secondly, it was not especially convoluted, and much of its strength lies in using common words in simple but beautiful ways which still communicate directly with the reader. Avery describes it as "enamel hard"; the image in my mind is of finely worked metal. (To me, it also contrasts with the spontaneous outpouring of Rumi's *Dīvān-e shams*, which has a different kind of strength and beauty [Kadkani, 1352]). Thirdly, Meneghini Correale's computerized analysis has shown that the vocabulary is not particularly large, and that the proportion of repeated words is quite high (Meneghini Correale in Glünz and Bürgel (1991: 105-136). Clearly, different translators will use different registers, and to some extent that is simply a matter of personal preference: Gray (1995) adopts a clear, direct style, Ordoubadian (2006) something more colloquial and lively. For a review of Bell (1897) and some discussion of trends in translation see Lewis (2001). I have gone for a slightly formalized diction, partly to reproduce the controlled elegance of the original, partly to reflect the court context and partly to distance the translations from the present; this also sets up a contrast with my prose annotations.

15 KH151. The word *taslīm*, which I have translated as submission, comes from the same Arabic root as Islam, and has strong religious connotations.

17 KH(91). The story of how Solomon sent the hoopoe with a message to the Queen of Sheba would have been known to Hafez' audience from the Koran (27: 21). In the first line there is a play on the two words *sabā* (spelled differently) the first meaning "east wind" and the second the kingdom of Saba. The hoopoe, which is a small bird, also plays a leading role in Attar's *Conference of the Birds*. B2: I have preferred KH *āsmān* (sky) to *āshiān* (nest) found in some other editions.

18 KH262. B9, final couplet: it is difficult to translate *tab' choon āb*, lit. nature/ability like water. I have chosen the lucid element whereas Alston (1996) emphasises purity. Khorramshahi relates it to the idea of *she'r-e tar*, fresh/moist poetry found elsewhere in the Divan. While *ravān* (flowing) seems to have a straightforward poetic sense here, it is a complex word that can also imply spirituality.

This seems an appropriate point to comment more generally on rhyme and meter. The rhyme scheme involves a rhyme between the first and second lines (hemistich/distich) and thereafter with every couplet/distich or second line. Some ghazals have a refrain where the same word or phrase is repeated throughout, but in the majority the rhyme involves only the final two or three syllables. Because in Persian the verb typically comes at the end of the sentence and therefore often the line, this is much less restrictive than it would be in English, where for example we have lost the form "did go." However, the rhyme scheme remains a tight one and Hillman (1972; 1976) has argued that it is an important element in the formal, aural unity of the ghazal. Since I find full end-rhyme often too obtrusive in English, I have made greater use of internal rhyme and assonance. The standard work on Persian metrics is Elwell-Sutton (1976). Most of this highly technical subject need not concern us here but a few general points should be made. Although Arabic terms are used to describe Persian meters, Elwell-Sutton shows that they are in fact native and may partly date from before the Arab invasion. The meters are based on patterns of short, long and overlong syllables in a ratio of 1:2:3. Hafez' lines usually comprise 14 or 15 syllables, though one also finds 13 and 16. These are all significantly longer than the typical English iambic pentameter, raising issues for the translator which are discussed later. However Hillman (1971) again argues that since Persian is an accented language, one can "hear" the rhythm or stride of a line over and above its syllabic pattern. This is a crucial part of the sound of Hafez' work, and may reflect the persistence of aural patterns from Middle Persian (see Lazard, 2006). In general, I have aimed at translations that are relatively patterned both in terms of sound and rhythm, though different poems have come out differently.

1 9 KH265v. The rhyme-scheme in many ghazals forms a refrain, but in English poetry the latter is found mainly in older, folk poetry rather than the lyric, where it can seem overdone. One way round the problem is to turn it into a root, as here. B7/2: I have translated *maqāmi* here as "stage." This is one of a number of words in the Divan which have a technical, mystical meaning as well as an ordinary language use; other cognate ones are *hāl* (state, condition) and *tariqat* (way, path). Those who espouse a spiritual reading of Hafez point to such terms as evidence for their interpretation; others think they are merely a matter of style. See Part VIII.

2 0 KH(289). Order changed. The candle metaphor is a familiar one in Persian poetry; see Seyed-Gohrab (2012b).

2 3 KH22. This well-known ghazal is one of the more "unified" ones and has been widely translated perhaps because of that.

2 4 KH408

2 6 KH16. B1: Avery (2007:594) has a useful note on *shāhed*. Its root meaning is to bear witness, but this was extended by Sufis to mean a witness to God's beauty and thence a beautiful person. I considered various translations (proof, testament, manifestation) but have ended up with "theophany" as giving the full spiritual force. This goes against Khorramshahi's worldly interpretation here, but I am persuaded by the association with *qodsi* (heavenly). The final couplet however implies that the entire poem is in fact addressed to a praised patron (*mamdooh*) rather than beloved *(ma'shooq)*, though it is possible that "master" is yet another metaphor for the latter: it all depends on whether one sees this as a love poem, spiritual poem, or court poem. The ambiguity is pervasive.

2 7 KH166. Order changed. I have translated *jān* here by soul, but it is sometimes better rendered as "life." It means that which gives life, the vivifying force; the word for spirit (as opposed to body) is *rooh*.

2 8 KH(452). The phrase "divine attributes" refers to the 99 divine Names, each of which identifies one aspect of God, but no one of which can express the divine essence. Sufi writers and poets tended to group some of these attributes under the two broad headings of *jalāl* (God's glory) and *jamāl* (God's beauty) and indeed Hafez brings them together in one line: *khosh mīdehad neshān-e jamāl o jalāl-e yār* (KH62:2): "gives joyful sign of the beauty and glory of the friend." Schimmel (2001:26) notes that poets liked to juxtapose such pairs of contrasting concepts but it is worth noting that in the ghazals *jamāl* occurs roughly three times more frequently than *jalāl* (21:7: Correale's figures; Seddiqian has 23:6; in both cases derivatives would add to these, though not affect the broad proportion). In the Bible (KJV) the word "glory" occurs over 400 times, in both the Old and New Testaments, while "beauty" occurs 49 times and only in the Old Testament. Its non-occurrence in the New Testament, and as far as I am aware, the rarity of the notion of divine beauty in subsequent Christian teachings or mystical writings, may make it more difficult for readers with such a heritage to hear the full spiritual resonances of *jamāl* in the Divan.

2 9 KH73. B1: I have preferred the alternative reading of *bahr* (sea) to *rāh* (road). *rend* is the subject of a later comment; I have paraphrased it here as "unreason," echoing Arberry's translations (1993).

3 0 KH69. The reed in the last line probably refers to one used for writing, although it could also be understood as a musical reed.

3 1 I have taken the description of the *majles* as something between a salon and forum from Jim Al-Khalili in his television series on Islamic science (see also Brookshaw 2003). Limbert describes three features of Shirazi society which are particularly worth noting: (1) the Turkish-Mongol ethos of the ruling courts which to some extent separated them from the rest of society, 2) the highly complex structure of overlapping social, religious and family groups, and 3) the extraordinary cultural diversity of a relatively small city of about 60,000 people (2004: 75; 96–7; 106). I sense that some of Hafez' ghazals are collegial and convivial rather than courtly in tone but the whole question of Hafez' audience or audiences remains problematic.

32 KH204

34 KII138. Final couplet omitted. B3: Petitioners would sometimes wear a shirt on which they had written their request. B8 (my final couplet): Persian music is based on a number of basic modes, which comprise a number of notes rather than a linear scale. Fouchécour indexes over 100 musical references in the Divan suggesting that music played a large part in the culture and that Hafez was very familiar with it. Indeed the term *hāfez* could also refer to a musician. While some of the references are to the conventional association with wine (*mei o motreb*) I sense that as a poet Hafez felt close to music. For a discussion of music in, and the musicality of, Hafez, see Lewis (2012).

35 KH(431). This is the second of two alternative final couplets, neither of which seems to have anything to do with the body of the poem, which comes in Part VII. The first couplet may have been dropped because of its implied criticism of the re-invading Mongols, who arrived in Shiraz near the end of Hafez' life; this one, by contrast, includes them. Sudi (1341–7) identifies the *turcān* as Tartars and they had a reputation for being handsome but cruel. By contrast, the Indian/Kashmiri references connote something more sensual and seductive. Hafez' poetry would have frequently been sung and sometimes danced to with a musical accompaniment; as noted earlier, the performance context was thus quite different from our modern, silent reading on the page.

II. THE GARDEN

I was already moving towards grouping the ghazals in sections as a way of managing a long text and bringing out the different facets of the Divan, but the idea was crystallized by Lewis's categorizing of Sana'i's work in a similar way (Lewis, 1995). That said, in neither case are the sections water-tight, and there is great fluidity both across and within the poems.

The "timeless orient" of 19th century Europeans was part fact, part fiction. In economic terms, these were stable societies, and for good reason. Middle Eastern agriculture is an unsung marvel. In Iran, man-made underground water channels carry water for miles from hill to plain, where it is carefully apportioned. In oases, a vertical system of cultivation is created, whereby trees shade bushes which in turn stabilize the soil. The Nile delta is one of the most productive agricultural regions in the world. Commerce was also highly developed. It is sometimes said that Muslim society has two poles, the mosque and the bazaar. The Koran provides the legal and moral basis for trade, and the necessary financial and physical infrastructure was also in place. People could and did travel long distances; there were 360 caravanserais in Egypt alone. Sharia law imposed a stable social framework, and although there was often hardship there was little outright destitution. Islam has its own social security system, far better than anything Christianity ever developed.

But over time what was stable became static. As Kuran (2011) shows, the legal frameworks that had initially enabled such societies to flourish gradually became a brake on their development. The arguments are complex (and Kuran distinguishes carefully between Islam and Islamic law) but factors related to inheritance, the role of trusts and nature of legal contracts meant that such societies found it difficult to modernize their economies, in terms of creating companies, accumulating capital, forming banks and investing productively. And while he rejects the common view that at some point in the past "the gate of interpretation was closed," he notes the long-term decline in *ijtihād*, leading to a degree of intellectual rigidity. Kuran underplays the redistributive nature of Islamic law, and is uncritical of capitalism, but his book is an important corrective to the view that external, colonial factors were largely or solely responsible for the Middle East's lack of development; indeed it has re-defined the debate.

These facts, however, underpinned a fiction. Said (2003) has argued that Europeans constructed an image of the Orient in order to create an image of themselves; for them the Orient was a defining other: exotic, opposite, an alter ego. The relative stability of middle eastern societies provided a canvas on which they could paint (sometimes literally) their own social, sexual and spiritual fantasies.

More than that, it provided a sanctuary from the major, often traumatic changes that were sweeping Europe itself in the 19th century. The notion of timelessness was thus deeply attractive to people who felt harried by time. All this post-dates Hafez by five or six centuries and is strictly speaking irrelevant to his work. However, it could affect how we read him, what we bring to him. Hegel (1975:370) cited Goethe's Hafiz as an example of "oriental serenity." We cannot know what he meant, and it is important to remember that "peace" is a fundamental concept in Islam, as in the daily greeting *salām aleikum*, peace be on you. But of all Hafez' images it is that of the garden which seems to summon up a kind of timeless repose. However, when we turn to the poems in this section, we find that far from always being peaceful, the garden is often a stageset for drama.

39 The Persian drinking-cup was typically oval-shaped, but with a handle, hence has been translated both as cup and bowl. This description is based on an actual miniature.

40 KH(44). The walled garden evokes the ancient Zoroastrian image of paradise. There may also be an echo of the Koran 80: 23–32.

41 This ghazal is not in the Khānlari edition, but is included in both Khalkhāli (295) and Qazvini and Ghani (p. 314) and I like it. Strictly speaking the *bolbol* is not a nightingale but a similar species, but since the word sounds rather ugly in English I have gone along with most translators in using the latter. The beautiful Arabic word is *andalīb*. In line 8, "gossip" could be translated as "inform," giving it a more sinister ring.

42 KH66. B4: the Water of Life refers to what was probably in origin a Greek myth which became assimilated into Iranian culture. It emerges from a spring in the deep dark realms, the sun passing through it each night so that it may be reborn again each morning. Alexander (not Great to Iranians!) wanted to drink it to become immortal but was prevented from doing so by the mysterious figure of Khezr, who is also associated with greenery and growth and, being "happy-footed," acts as a spiritual companion or guide. B6: this is a deeply problematic *beyt*. There was no punctuation in Persian in Hafez' time, but here Khanlari unusually introduces a comma before *khamūsh* at the end of the first line and after *ei modd'ai* in the next. This creates an enjambment which although rare in Hafez does sometimes occur, for example after the word *vali/likon* (but). Translators generally have accepted this, but the problem is that it makes the first line read literally "what does the sky know of the secret/mystery behind the curtain?" when one might expect the sky (as heavens/firmament) to know precisely that (Fouchécour indexes destiny/sky together). However, one must distinguish between two different senses of "fate" in Hafez. The first is the religious notion of predestination as the working out of the plan of an omnipotent and omniscient God, and the previous couplet suggests that Hafez was destined from pre-eternity to be a lover. This might be taken as absolving him of responsibility and implies a certain fatalism, but the religious counter-argument is that he was also predestined to think and act, and the Divan is also full of examples of personal consciousness and agency. The second sense of Fate is of a blind, arbitrary and sometimes cruel force, for which various images (*falak, gerdoon, charh*) are used. This sense seems to have different origins from that of predestination and is much closer to the Greek sense of "the fates." It pervades Persian poetry from Ferdowsi onwards and as Feldmann (1996) explains is expressed in the same terms in later Turkish poetry also. The sense that fate or life plays games with us—*bāzī*—is also common. (See also the articles on "Astrology and Astronomy," "Cosmogony and Cosmology" and "Fatalism" in *Encyclopaedia Iranica*.) An alternative reading of the couplet is that *che dānad* refers forward to the *modd'ai* in the next line and *falak khamoosh* goes together as "the heavens are silent" perhaps as a cheville. However this is syntactically unlikely so I have gone for the first reading but added "even" to accentuate the ultimate unknowability of the divine mystery to which even Fate does not have access. Morris (2007) offers a general analysis of this ghazal which, as with some others, he interprets in terms of both the syntactical perspectives (I/you/he) and semantics of the Koran, seeing this and other poems as climaxing in the key root of h-f-z of which the name/title *hāfez* is one form.

44 KH342. Hafez frequently uses the word *bot* which translates as idol. It is provocative since Islam in its early stages had to fight precisely against such idolatry in pre-existing cults. That said, Shabestari in *golshan-e rāz* (The Garden of Mystery/Secrets) argued that as long as idols were used simply as a means on the way to true spirituality, they were allowable (Darr, 2007: 154–157: lines 865–74). Khorramshahi is curiously reticent about *botān*. Rumi famously invokes the wooden flute at the start of his great mystical poem the *Masnavi*: "listen to the *nei* as it tells its story . . ."

47 KH77. May: *Ordibehesht* is an ancient Zoroastrian month, as are several others still used, and runs from mid-April to mid-May, the most temperate period of the Persian year. The reference to the synagogue (*kenesht*) in B4 is unusually harsh; Hafez seems generally tolerant of other religions. The black ledger is the book of judgment which will be referred to when a person dies.

48 See Broms (1968) and Hameen-Antilla (n.d.). The question is about poetic forms, not cultural invariants. Persian narrative poetry is linear, and a lot of modernist western poetry is non-linear. One might also ask whether Bach's *Diabelli Variations* or Schubert's *Trout Quintet* "go somewhere." Indeed the musical form of theme and variation may offer a better insight into the ghazal than literary forms.

49 KH456. Hafez regularly uses the word *madār* (turning, revolving) to describe the world, but this would have referred to the heavens rather than the earth. In B4/2 the syntax is ambiguous but I have taken the *nah* in the middle of the line to refer both to what precedes and follows it, as does Fouchécour but not Avery. This is an interesting example of the kind of prosodic symmetry one finds.

50 KH(13)v. A shortened version of another refrain poem, which I have omitted for the reasons given in Note 19. I have translated *chaman* here by lawn in its older broader English sense, but see note 55.

51 This little poem is not in the Khānlari edition but is included by Qazvini and Ghani (p.78), and is No 60 in an older Khalkhāli edition. It seems a little light for Hafez (though Lahuri predictably finds symbolism in it) but I like its delicate touch and decided to include it.

52 KH(44). I have read *āhang* as meaning intention here, not song. We should be open to the possibility of a court reading of this, as referring to a departing prince or patron.

53 KH249. This relatively unified poem will serve as a typical example of the process of "triage" mentioned earlier in the introduction. One chooses a dominant theme, and couplets are then classified as core, related or unrelated, giving us some purchase on the structure of the ghazal. If we choose Love as the key theme, we (arguably) get

	+	?	–
Love	1,2,4,5	3,7	6

However, if we choose Absence, the configuration looks different:

	+	?	–
	3,4,7	1,2,5	6

with a shift of emphasis in beyt 4. In both cases, beyt 6 seems to stand on its own, perhaps directly addressing the audience; the reader could indicate this in his performance. The whole process is tentative, providing a basis for reflection and discussion, not a definitive reading.

55 KH9. B2: As both Dehkhoda's and Anvari's dictionaries indicate, *chaman* has various senses, and gets translated in various ways. Khanlari (1362: 1174) has a note on it in the light of which I think "arbor" best captures the connotations of trees, greenery and seclusion. The "young saplings" are probably a metaphor for young princes or members of the court. B4: Like Avery and Fouchécour, I understand *sar gardan* here not as the compound verb "to wander" (as Meisami has it) but literally as "head-turning/spinning": the image is of the lover's head as a polo ball, a conceit which is quite common in Persian poetry. B6: Adam's clay: the belief was that Noah brought Adam's remains onto the Ark as a guarantee of ultimate safety. B10: in the final couplet, Hafez attacks those who misinterpret the Koran for their own hypocritical ends. Although he often plays with other religious symbols, he always treats the Koran with reverence.

This complex ghazal has been analyzed by Bausani (1958) who sees it as typical of the "incoherence" of Persian poetry; Hillmann (1976:125-130) who finds it at best only loosely unified by the final couplet; and Meisami (2003: 50-54) who argues that it is a perfectly coherent court poem, centering on the middle couplets, giving advice to a prince. The problems of interpreting Hafez are compounded by the absence of a contemporary theory of poetics. However Meisami (2003) does cite various relevant sources of the time and also brings to bear the European medieval framework of Geoffrey de Vinsauf's *Poetria Nova*. Using this she argues that there is an underlying didactic purpose and progression in the ghazals which belies their apparent incoherence, and allows us to decode them as court poems. In this case that means privileging the middle, moralizing couplets (6-8). People may well have nodded their heads at these (such moralizing was *de rigueur*) but I suspect would have been delighted by the earlier couplets. I find Meisami's ideas interesting but some of her actual translations questionable, as indicated in several places in these notes.

57 KH81. B1: While Dehkhoda gives *morgh-e chaman* as nightingale, Steingass also translates it as forest bird. *no khāstē* means newly risen, which is consistent with daybreak, hence "awakened," but Steingass also notes that it can mean "a youth whose beard begins to appear." B5: the garden of Iram was a legendary garden of the Arab king Shaddād, referred to in the Koran (89:7–9) whose pride led to its destruction. Jamshīd was a legendary Persian king who possessed a cup in which he could see everything (in Persian this is neatly *jām-e jam*) and is a key figure in Persian mythology. The name is derived from the Zoroastrian figure Yima Khshaeta (Boyce, 2001: 12–13) and Jamshid was believed to be the first king of Iran who unified and developed the country and who ruled for several hundred years in what was, until his fall, a golden age. What we know by its Greek name Persepolis is known to Iranians as *takht-e jamshīd*, the Seat of Jamshid. Although he is thus a standard reference in Persian literature, Hafez refers to him and his cup over 30 times in the ghazals, and it is important to ask why. First, Hafez seems to be situating himself in a specifically Iranian mythology and indeed after Ferdowsi could be regarded as the most national of Persian poets. (See Meskoob [1992: 34ff] on the incorporation of pre-Islamic Iran into Iranian historiography.) Some see this as an alternative to the Islamic heritage, but that is too simple: the fact that in this single poem he could make both a Koranic reference (above) and invoke Jamshid suggests an eclecticism which I find characteristic of the Divan generally. Secondly, Hafez uses Jamshid's cup as a symbol of special, extra-ordinary knowledge. While this could simply be written off as a literary trope, it does form part of the more general evocation of the hidden, esoteric or supra-sensible realm; even the literal-minded Sudi treats it as such.

Meisami (1987: 286–294) in a detailed analysis argues that this is clearly a court poem which falls into three segments. However, this involves reading B3 and B4 as continuations of the rose's reply. As my indentation indicates, I see nothing to warrant this and in any case in Hafez each image (e.g. rose/nightingale; wine/tavern) remains distinct: he does not mix his metaphors. Also, B7 seems to me a direct comparison of speech and wine, what can be articulated and what remains ineffable, and it strains the text to read it in a purely courtly context. That said, I have tried in my translation of the final couplet to capture some of the ambiguity of reference, never far away in Hafez.

60 KH113.

61 KH406.

62 KH477. The beginning and end of this poem may evoke Rumi, who lived about a century before Hafez, usually known to Iranians as *molavi* or *moulānā* (master). (I prefer the poet Robert Duncan's evocation of Rumi in his "Circulations of the Song" [1984] to any of the better-known scholarly translations.) Khosrow was an ancient Persian king of the Sassanian era who acquired semi-mythical status in poetry. B1: the reference to Pahlavi at the beginning may refer either to the old Persian language or to a musical mode. B2: Meisami has "come, for Moses' fire has put forth a rose" whereas my translation and those of Avery and Fouchécour understand the rose to be the agent (i.e. the syntax is the reverse of the word order). The reference is not to the burning bush familiar from the Bible but to a different revelation described in the Koran 28:29-30. B8: again my text follows those of Avery and Fouchécour in translating *dehqān* as farmer or peasant, not gardener as Meisami has it. Fouchécour also notes the reference to all four religions (Zoroastrian, Jewish, Christian and Muslim) in this one poem.

63 KH468. B1: There is a basic textual disagreement here. Most editions have *zīrak* (clever, sharp) which as Dehkhoda notes is one of the characteristics of the *rend* and so would be perfectly appropriate. Despite this Khanlari (1362: 1232-3) prefers *nāzok* (attractive, alluring) citing several other examples of its use in this context. Either word could be translated in various ways, but I have compromised with "engaging." B2: In the light of Qazvini and Ghani's paraphrase of the poem (1379:518) which uses the word *takfīr* I have interpreted *anjomani* as being an orthodox religious group outraged at Hafez' epicurean lifestyle. This poem may well refer to the second Mongol invasion, near the end of Hafez' life; the first had taken place in the previous century and both were unimaginably destructive. However, the sacking of Baghdad in 1258 had the side-effect of reducing its religious hegemony over Iran and meant that there was considerable cultural fluidity in Hafez' time in the 14th century, which helps to explain the variety of religious references in the Divan. For an overview of the period see Axworthy (2007:101-121). B4: *fesq* could be translated more generally as "sin" but the word has strong sexual connotations (as in the phrase *fesq va fojoor*, iniquity and debauchery) which I have decided to retain here ("lecher") although on the whole sexuality is not explicit in the Divan. B8: as often elsewhere, Hafez uses *ahriman*, which was the Mazdean/ Zoroastrian principle of evil, rather than the Muslim *sheitān* (cf. our Satan) and which I have translated as "devil."

III. THE TAVERN

It will have become clear by now that there are a lot of different things going on, often in parallel, in many ghazals, and part of the complexity of Hafez arises from the fact that he uses not one but a number of symbolic registers. The main ones are those of love and the beloved, the garden with the rose and nightingale, and in this section the tavern, populated by the *pīr-e moghān* (the host or master) the *moghbachē* or *sāghi* (the acolyte or serving-boy) and the other drinkers or clientele. However, there is also the quite different symbolic register of the way or path, with its stopping-places, dangers and destinations and also the elemental register of earth, air, fire and water (*khāk, havā, ātesh, āb*). Without a systematic study of the latter references one must hesitate to say much about them, although fire seems to be the most important. And while it would be simplistic to relate them directly to Zoroastrian cosmology they do suggest that Hafez' sense of the world was to some degree, perhaps even unconsciously, grounded in them.

I have tended, like other translators, to use the word "tavern" for the Persian *meikhānē* or *meikadē*, literally winehouse. It is unfortunately rather old-fashioned but the other options, such as inn, pub or bar all seem to me worse in one way or another, although "den" captures some of the marginal, low-life connotations of the original. Khorramshahi (1387:1006) characterizes it as an *'eshrat-kadē*, pleasure-house, with suggestions of illicit sex, drugs and even gambling as well as drink. Such places were usually on the edge of town, housed in broken-down buildings or remains; hence the related term *kharābāt* (ruin). The point to make is that Hafez is deliberately choosing an earthy, pejorative word to form part of his system of idealized, even spiritual metaphors and meanings, as he also does with the originally low-life term *rend* (see below).

6 7 KH(13). Whether the taverns were open or not depended on the ruler of the time, some of whom were strict in this respect, others more relaxed. Hafez lived through several such changes of regime. Generally, wine was forbidden on religious grounds, although some jurists argued that as long as it was sufficiently boiled down to reduce the alcohol, it was lawful, as implied in this ghazal. However, only non-Muslims (i.e. Jews, Christians, Zoroastrians) were allowed to make or sell it. That said, wine-drinking was fairly common practice in the courts. This could be seen as a carry over from pre-Islamic Sassanian times, or even an echo of the ritual use of wine in Zoroastrian ceremonies. The whole

iconography of wine was a common one in Persian poetry and in this as in many other ways Hafez shared in the general poetic conventions.

6 9 KH25. Order changed. B2: *zohd* (asceticism, puritanism, here restraint) is one of the key negative terms in the Divan; *zohdforūsh* can mean hypocrite. As Khorramshahi (1387: 365ff) points out in a lengthy note, it is not the piety of such people that is the problem but their motivation: a concern with appearances, pride, adherence to the form rather than the spirit and a fundamental absence of love. *zohd* is closely linked to another word in the poem, *rīā*, hypocrisy.

7 0 KH(10). Since the Ka'ba in Mecca provides the point of orientation for Muslim prayer, there is explicit impiety here, meant to shock.

7 1 Boyce (2001:157) notes that the word *mogh*, which Hafez uses for Magian priest, had already fallen out of use several centuries before, which supports the view that what we have here is merely a literary conceit, not a real affiliation with Zoroastrianism. (Of the scholars I have read, only Burgel [1991] takes this aspect of the Divan seriously, although there is also some material on the internet.) I have used the term Zoroastrian to refer generally to the pre-Islamic religion of Iran, but it evolved in various ways and stages from its beginning in (probably) the late second millennium BCE, and the history is much too complex to be explained here. The terms Mazdean (after Ahura Mazda, the principle of Good) and Mithraic are often used of the first millennium BCE, and Zoroastrian tends to be applied from the Sassanian period in the early Christian era onwards. The Magi were the priestly caste who became more organized, centralized and powerful in the latter period, which also saw the spread of their fire-temples (*āteshkadē*). There was an important one at Istakhr, not far from Shiraz, though by Hafez' time it had been destroyed.

7 2 KH11. The final couplet (*maqta'*) is a typical expression of gratitude to the current patron, and like many others is only loosely linked to the rest of the poem. For a useful general discussion of the *maqta'* see Losensky (1998a).

7 4 KH154. One of the dangers of labelling Hafez as a lyric poet is that we may miss the tone of irony, nicely exemplified here. B5: I have translated "the way of" rather than "the way to" the tavern to try to get the sense here of *rah* as a type of behavior.

7 6 KH(48). The reference is as always to Jamshid's visionary cup on which there were several lines of mystic writing. The cup is mentioned in the founding Persian epic, Ferdowsi's *shāhnāmē*, The Chronicle of Kings, although it was not always associated with Jamshid. Writing, *khat*, has one of the longest entries in the dictionary, and there were and are various different kinds of script, signalling its importance in the culture. The reference to head-dress probably relates to the Sufi bonnet. Hafez' final reference to "reason" can be seen in the light of the major debate that went on in preceding centuries about the relationship between reason and revelation, which swung definitively towards the latter in the 11th century with Al-Ghazāli's *Incoherence of the Philosophers* and was not effectively countered by Ibn Rushd's (Averroës) Aristotelian *Incoherence of the Incoherence* a century later. The abandonment of *falsafe*, together with the terrible Mongol invasions, arguably marked the end of the golden age of Islamic culture. More pertinent here is Hafez' rejection of reason which helps explain why Sufism has sometimes been regarded in Iran as socially reactionary and backward-looking.

78 KH201. I have translated *hemmat* here by guidance in achieving the "high ambition" of a spiritual goal. It is one of various words in the Divan which has both an ordinary and a spiritual meaning: for a discussion of the latter see Fouchécour (2006: 406–08). In the final couplet Hafez atypically uses the feminine *ma'shooqē*, rather than male *ma'shooq* (beloved) but in his appendix volume Khanlari (p.1228) argues that we should not read too much into the feminine form when it occurs. In fact there are only about 15 female references in the entire Divan, including figures of speech (e.g. Lady of Victory/Daughter of the Vine/Bride of Fortune). There is thus little support for the "feminizing" of the text which some translators have imposed (perhaps for reasons of sexual correctness) but that said it is quite possible that Hafez was read in the female quarters of houses and palaces as well as in male, public life (Fouchécour, personal communication). On the subject of gender, the translation of the poems of the contemporary princess Jahān Mālek Khātūn by Davis (2012) was a revelation to me and I suspect many others.

79 Khorramshahi (1387: 403ff) notes that this is one of the most important but complex terms in Hafez, used some 80 times in the ghazals, and with 15 distinguishable aspects. Its social origins seem to have been dissolute, low-life (Limbert 2004: 90, 104–06) not unlike *ayyār*, often translated as ruffian or rogue, another term found in the Divan; indeed Hafez uses them together in one line. Early references in poetry to the *rend* or *rendi* were thus purely pejorative, but gradually the meaning widened to include a certain admiration for the *rend*'s freedom of spirit and disregard for hypocritical conventions and appearances. The term gradually evolved in the work of Sana'i, Khayyam and Attar, and is found in Shabestari, but it was Hafez who really developed its paradoxical sense: as Khorramshahi puts it *malāmati* (shocking) on the outside, *salāmati* (virtuous) on the inside. For a detailed discussion of *rend* and related terms see Lewis (2002).

80 KH258

82 KH(430). I have translated *zekr* by "repeat" but it is also a Sufi ritualistic term which refers to the repeated invoking or intoning of a divine word which is intended to empty the mind of everything else. In this and some of the poems that follow the object of Hafez' affections is clearly the serving-boy (*sāghi*). Elsewhere he simply refers to boys (*pesar, pesarān*) and on two occasions specifically to 14 year-old boys (KH251 and KH284). There are also a number of references to the down of a growing adolescent beard (*khatt*). Those who regard Hafez as a worldly poet see these as examples of the pederasty that seems to have been a common enough feature of Persian court life, not only before Hafez in Sassanian times, but after him: a recent Safavid exhibition in London included a tender little portrait of Shah Abbas and a page-boy (see also Yar Shater, 2002). As Davis (2012: xxvi) notes, there are also parallels with homoerotic elements in ancient Greek culture. Those who read Hafez in mystical terms see the *sāghi* as the symbolic dispenser of the wine of the spirit in the symbolic tavern. Khorramshahi (1387: 257-9) discusses same sex (*hamjens*) references in Hafez. While he allows that some minor Persian poets have been homosexual, he argues that praise of young boys has been a literary convention in poetry ever since Rudaki, and should be treated as such in all the major poets including Hafez. In any case, as Bate (2008: 200-235) has argued in his analysis of homoerotic references in Shakespeare's sonnets, we need to be cautious about arguing from literary convention to biographical fact.

83 KH273. Bahram the famous hunter also appears in Fitzgerald's Khayyām. In B4, as Avery notes, the word *goor* can mean either "wild ass" or "grave." I have chosen the first.

85 KH(41). The difficulties of interpreting and translating Hafez are encapsulated in the last two lines of this extract (the rest of the poem is on p.238). The word *haqiqat* means what is real or true, but can also signify Reality or Truth (though Persian has no capitals) and *majāz* is often translated as metaphor, although that is not an exact equivalent. So these lines could refer to the wine of Reality as against the mere phenomenal manifestation of earthly wine, giving the poem a strongly spiritual flavor. However, this seems to me to go against the grain of the preceding lines, so I have opted for the wordly interpretation in this case. In other poems, however, the grain seems to me to dictate a spiritual reading, and I have translated accordingly. Meisami (2003) provides a detailed discussion of *majāz* and other kinds of "ornamentation," but it is worth quoting Dabāshi (2003) at length on this. Contrary to most commentators, Dabāshi believes that Persian lyric poetry had initially developed along worldly lines until it became infiltrated and subverted by Sufism, notably with the "conversion" of Sana'i. This led to a displacement of its sensual realities by a system of metaphors which gradually replaced those realities: "The paradoxical binary between Haqiqat and Majaz, or between Truth and Metaphor, in Persian poetic parlance, so radically tilts in favor of the immaterial Majaz (or Metaphor) that it in fact takes over for the Haqiqat (or Truth) that it was meant to characterize. Persian literary metaphors, like Platonic ideals, have emanated and ascended from the sensual realities that originally suggested and sustained them, and thus in the air of their immaterial majesty have begun to form a conspiracy of verisimilitudes against the sensual evidence that had politely asked them to please represent them in polite conversations.... What is real becomes unreal, what is unreal becomes real. If ever there was a transvaluation of values, as the madly wise man used to say, this was it: where what we touch, feel, love, embrace and ultimately mourn is not real; and what we will neither hold or behold becomes real, paramount, persistent. What was in full public view and thus palpably evident was denounced and dismissed as metaphoric and ephemeral, and conversely what was so private and exclusive that [it] had become sacred was celebrated as Truth Everlasting" (pp.942-3). The question for us is whether Hafez "tilts" in this way; I see him rather as the supremely balanced tight-rope walker.

86 In one poem (KH304/2/3) we even have the feminine and masculine forms in succeeding lines although the first—*ma'shooqē be kām*, meaning roughly "the beloved who fulfils my desire"—might have been a common expression.

87 KH343

89 KH42. *mohtaseb*, chief of the moral police, which was also the nickname for one particularly unpopular ruler, Mobāraz ad-din Mohammed who imposed a cruel, puritanical regime, reportedly executing many people himself. The

sleeves in Persian gowns were full and capacious enough to contain or hide things, and there are various expressions associated with them. Eraq was a province in central Iran, not to be confused with modern day Iraq.

9 1 KH(426)v. I have paraphrased the first couplet of this powerful but very disjointed ghazal. The ten couplets in the Khānlari edition comprise six from Khalkhāli 445 and four from Khalkhāli 455. Other editions are different again. This kind of collation is only an extreme example of the general textual problems that beset Hafez' work, which seem to go right back to the author (for a history of the various editions, see Neisāri 1367). Not only did he not (it now seems) compile any Divan in his own time, he does not even seem to have standardized the various texts which must have been circulating, or the various interpretations to which they were subject. We can only speculate as to the reasons for this apparent detachment. Was it simply fatigue or disillusion at the end of a long life? Was he preoccupied always with the next poem, the next commission or occasion? He was after all a "working" poet. His first editor, Golāndām, says he was simply too busy with court duties. Or was he actually happy to leave things open, to let the reader generate a range of possible meanings? Did he think that his essential message would get across anyway, regardless of the textual variations? As Meisami (2012) notes, a *dīvān* could be a selected rather than collected poems, put together for a particular patron or perhaps audience. As the variants were gradually collated after his death, editors probably included rather than excluded any couplets they found (it would be a brave man who would leave anything out!) thus leading to longer, inflated and more disjunctive poems.

9 2 KH146. B7/2: *sang be jām andāzad*. Others have translated this as "throws a stone at the cup" but this seems to me unlikely and I have preferred the explanation offered in Karimi-Hakkak and Wolak (2009:145). It was apparently the custom after drinking wine to return the cup with some token of appreciation in it, such as a flower; returning it with a stone was the height of ingratitude. Either way, the police-chief does not come out well.

9 3 KH414. In B5/2 I have followed Fouchécour in translating *tashrīf* as a verb (to honor) rather than a noun because of *makon* at the end of the previous line. Others have translated it as a noun, i.e. the robe of honor of youth.

9 6 KH306

9 8 KH(47). B8: I interpret the second line here in the light of the following couplet where Hafez expresses, as a *rend*, his disregard for public approval.

99 KH54. An enigmatic ghazal, which might be placed anywhere. Fouché-cour interprets the final couplet in theological terms, but to me the word *adab* implies some court situation, unknown to us. Modern Persian still uses the terms *mo adab* and *bi adab* (polite and impolite). Interestingly the word for literature or letters, *adabiāt*, has the same root.

100 KH230

101 KH349. The *hajj* is the pilgrimage to Mecca, and each group of pilgrims had its own leader. There was commerce between Iran and China along the silk route for many centuries; the latter is sometimes referred to as Khotan, which is located in north-west modern-day China. It has a distant, quasi-mythical status in the Divan. Marco Polo's "Cathay" was a corruption of Khotan. Sudi, as usual, offers a non-spiritual interpretation of this poem but I am not convinced.

102 KH(418). Magic is a recurring if minor theme in the Divan. Clearly it had some place in the culture, although it is difficult to know exactly how prevalent it was or what forms it took. Hafez refers at various points to superstitious practices, which he always disparages, probably on religious grounds, since they are clearly condemned in the Koran.

103 KH107. "Compass" here as elsewhere refers to what we now call a pair of compasses, not a magnetic compass.

106 KH457

107 KH388

108 (KH197). As Fouchécour notes, this poem almost certainly refers to the regime of Mobaraz ud-din Mohamed (1353–63) which was characterized by a rigid, puritanical imposition of the religious law.

109 KH135. Wine was conventionally referred to as the "daughter of the vine" from the earliest days of Persian poetry.

110 KH367. On the first couplet Khorramshahi has a long note on Hafez and free will but it seems to me primarily a literary echo of Khayyam. The various translations of this ghazal demonstrate the subtle differences and choices that exist in many and the impossibility of arriving at a definitive version: see Alston (1996: 168); Ordoubadian (2006: 161); Avery (2007: 450); Einboden and Slater (2009: 1).

111 KH293. The six exits refer to the four directions plus up and down.

The interpretation and translation of lines in this as in other sections draws on various Persian commentaries on the Divan. Such commentaries (*sharh*) typically work couplet by couplet, explaining any words or phrases in them that are obscure or difficult. This was the original approach of the 16th century Bosnian Turkish commentator Sudi and is also that adopted by more recent commentators such as Lahuri, Khorramshahi or Heravi. Some editions, such as Qazvini and Ghani, offer entire paraphrases of ghazals, whereas Khanlari concentrates on explanations of problematic words and phrases. While such commentaries are obviously essential to an understanding of the text, they lie within an exegetical rather than literary tradition, and although they make technical or prosodic comments about meter and rhyme they tend to say little about the poems as poems. There may be several reasons for this. First, the history of Koranic exegesis provided a powerful model for the hermeneutic analysis of texts. Secondly, Hafez provides ample scope for such exegesis because of his ambiguity. Thirdly, the regard in which he is held may inhibit the kind of literary criticism which asserts that one ghazal is better than another. Whatever the reasons, I cannot help feeling that, with all the emphasis on understanding what Hafez "says" or "means" (notions which take us away from the actual text) the poetry somehow, to some degree, gets lost. So while Khorramshahi makes some interesting general comments about Hafez' style and prosody in the introduction to his *hāfeznāmē*, he does not analyse specific ghazals in these terms. Indeed I have not found any Persian commentator or writer who systematically treats the ghazal as a whole: a major difference between Persian and western approaches. The issue is, however, not simply a part/whole one. Exegesis should surely constitute only one element in the more general cognitive, ethical and aesthetic *response* to a poem, and it is that response which underlies a poetic, rather than merely lexical, reading or translation of the original.

115 KH71. B1: the word *zekr* ("repeats") refers to the ritual incantation of a divine name practiced in particular by Sufis. It is difficult to translate the various different forms of Muslim prayer. These do not correspond to the various Christian prayers, so I have typically had to use the generic term, which is not satisfactory since as Khorramshahi (1387:500) notes Hafez distinguishes carefully between them. This poem makes a number of religious allusions: the second stanza refers to the circumambulation of the Ka'ba; the angel of heaven refers to Gabriel; breathing life into someone was believed to be one of Jesus' miracles.

117 KH317

118 KH308. B4: *'eish,* which I have translated here by "sensuality," ranges in meaning from worldly comforts—the good life—through to pleasure or pleasures; the word *'eshrat* which Hafez also sometimes uses is more sensual. Although Persian poetry in Hafez' time was in general highly refined there were also poets such as Obeid who were cheerfully obscene, and sexual pleasure never carried the guilt in the culture that it has often had in Europe. (The distinction between shame cultures and guilt cultures may be relevant here.) It is difficult to know quite what register to strike, and some might opt for a more explicit one, but I have tried to preserve the delicacy and obliquity of Hafez in these matters. One other point: the use of both "dust" and "dirt" in this poem illustrates the difficulty of translating *khāk,* which is an important word in the Divan. The two English words have different associations and I have usually employed the first.

120 KH393

122 KH248

124 An earlier example of this kind of code is Ibn Al-Arabi's commentary on his own *tarjomān al-ashwāq* (Mystical Odes, translated by R.A. Nicholson; see the bibliography). This was added by the poet, philosopher and mystic after the poems were circulated, to stem criticisms that such love poetry was unbecoming in a religious figure. Nicholson did not doubt his sincerity, but found some of his glosses absurd. Shabestari is often associated, rightly or wrongly, with his contemporary Hafez, but the more general point has to do with "mystery." By now readers will have noticed regular references to it or "secrets." Hafez uses both the old Persian word *rāz* and the Arabic *serr*: there is no consistent difference between them and together they occur over 100 times in the ghazals. In addition, Fouchécour indexes 49 references to veil/curtain and 38 to revelation/hiddenness. Schimmel's wider study of Arabic and Persian mystical poetry corroborates such figures (Schimmel 2001). However, there are two kinds of mystery. One relates to the inner workings of the court and the person of the ruler. This reflects the secrecy of much policy-making and patronage, but the attribution of mystery may also have been a subtle form of flattery. The other kind of mystery is spiritual. Sufism, and the possible influences of gnosticism and neo-Platonism are discussed in Part VIII, but the notion of mystery is inherent in its esotericism. In *Orientalism*, Said (2003) is critical of the notion of the "mysterious Orient" (p.26). However, the basic methodological weakness of his thesis is that as he himself admits ("I have no 'real' Orient to argue for" p.xiv) he does not offer any authentic, indigenous picture of the East against which the orientalists' stereotypes can be tested. One searches the index in vain for references to many of the key figures, events and ideas that might help one to do this: for a book on Orientalism, it has surprisingly little about the Orient in it (only about 60 direct index headings out of over 1600). So at least in relation to Persian poetry, the orientalists, wrong-headed in other ways, got "mystery" right.

125 KH467. B5: Fouchécour has the sword imagining, which is also possible. B7/2 I have translated *hadith* by "lore" here because of the context but the religious connotations would not have been lost on his listeners.

127 KH(47)

128 KH473

130 KH(43). B3: *shab-e qadr*, literally "night of power" is a Koranic phrase referring to the initial revelation of the Koran to the Prophet (97: 1–5). Avery has a useful note on this, and its connotations of blessedness; I have translated it here as "transcendent" to try to capture its spiritual significance, but no translation can be adequate. B4: *dor softan* (to thread a pearl) can also mean to compose a poem. B6: following QG I have moved the penultimate couplet to second ("to sweep the road") so that it does not disrupt the flow. I have also, after some agonizing, omitted the final couplet which reads: "how I wish I could write a shocking poem such as Hafez has/to spite those who claim to be pious." It is a salutary reminder of just how literary and social the context was, but I think it subtracts from rather than adding to the poem, which is true of quite a few *maqta'*.

131 KH18

134 KH(60)

135 KH466. There is an untranslatable play on words at the end, with the word *mardom* meaning both "people" and the "pupil of the eye": people give him the brush off like a tear is brushed away. As a translator, one has to resign oneself to paying a kind of import tariff which means one rarely gets the full value of the original.

136 KH301. Al-Hallaj was a Sufi executed in 922 for heresy and notorious for exclaiming *ana al-haq* (I am the Real). It was just about acceptable to claim to be mystically *at* one with the divine reality, but not to claim to be that one: the ultimate expression of immanence. The "lawyers" in my translation refers to al-Shāfi'i, founder of one of the four Sunni schools of *shari'a* (see Kadri, 2011: 36–52) contrasted here with the ecstatic, heretical Hallaj. Hafez was not the only one to be critical of lawyers: Al-Ghazali (2003) argued that the heart lay beyond the scope of the law and, while admiring the founders of the various schools of law, derided some of his contemporaries as no better than "blacksmiths." B7: *looh-e sīnē* ("the tablet of my breast") is surely an echo of the "well-guarded tablet" on which the Koran is preserved in heaven (*al-looh al-mahfooz*, Koran 85:22). The English phrase "tablets of stone" comes from the ten commandments of the Old Testament.

138 KH300

139 KH311. B7: I have translated *jān o del fadā kardam* by a translation of the French expression for orgasm "le petit mort." The final couplet suggests that this is a court poem addressed to the patron.

141 (KH309). The form of this poem is unique in the Divan.

142 KH243

144 KH277

145 KH(323)

146 KH341. Salmā is the personification of female beauty in classical Arabic, and the abandoned encampment a standard trope of Arab poetry, sometimes picked up and used in Persian poetry also, although it was a much more settled and urbanized country even from early times. However, the constant evocation of beauty in the Divan goes beyond this, or what we are used to in western romantic poetry. Beauty was not only an aspect of the beloved, but was also attributed (however improbably) to the ruler or patron, as a form of compliment. Even more importantly, it had divine resonances.

148 KH234. B2: I have translated *khīāl* here as "fantasies" to capture the sense of the impossible, but as Khorramshahi notes it is a complex word, and in other cases imagination or even vision would be the appropriate equivalents. Just as wine can be interpreted as a spiritual elixir, so the Water of Life can be read as earthly wine.

150 KH131. The ancient covenant (*ahd-e alast*) is between God and man.

God asks: am I not your Lord? Mankind replies: yes, we bear witness to it (see Koran 7:172). Hafez repeatedly refers to this as determining subsequent events, including his own inescapable destiny as a lover, although as noted elsewhere he does sometimes assume free will. Hafez' references to Islam are a complex and contentious issue. The majority of inhabitants of Shiraz in Hafez' time were Sunnis, and Hafez was probably also one, although there was a small Shia minority. As Burgel (1991:7–39) points out, he does not mention the Prophet Mohammad once by name, although there is one use of the variant Mustafa (KH 65) and a number of implied references. Moreover, Hafez treats many of the major symbols and rituals of his religion with levity. It seems likely therefore that in his own time he was accused of impiety, and his moral and religious reputation seems to have remained rocky for some centuries afterwards; a striking reference to Ali as the master of Najaf (*shāhneye najaf*) in one poem (KH290) may have helped to make him more acceptable to the Shia Safavids in the 16th/17th centuries. Dig deeper however and the Divan is permeated by echoes of the Koran and the *hadith* (sayings attributed to the Prophet, or in the case of the *hadith qodsi*, regarded as forming part of the revelation of the Koran itself). Khorramshahi (1387: 1279–81) notes references or allusions to over 130 verses of the Koran and over 40 *hadith* in his edition (see also Zarghāmfar 1345). Thus it is not surprising to find Hafez claimed by both the orthodox and the unorthodox, with the former pointing to the implicit core of his work and the latter invoking the mystical traditions of Sufism and in particular the radical *malāmatiye* movement, which employed shock tactics to destroy personal pride and everything that was not deemed to be of the spiritual essence.

151 KH(34)

152 KH260. B1: in the dictionary *loolī* is given as a kind of travelling gypsy, perhaps originating in India, and also a dialect group in western Iran, although there may be some confusion with *loorī* (from the center-west region of Luristan). (Sudi claims he got to know one.) These people were known for street performances of music and dancing, and I follow Alston (1996) in highlighting this aspect, which is surely what captivated Hafez. Thus I think *rang āmiz* may refer to their make-up as well as their "mixed character" (although *rang* means color it can also have a figurative sense in Persian). B3: Angels, although higher in the spiritual order than human beings, were believed to be incapable of love; hence the identification with Adam as the first man.

154 KH82. There is a play on words in B1, where *khatā* means both China and mistake. The word "canon" translates the Arabic *qānūn*, which is strikingly similar.

156 KH(94). A case where I would like to have translated the ghazal as a whole but could not make it work. In B5/1 *rasm* could be translated as law but I have preferred "custom" since that seems the more common sense in Hafez; the line reminds me of Yeats' "great discourtesy of death."

157 KH(383)

158 KH229

160 KH216

161 KH106

162 KH29

163 KH(3). At the end, *ke bar nazm-e to* is ambiguous. Here, I have translated *ke* as "for" rather than "so that," on the basis that Hafez is, as the convention was, extolling the existing virtues of his art, rather than envisaging some future reward; although if we construe the heavens as the earthly power (i.e. his patron) the latter is possible.

V. THE AGE

The poems in this section are more obviously contextual than many of the others, but much of Hafez can be read in court or social terms. As noted earlier, my headings are not meant to preclude that, simply to bring out the range and scope of the original.

Hafez refers to various patrons at different times in his life and as a court poet played a role in legitimating their rule or claims to the throne. One of the most important of these kings was Shah Shoja who ruled Shiraz from 1363 until 1384, near the end of Hafez' life. Fearing that their father, Mobaraz ud-din, might allocate the succession to one of his grandsons by another, deceased brother, Shoja and another brother blinded and overthrew him. However, the brothers then quarrelled and Ferdowsi (unpublished notes) argues convincingly that a number of ghazals relate to Shah Shoja's temporary overthrow and exile from about 1364–66 and subsequent regaining of the throne, using the story of Joseph's exile in Egypt as a legitimating narrative of exile and return.

That said, Fouchécour (2006: 47) states that only 89 (18%) of the ghazals can be dated, and even then only in broad terms. This figure tallies with my own count. The lack of historical markers means that the kind of stylistic evolution proposed by Arberry (1993: 28–33) or substantive shift from poet to *rend* proposed by Shayegan (1995) must remain speculative. As noted earlier, we are faced with a largely unknown chronology.

Also, a parallel from a quite different tradition. Carney (1985) in his book on *Medieval Irish Lyrics* notes how "Irish bardic poets, when praising their princely or royal patrons, could assume through a well-established conceit the completely feminine role of 'king-lover'" (p. xxv). Again, it is important to recognise the importance of convention in understanding court poetry in any culture.

167 KH463. Hafez in panegyric mode. This poem, and some others, could be considered a *qasidē* or ode, but shows to what extent the ghazal had become a multi-purpose form in Hafez' hands. In B1/2 I have read *ezāfēs*, signifying *ibn* (son of), after both *ahmad* and *oveis*. B3: this is an ambiguous line and Avery (for example) translates differently.

169 The figure quoted is from Meneghini Correale (1988); Seddiqian (1383) has 76. There are some discrepancies between the two concordances, which may be due to the process of "lemmatization," that is, how one identifies a distinct "headword." For example if one counts words with an enclitic ending such as -i, -esh, or –am as examples of the headword rather than distinct words one will arrive at a higher total; and this is a matter of methodological choice.

170 KH(274). The two halves of this ghazal (this is the first) seem quite different, with the second praising the attractions of a *looli* (gypsy).

171 KH302. I have had to rely on translations of several Arabic lines in this as in other poems where they occur, since my own Arabic is limited.

172 KH435. The Persian new year (*no rooz*) which dates from pre-Islamic times is at the spring equinox, March 21/22.

175 KH378

176 KH382. B3: Solomon's seal, which was said to have the name of God inscribed on it, is often called Jamshīd's in Persian poetry, as here. This is a complex couplet, with a play on the first word of the first line (*khātam*, meaning seal) and the last word (*khātamat*, meaning outcome). In the second line *kutāh dast-e ahriman* literally means to cut short the devil's hand, but metaphorically means to overcome. The devil was believed to have stolen Solomon's ring at one point, and the implication is that it has now been regained through the accession of the ruler. The "son of Pashang" refers to an autonomous prince of Luristan, probably on the occasion of his enthronement in 1356, but also harks back to Ferdowsi's *shāhnāmē* (The Chronicle/Book of Kings) the great Persian national epic. Both Avery and Fouchécour have detailed notes on the historical context of this ghazal. B8: the reference here is to the plains of Izaj which were boiling in summer, very different from the original temperate habitat of the musk-deer. B11: *zar feshān* means "gold-scattering," implying (hoped for) generosity but since it does not flow well in English I have compromised with "gilded."

178 KH(5)

179 KH170. The harbinger was the hoopoe and the distant land Sabā. I have translated *'āref* here as wise man rather than gnostic or mystic, picking up the Biblical description of the Magi.

180 KH278. This is one of some 20 ghazals that relate to Shah Shoja. The "regime" refers to the previous rule of the cruel and puritanical Mobaraz ud-din (see above). B8: the name Soroosh is derived from Zoroastrian angel Shroasha (see Avery 2007: 69) although subsequently identified with the angel Gabriel who brought the revelation of the Koran down to the Prophet Mohammed. Hence perhaps the reference to "divine illumination." This is one of the most "unified" ghazals, with a triage showing only one moralizing couplet in the unrelated column:

KH278	+	?	−
Shah Shoja	1,2,3,4,5,7,8,9	6	

182 KH(145). Final couplet.

183 KH362

184 KH400. The second line is a simplified, unsatisfactory version of a very complex image.

186 (KH117)

187 KH286. The last line refers to the millennial mythical belief that Jamshid will finally return to claim the throne of Iran again.

188 Time winnows, and there is an understandable tendency now to see figures like Hafez in isolation, although recent scholarship is correcting this. But in his own time, Hafez would have been viewed in relation to other court poets of whom two, Khājū Kermāni and Salmān Sāvaji, are firmly put in their place at the end of KH251.

189 KH203. B2: I have translated *sohbat* by closeness here. In modern Persian it means conversation but in Hafez' time implied real intimacy and friendship. The contrast is between the open lily and tightly-packed rose. B3: the language is of textual exegesis of the kind applied to the Koran (and later to Hafez' own poetry). A *mufti* was a senior religious judge who had the authority to issue *fatwas* (from the same Arabic root). Hafez is sometimes described as an antinomian poet (from the Greek *nomos*, meaning law) and it is important to place this in context. In Islam religious ideas form the basis for religious law (*shari'a*) so senior religious figures thereby also have a legal role (for a detailed account relating to Iran see Mottahedeh, 2008). Sufism can be seen partly as a reaction against legalism, in the name of the spirit rather than the letter, and although he is often critical of Sufis, Hafez shares this suspicion of the externalities of religion and hence "reason." Abu Eshaq was a pleasure-loving and politically naive ruler who was a patron and friend of the poet, but who was in due course overthrown by the much more severe Mobaraz ud-din Mohammad. B5: Khanlari's variant *sar dar gel bood* (head in the mud) makes more sense than the variant *pā dar gel* (feet in the mud) which Meisami uses. B8: as Fouchécour points out, *dīdī* which literally means "you saw" can mean "you heard" which seems better here.

190 KH374

191 KH(12). This said, Hafez did not have a happy stay in the central Iranian city of Yazd (which he insults in one ghazal as "Alexander's prison") and soon returned to Shiraz.

192 KH(325)

193 KH232. This translation illustrates one of the problems of turning Hafez into English. As noted earlier, the typical line in a ghazal contains 13–16 syllables (Fouchécour 2006: 1183) substantially more than the 10 or 11 of the iambic pentameter which arguably remains the default line of English verse, although one cannot simply compare syllables across languages; because of its Anglo-Saxon element, English is a particularly compact language in this respect. Davis (2012) solves the problem by using the older "fourteener" line, often in 4/3/4/3 ballad form and this can work well. However, it assumes a basic iambic foot, and can lead to over-rhyming compared to the original, risking a kind of jingle. The alternative is to create longer pentameters by using some trisyllabic (anapaest/dactyl) or tetrasyllabic feet. In this ghazal I have managed to create some long lines, but not all. Part of me regrets that I have not always been able to reproduce the gait and grace of the Persian; part of me thinks that it would just seem artificial in English.

194 KH(381)

195 KH225. The patched gown refers to the patchwork Sufi gown, a supposed public manifestation of poverty. In the last line, it is difficult to translate *gooshē* (corner) and its compounds *gooshē neshīn* and *gooshē gīrān*. Hafez often implies a kind of social or emotional withdrawal, but it was also Sufi practice to go into such retreats or isolation for 40 days, so the phrase has dual associations.

198 KH231. B2: I am persuaded by Fouchécour's contention that there is an allusion here to chess, with the knight/horse being taken by the king, but my reading of *veyam* in B7 differs from his.

199 KH102. In the first line *nāz* is a lovely Persian word but difficult to translate: see Fouchécour (2006: 680) on its multiple meanings. Often used of a beloved's charms, with "ministrations" I have tried to catch something of the airs that doctors can give themselves. Wild rue was burned in order to ward off evil spirits.

200 KH294. B4: here *khīāl* (image) has a positive sense.

201 KH(174)

202 KH164. I have altered the order here. The sure-footed (actually "happy-footed") guide is Khezr.

205 KH(335). Again, a ghazal that seems to fall into two quite different halves, of which this is the second. B5: I have translated *havā* here as fondness rather than air, which is another common meaning, but the latter is possible. Turanshah was a vizier of Shah Shoja and protector of Hafez. Shiraz is the capital of the province of Fars and Hafez expresses his disillusion with life in the court there in KH286 also.

206 KH(130)v. One of the very few poems with a probable autobiographical element. The commentator Sudi and others think that it refers to the death of a young son.

207 KH228

209 KH(287). B7: I have translated *honar* as "art" here because of the relevance to poetry but it is a complex word which also has connotations of virtue.

210 KH46

212 See Arberry (1994: 329–30) who traces this story back to 1427. Despite his barbarity, Timur Lang was appreciative of the arts.

213 KH(298). I have omitted two couplets in the middle which would require inordinate unpacking to make sense in English. "Defender of the faith" can be translated as part of the king's name, as Avery does.

215 KH(111)

216 KH235. The opening couplets are not about Jesus but use his coming as an analogy.

217 KH(486). The very last couplet in the Khānlari edition of the Divan.

218 KH(20). Hafez uses the Persian-origin words *hast* and *nīst*, which I have translated as "being" and "nothing." These provide a powerful set of opposites in the original, and all the more so because they are rooted in ordinary speech. In other places he sometimes uses the Arabic word *vojood*, which I have tended to translate as "existence" although the Arabic phrase *wahdat al-wojood* is sometimes translated as the "unity of being." *āsaf* was Solomon's vizier in Persian mythology, and was referred to as a form of compliment to any high official.

220 KH99v. This ghazal has a refrain which I have only partially reproduced as a stem. The reference to Isfahan may or may not imply a stay there. B6: the way one translates Hafez' frequent references to *rāz* reflects one's reading of the whole poem: "confidences" would imply a social interpretation, "mysteries" a spiritual one. Here I have stayed with "secrets" as allowing either.

221 KH330.This poem has an obvious autobiographical element. One occasionally gets these flashes of anger or disillusion.

222 KH143. The reference to Shah Mansur indicates that this stately ghazal was composed towards the end of Hafez' life. B2: I have preferred the variant *pāk* to *chāk*. I have paraphrased *rezvān* as the "keeper of heaven." B5: the "felt bonnet" was the Sufi head dress and the line is a reminder of their supposed power, a warning reiterated in other ghazals.

223 KH(150).

224 KH76. B6: Hafez' recasting of the *shari'a* law might be read as just another instance of poetic hyperbole to be greeted with a knowing smile. However to reduce the entire, complex edifice of laws that had been built up over the preceding centuries (see Kadri, 2011) to a couple of maxims must have shocked some of his audience and this is one of the most arresting statements in the Divan. While the common view is probably that legality codifies morality, Hafez seems to be counterposing the two and reinstating moral values rather than religious law as the central concern. This helps to explain why (see Section IX) some see him primarily as a moral poet with an ethical message based on love. B9: the final line in the poem is probably an insult directed at a rival poet. There was a slave trade conducted by the Arabs along the east coast of Africa, in particular Zanzibar, but the word *siāhi* (black person) could also refer to an Indian.

225 KH(124)

226 KH(380). Hafez here uses *yazdān*, the Zoroastrian word for God or principle of good, which contrasts with *ahriman* which is the Zoroastrian principle of evil.

227 KH(384). Final couplet.

228 KH176

VI. THE BELOVED

I had originally intended to make two sections out of this (The Beloved; The Friend) but found it impossible due to the mixture/overlap of terms related to love and friendship not only from one ghazal to another but even within ghazals. Khorramshahi subsumes both *doosti* (friendship) and *yār* (friend/beloved) under *'eshq* (love.) Those who read Hafez primarily as a worldly poet will see these as deferential court poems addressed to patrons, and explain the amatory language in terms of the stylistic conventions of the time, though that simply pushes the question back a step: why did the language of love become transferred/applied to a power/patronage relationship? Likewise, those who view him as a spiritual poet will see both love and friendship as two aspects of our relationship with God (but again, why did the language of love become a spiritual metaphor?). These two interpretations thus each resolve the ambiguity in their own way.

231 KH85

232 KH398. The references are to two legendary Iranian kings mentioned in Ferdowsi's epic the *Shāhnāmē*, both of whom exemplified the transitory nature of earthly power.

2 3 4 KH282

2 3 5 KH409. The "Elders" refer to mystical masters (*pīrān*), the "Sheikhs" to Sufi leaders. Given the problems of translating *rendi*, I have used various terms and phrases, here "goings-on."

2 3 6 KH92v. Order changed and one couplet omitted. B1: the opening phrase, *ei ghāyeb az nazar* could be translated (socially) as absent from view or (spiritually) hidden from sight. I have gone for the latter given the powerful mystical connotations of the two words (one of Hafez' soubriquets was "the tongue of the hidden") but the ambiguity is there. The Babylon of pre-Islamic times was associated with magic and sorcery.

2 3 7 KH90.

2 3 8 KH(41). The second part of this ghazal (for the first two couplets see p.85) which I find problematic in terms of the sequence of couplets, although the texts show no variants. B3: I have dealt, not very satisfactorily, with the ambiguity of *vei* (as "it" [the wine] or "him" [the friend]) by using "the other." The couples referred to in the poem are two of the great love stories of Persian literature, the first heterosexual, the second homosexual.

2 4 0 See Kreyenbroek (2004).

2 4 1 KH244

2 4 3 KH68. In B4 I have translated the double sense of *parvānē* as both letter of authorization and moth.

2 4 5 KH(110)

2 4 6 KH61v

2 4 7 KH420. In B1/2 the word *ramidē* suggests an elusive, fugitive wild animal. Final couplet omitted as unrelated.

2 4 8 See in particular KH79, p.379.

2 4 9 KH433. I have translated *pīshkesh* as "gift." The hyperbole lies in the fact that this is given to the beloved's servants rather than the beloved, but it could also be construed as a bribe.

2 5 0 KH(450)

2 5 1 KH394

2 5 3 KH202. B9: The Night of Power (*shab-e qadr*) was when the Koran was revealed to the Prophet Mohammed, although the phrase was used by Sufis more generally to refer to any transcendent experience. Still, one can see how this couplet and other parts of the poem might have seemed blasphemous to orthodox Muslims. B10: the final couplet is a nice reversed conceit.

255 KH210. Fouchécour thinks this complex, delicate ghazal is an elegy on the death of someone close.

257 KH465. "The angel kneeling before Adam": God commanded the angels to revere Adam as His creation. Satan refused on the grounds that angels were made of fire whereas people were made merely of earth, lower in the order of being.

260 KH100. The bird of good omen is the mythical *homāī* (osprey) which gave protection to those rulers who came under its shadow. Birds play an important part in Persian poetry generally, above all in Attar's *Conference of the Birds*.

261 KH313

262 KH123

264 KH139

265 KH427. The ending is one of a number of places where Hafez meditates on the issue of predestination versus free will. Fatalism is one of the stereotypes of Orientalism, but I think in Hafez it is sometimes merely a pose, employed to excuse some of his excesses or as a form of flattery to emphasize his subservience to his patron. The sheer energy and ingenuity he displays vis-à-vis "the beloved" belies it.

267 KH448. *hāfez* here refers to the religious title and role of those who, like Hafez, knew the Koran by heart, and he plays on his own name/title in several poems. This poem, with its references to both *yār* and *'āsheqān*, exemplifies the overlap of the registers of friendship and love.

269 KH93. The first couplet of this poem was analyzed at the beginning of these Notes and the ghazal provides a useful peg for a discussion of Hafez' rhymes. Kasravi (2006) in his diatribe *What Does Hafez Say?* argues that the incoherence of the poetry stems simply from a desperate search for rhymes to fulfil the strict requirements of the form. (I have to say that in a few cases I think this is true.) There are many more verb-rhymes than noun-rhymes in the ghazals. This is not only because the verb normally comes at the end of the sentence but also because Persian has a very large number of compound verbs, consisting of a noun combined with a range of common verbs, such as do, have, put, bring.

This creates numerous rhyming options, and even though Hafez would only have considered a subset of these for semantic and stylistic reasons, it still allowed him great scope. However KH93 is interesting in that the rhymes here consist of Arabic nouns ending in *āyat* (e.g. *'enāyat, velāyat, hedāyat, nehāyat*). This is obviously more restrictive but I still get no sense of the poem being rhyme-driven. It is unlikely that a poet who was so patently skillful in the construction of his lines would not be equally skilled in making his rhymes, so I think Kasravi's general thesis is invalid. I think the real reason he disliked Hafez so much was that he saw him as a reactionary influence, holding back the development of a modern, secular Iran.

272 KH190. Judas-tree translates the Persian *arghavān*, which is an ancient word with Sassanian (not Christian) associations.

273 KH(187)

274 KH455. B1 is so condensed that I have unpacked it into two stanzas.

275 See KH431/3, p.294.

276 KH38. In fact the dot in the letter *jīm* is within the letter.

277 KH(310). The first letter of the Arabic and Persian alphabets is *alef*, which is an almost vertical line.

278 KH39. Last couplet, which seems circumstantial, omitted.

280 KH(245). This is a striking but disjunctive ghazal and I have omitted *abyāt* 5–7 since I can find no connection between them and the rest.

281 KH(26)

VII. THE FAITH

This and the next section were originally one, and can be read together. However, I have tried to tease out the various different threads in the Divan and at the risk of over-elaboration, decided there were sufficient differences among the ghazals to warrant creating the two sections, the first concerned with what might be labelled orthodox piety and the other with unorthodox mysticism. Most of the religious aspects of the ghazals have already been addressed in previous notes, so only a few points remain to be made here.

Another well-known Persian classic, Sa'di's *Golestān* (2008) written about a century before Hafez, begins with praise of God, followed by praise of the

Prophet (*na't*) and then praise of his patron. This was the expected preface not only to high literary works but also more mundane, everyday documents. In Hafez' Divan we have the first and third but not the second. Although there are only two explicit references to *towhīd* (KH374/3, KH477/2) the formal profession of the oneness of God, there are 165 other references to God in the ghazals (see Seddiqian); but there is no explicit reference to *na't* anywhere in Hafez, although there are several allusions to the Prophet in the ghazals. Schimmel (2001: 171–211) has discussed the place of poetry in praise of the Prophet in, among others, the work of Sana'i, Attar and Rumi, and Vitray-Meyerovitch (1995: 211–29) has explored the associated concept of "the perfect man" (*ensān-e kāmel*). And as Einboden (2005) points out the situation is complicated by the fact that Hafez does often refer to other religious figures such as Moses and Jesus.

The absence of *na't* is surprising and Burgel (1991:32) sees it as part of a more general omission: "[I]t strikes the reader of Hafiz that there is so little truly Islamic in his poetry, and almost no trace of unblurred Islamic piety." Nor does he allow the common explanation of this in terms of the esoteric traditions of Sufism: "Hafiz' 'religion,' confession, or order thus hovers above, or beyond, not only exoteric Islam but also above Islamic mysticism" (p.27). As this section will show, there are in fact some ghazals and lines that do manifest such piety, but the absence of *na't* has led some to conceptualize Hafez' faith in terms of a vaguer, more inclusive "religion of love," perhaps most memorably expressed in Ibn Arabi's *Tarjumān al-Ashwāq (the Interpreter of Desires)*:

> My heart has become capable of every form; it is a pasture for gazelles
>> and a convent for Christian monks
> And a temple for idols and the pilgrim's Ka'ba and the tables of the
>> Tora and the book of the Koran.
> I follow the religion of love: whatever way Love's camels take, this is
>> my religion and my faith. (1911: 67)

The notion of a religion of love has also had more recent advocates: see for example some of the chapters in Lewisohn (2010). However the actual phrase *mazhab-e 'eshq* occurs only once in the ghazals (KH119/7) and that is as a playful literary trope, hardly a sufficient basis on which to build an entire interpretation.

Against these doubts and problems we should set two things. The first is

Hafez' regular attacks on religious hypocrisy, exemplified in some poems in this section. If he really did not care about his faith, the argument goes, he would not have bothered. Secondly, there is the ubiquity of prayer in the ghazals, of which Fouchécour lists over 90 instances. As noted earlier these cover a range of different kinds of prayers. Some are simply conventional phrases such as "morning reading and nightly prayer" and sometimes it is the beloved's face or hair that are the object of such devotions. Hafez asks people to pray over his tomb, which many indeed still do. Prayer is repeatedly invoked for his various patrons, although it may also be associated with the hypocrisy of the "devout cat" (KH129). That said, there are many genuine and powerful references to prayer, in particular to *do'ā*, which is an informal prayer with the arms held out or raised (*bar āram*) often invoking or asking for God's blessing. The beautiful Muslim image of the first text is an example of this.

285 (KH118). The text is however problematic. Some translators have understood the hands as belonging to the angel on the syntactic grounds that the phrase *be do dast-e do'ā* ("with two hands of prayer") follows on from *fereshtē-at* (angel) although one can argue that it follows most immediately on from the enclitic object pronoun *"at"* (you). In a comprehensive article, Jadaane (1975) refers to angels glorifying, but not praying to, God but also refers to Koran 40: 7-9 which speaks of angels asking God for forgiveness of believers. An alternative translation of the last line would thus be: "the angel will catch you with hands held out in prayer." However, in his long note on this couplet Khorramshahi (1384:500-03) argues that *do'ā* is one of the key words in the Divan (Seddiqian lists 65 instances of it and derivatives) and cites numerous examples of it related to human supplication (see for example Koran 2:185-6). On balance, I am swayed by the poetic link between foot and hand: foot stumbling, hands held out: not a bad summary of the human condition.

286 KH368. B7/1: I have translated *roozē-ye rezvān* here as "gardens of heaven." In Persian poetry *rezvān* was the angel who guarded the entrance to the gardens of paradise. In a text which, as we have seen, expresses a variety of ideas and attitudes Hafez' dislike and distrust of Sufis is a constant. It is possible that this reflects some vendetta with a powerful local Sufi figure, but the charges are more general: pride, insincerity, trickery, corruption and the double standards or hypocrisy cited in this ghazal. However, there may have been an even deeper reason. By Hafez' time, much Sufi practice had become organized, formalized and codified into a kind of procedural mysticism, very different from the ecstatic visions of (say) Ruzbehan Baqli. It may be that in his distinction between appearance and reality Hafez was contrasting such routinized mystical practices with the wider *mysterium* which arguably his poetry bears witness to.

287 KH(194)

288 See Limbert (2004) on the religious orders in Shiraz in Hafez' time. Khorramshahi (1387: 165) notes that Hafez was not alone in making this distinction: Sa'di did too.

289 KH78. B7: it is difficult to reproduce the subtle distinction here between *nehād* and *seresht*, but the first has the sense of a foundational principle and the second the sense of intrinsic nature, i.e. behavior and being.

291 KH(155)

292 KH373. B5: I have tried to reproduce Hafez' play on the word *'aib* which can mean both fault/blame and stain/blemish. The multi-colored (*molamma'*) patchwork gown was worn by Sufis as a sign of poverty. Curiously, the term is also used of poetry written in a mixture of Persian and Arabic, as some of Hafez' ghazals are.

293 KH(169)

294 KH(431). B4 omitted. I used the *maqta'*, which seems circumstantial in relation to the rest of the ghazal, at the end of Part I.

295 KH(474). B2: the 40 days may refer to the spiritual retreat mentioned earlier in relation to *gooshē girān*. B8: the phrase *dard-e dīnī* literally means the pain of religion, but perhaps expresses the mystical idea of the passion or travail involved in true faith.

296 Ibn Arabi was a key figure in bringing the notion of emanation into mainstream Islamic thought, although it remains unorthodox.

297 KH481. The temple in the first line refers to the Magian ruins, i.e. the tavern. It is thought that Hafez put the final, provocative, self-justifying lines in the mouth of a Christian to avoid a charge of apostasy (*kofr*) brought by some of his enemies at court. (According to the later historian Khandamir the incident arose out of a quarrel with Shah Shoja, although it was not documented at the time.) In Sufi terminology, "today" meant this life, and "tomorrow" the next, which I have tried to indicate here by using a capital letter.

299 KH(195)v. I have obviously altered the form here. In B1/2 *takfīr*, from the Arabic root k-f-r, implies a religious rather than purely legal prohibition.

300 KH(441). Metal: the usual meaning of *gohar* is jewel, but it can also mean material: Fouchécour translates it as the French *substance*.

301 This was in relation to the apparent denial of the Day of Judgment (see note 297).

302 KH366. Qalandars were and still are a branch of wandering Sufis who were notorious for their wild behavior, so Hafez is going to extremes here. Bayazid Bestāmi was an earlier Sufi mystic.

304 KH(141). The contrast here is between the Magian elder and Sufi Sheikh.

305 KH(188). The references to eye contact (*nazar-bazi*, lit. eye-play) are difficult to translate; terms like wink or ogle seem trivial or distasteful. But clearly they were part of the convention of courtly love in his day, and carried the suggestion of shared (perhaps spiritual) secrets. See Fouchécour (1996a). The last line is obviously a reference to himself.

308 KH478

310 KH(129). The egg refers to a folk story about a man who stole some eggs and hid them under his hat. When challenged, he gesticulated his innocence and in the process knocked his hat, breaking one. This and some other acerbic anti-Sufi poems may have been aimed at an influential Sufi, Emād ad-din Ali Faqih Kermānī, who moved from Kerman to Shiraz in Hafez' time (see Fouchécour 2009b). He should not be confused with Khāju Kermānī, an older poetic contemporary and friend of Hafez, who wrote in a style similar to, though less accomplished than his, and who formed part of the same court circle. But the attack on hypocrisy goes well beyond any individual, and may also reflect the ancient Zoroastrian preoccupation with right speech and the avoidance of lies, *doroogh*, still a powerful word in contemporary Persian.

311 KH(238).

312 KH64. This poem is often seen as an expression of Hafez' religious tolerance, although as pointed out in the general notes, we need to be careful about reading things into Hafez. B1: although some have translated the first line as meaning "you attract a thousand rivals to me," the primary sense of *raqīb* is that of a guardian, a person who keeps an eye on someone. B4: These two lines parallel each other: the relationship between lover and beloved is similar to that between patient and doctor, and I have expanded a little to make this clear. In the last line, Hafez uses the word *hadīth* (which I have translated as "lines") well aware of its religious connotations as the "sayings" of the Prophet.

314 Hafez' poetry is too bound up in meanings to be simply sensual in stereotypical orientalist fashion, another way in which first impressions are confounded by deeper acquaintance. The only orientalist stereotype that is really borne out in his work is that of mystery, which is integral.

315 KH250. The word *gham* is often translated as grief or sorrow but has a very wide range of resonances in Persian, from "worry" right through to "despair." I have used the latter here since it forms a powerful refrain in the original. This fine and cohesive poem may nevertheless be read in several ways. The initial reference to Joseph here could be a personification of Shah Shoja, suggesting a historicist reading of the text in terms of the narrative of exile and return. On the other hand, if one reads back from the end, the poem may be seen as an expression of religious faith, or even (unusually) a personal statement of despair and hope. However, Hafez may have built the poem on its refrain, which suggests that one should give fairly equal weight to all the couplets. Whatever the *pretext* or *context* of a ghazal, one must also respect its *text*, and its internal dynamic and direction; back to our original *problematique*.

VIII. THE MYSTIC

Any discussion of Hafez' "mysticism" needs to be prefaced by some reference to Sufism. The subject is extremely complex, with an extensive literature in its own right, and the brief remarks that follow are intended only to help us consider Hafez' work in this context. Sufism has been characterized in various ways. Some see it as an esoteric tradition which complements or contrasts with the exoteric elements of Islam. Others point to its search for hidden rather than explicit meanings in religious texts, or even its emphasis on the non-verbal (dance, music, the "taste" of gnosis) rather than the verbal. Others again describe it as being concerned with the "spirit" rather than the "letter" or the "heart" rather than the "head." Some Sufis seem to have leaned towards a belief in immanence rather than transcendence and focussed on the development of an "inner way." Some commentators refer back to neo-Platonism and others have used the word "gnostic." Such general terms allow Sufism to be related to other mystical traditions, but Dabashi is critical of the tendency, particularly among Western Orientalists, to speak of Islamic or Persian mysticism *in vacuo*, and stresses the need to contextualize it historically (see Dabashi 1999, especially chapter 3). He argues that *'erfān* or Sufism emerged in relation and reaction to the dominant nomocentric and logocentric discourses and structures of the time, and characterizes it as theo-erotic and homocentric (Dabashi, 2003).

Another interesting approach is in terms of the distinction between "faith" and "belief" (Smith, 1979; Lewisohn, 1995). This is itself a problematic distinction, which cannot be absolute. Faith must be faith in something, and belief has to be sustained by something. And there can be a dialectical relationship between the two. For example, this might throw light on Abu-Hamid al-Ghazāli's "crisis," documented in his autobiography, *Deliverance from Error*. In English, the two words are sometimes used interchangeably (and confusingly "faith" can also mean an entire religion). And as Smith notes, the distinction does not translate directly into Muslim terms and indeed would be rejected by many, although "faith" suggests the Sufi term *sālek*, often translated as "seeker" or "wayfarer." Nevertheless it may be useful to distinguish between (1) a belief system comprising the propositions, ideas, narratives and symbols of a religion which constitute its doctrine and (2) the engagement or trust that an individual brings to the search for God. In a nutshell, Sufism often seems to accentuate the latter, in terms of personal devotion, commitment, search or surrender to the point of self-annihilation. Conversely, the belief system often seems less salient, with a rejection of rational thought (*'aql*), a suspicion of mere formal observance, a playful use of religious symbols and an implicitly nominalist view of language, all of which can be found in the Divan. One can readily see why Sufism has long been distrusted by more orthodox believers and why, by extension, Hafez' piety was and remains still in question.

Even in his own time, Hafez' "Sufism" was an issue. The poet Jāmī, whose father may have known Hafez and who himself lived soon after him, avers that although Hafez did not belong to any Sufi sect (*tāyefeh*) nevertheless '*hīch divān beh az divān-e Hāfez nīst agar mard sufī bāshad*': "there is no divan better than

Hafez' divan if a man is a Sufi" (quoted by Khorramshahi 1387: 29). The debate has continued ever since and scholars can be lined up, rather like two football teams, comprising those who read Hafez in worldly, courtly terms, and those who see in him one of the greatest representatives of the long, mystical tradition of Persian poetry. The 16th century Bosnian commentator Sudi took the first view; most but not all Iranian scholars espouse the second. Many western scholars initially leaned towards the mystical interpretation, often reflecting stereotypically Orientalist assumptions, but latterly the court poet reading has tended to prevail, reflecting a more "situated" or "grounded theory" approach to literary studies which in turn draws on Marxist theory or the sociology of literature.

The mystical interpretation is based on several kinds of arguments. First, Hafez regularly uses a number of terms which form part of the vocabulary of Sufism, for example *hemmat* (spiritual purpose) *tajalli* (manifestation) *tariqat* (path) and *fanā* (annihilation). Some of these words have an ordinary language meaning as well as a technical, mystical denotation: for example *hāl* can mean "state" and *maqām* "position" in both general and spiritual senses, *manzel* can mean a stopping-place as well as a spiritual stage, and *vaqt* means time as well as the Sufi "moment." On their own, any one of these words could simply be interpreted in terms of its everyday use, but together they form a family which reinforces each of them and points towards a specialized, spiritual interpretation. For example, Hafez' vocabulary includes a number of the terms listed in 'Ayn al-Qozāt's lexicon (Arberry, 1969:53). Conversely, Meisami argues that such vocabulary shows that Hafez' "mysticism" is largely "a stylistic feature of his ghazals" (Meisami 2003:50). But it is the existence of this cluster of terms that has allowed people to interpret the ghazals in a mystical way if they are so inclined, and the Divan has in fact been used in Sufi circles for many centuries. And it is worth remembering that Hafez could have avoided using at least some of these terms if he wanted to preclude a spiritual reading, but he did not.

Beyond that, there are possible links to particular figures. One such is the Shirazi mystic Ruzbehān Baqlī who died just over a century before Hafez was born. The possible relationship between him and Hafez has been discussed by Corbin (1971) and Ernst (1996) and some sources suggest that Hafez belonged to a chain (*selselē*) of mystics going back to Ruzbehān; others doubt this. If there was such a relationship one might expect Hafez' language to show the influence of Ruzbehan's terminology. Some of the range of terms indexed by Ernst do appear in the Divan, but it is arguable that they are part of the common language of Sufism with which both figures would have been familiar. Khanlari specifically relates several phrases (e.g. *mast o mastur*) back to Ruzbehan but there is no reference anywhere in Hafez' work to Ruzbehan's key concept of *eltebās*. This derives from the Arabic root to do with clothing, and Ernst translates it as "clothed with divinity" (1996: 35). Beyond any specific terminological links, one has also to consider the general tenor and style of both writers. There are certainly affinities, for example in terms of the iconography of the rose, but in other ways the two seem to me very different: Ruzbehan is a manifest visionary, and his writings are full of spiritual figures, oceans and deserts, whereas Hafez is much more refined, oblique and literary.

Another possible link rests on the set of equivalances set out by Hafez' near contemporary Shabestari in *The Rose Garden of Secrets/Mystery (golshān-e rāz)* which allows one to decode Persian erotic and bacchic poetry in a spiritual way. One cannot rule this out on historical grounds—the timing allows it—and it does provide a key that fits, but it was asserted (and not contested) at the 2007 Exeter conference that there is no hard evidence linking Shabestari to Hafez. Although Shabestari does use many terms (including *rend*) which are also used by Hafez, he seems to me too neat, too pat; the texture of Hafez' ghazals is simply not as programmatic or formulaic as this. There are other possible influences. Hafez would surely have been familiar with a wide range of Sufi writers, including for example the 12th century thinker 'Ain al-qozāt Hamadāni whose inclusivism and ecumenism find echoes in the ghazals (Arberry, 1969; Dabashi, 1999). However, influence-tracing is a tricky business unless one can single out distinctive phrases or terms and many Sufi ideas would have entered the general, cultural bloodstream by Hafez' time.

Beyond such possible specific links, the mystical interpretation relies on the internal evidence, such as it is, of the text itself. The ghazals do include a number of apparently ecstatic poems, some of which are translated in this section, and which in the root sense of the Greek word ἔκστασις, standing outside the self, seem to manifest Hafez' preoccupation with transcendence of the self (*khod*). Whereas it is possible to read Hafez' references to *'āref* (gnostic, mystic) and the associated noun *ma'refat* non-transcendentally or even ironically, *khod* and its various compounds such as *khod bīn* (self-regarding) or *khod parasti* (self-worshipping) are unambiguous. I find it difficult to read these "ecstatic" poems in any other way, and indeed *masti* might be better translated by "ecstasy" rather than drunkenness or intoxication, which in English tend to have downbeat connotations.

There is also a more general textual argument, to do with language itself. Bürgel (1991:36) argues that Hafez is not merely ambiguous, but *about* ambiguity. (This makes him sound not merely modern, but post-modern.) Clearly, Hafez delighted in language and had a real feeling for words, but that is not what Bürgel is saying. He suggests that Hafez was alive to the inadequacy of language *per se* and the dangers of treating it as unproblematic, which can lead to conceptual and moral absolutism and hence intolerance, a point made all the sharper by the centrality of language in the Abrahamic religions as religions of the Word or Book. Hafez' attacks on reason (*'aql*) can be understood in this light; indeed the case for a mystical reading can also be made in terms of the words Hafez uses pejoratively such as *'aql* (reason), *khod* (self), *salāh* (virtue) or *modda'i* (pretender) although secularists would interpret these in ethical (*akhlāqi*) rather than spiritual terms.

My own, final point is related, though slightly different. I think it is no accident that I have found some of the poems in this section the most difficult of all to translate, because they push right up against the edges of the sayable, recalling Walter Benjamin's "fragments of a greater language" (Benjamin, 1970: 78). A concern with the limits of language does not necessarily imply mysticism but it has been a characteristic of many mystical traditions, and seems to me to go well beyond the domain of worldly, court poetry. The poems that comprise this section include most of those commonly regarded as "mystical." But, as I have noted many times now, ambiguity is never far away.

319 KH240. The parrot is an image of the poet, and sugar means money. However, parrot-stories are among the oldest and most widespread in the world, having probably originated in ancient India. The parrot is the unpredictable speaker of awkward or gnomic truths, and Hafez would have been aware of these connotations, although the emphasis in the Divan is on the parrot as a mere mouthpiece, speaking what he has been divinely or humanly taught. So although this poem seems to belong in this section, it could also reflect Hafez' sometimes ambiguous position vis-a-vis his patrons. I have rendered the neat Persian phrase *zoor o zar*, literally power or gold, as fear or favor. Although the text refers to a Chinese figure, I have taken it to be the invading Mongol.

3 2 1 Khorramshahi (1387) has a very useful note on this term: see his word index.

3 2 2 KH(37). I have split this ghazal between this and the next poem since although it is quite coherent, it is difficult to accommodate the internal shifts within a single translation. Some couplets omitted.

3 2 3 KH(37). My line 5 is an attempt to translate the untranslatable *kabood*.

3 2 4 KH(199). The compass image here again refers to what we now call a pair of compasses rather than a magnetic compass. These center/periphery images occur several times in the Divan. They are primarily a literary trope but as noted earlier can perhaps also be understood theologically in terms of the human impossibility of apprehending the divine and the distinction between *tanzīh* (pure being, transcendence) and *tashbīh* (comparison, similitude). Hafez' ghazals sometimes seem to circle around and around, throwing a different light on their apparent disjunctiveness; a pattern of theme and variation, except that the theme is never, and cannot be, fully stated. I do not regard such circling as necessarily "Oriental" but rather as characteristic of certain examples of spiritual verse, and I find elements of it in, for example, T.S. Eliot's *Four Quartets*. Later in this complex ghazal, Hafez refers to his "rose-colored elder/master" (B8: *pire golrang-e man*). This sole reference has given rise to speculation about two things, which can only be touched on here. The first is possible color symbolism in the Divan. The usual color associated with Sufism is blue, although strictly speaking it was related to lower levels of spiritual rank or development, hence possibly Hafez' disparagement of it. It is possible that the color red was associated with a higher level of development or a different Sufi order, or indeed an older mystical reference in Sohrawardi to a "crimson angel" (see the extended note in Fouchécour, 2006: 557). Going back even further, color symbolism was also a feature of Zoroastrianism. The other issue is whether Hafez did have a spiritual master, and (as discussed above) even belonged to a "chain" (*selselē*) of Sufi initiates: *selselē*, interestingly, is also the word for a strand of hair. Those who tend towards a spiritual reading of Hafez have explored such links, though Fouchécour, who also sees Hafez in spiritual terms, argues that his master was "internal." In one ghazal, however, Hafez does express the need for a master before setting out on the path of love (KH166). There is of course a much simpler explanation of *pir-e golrang*, advanced by one Persian scholar, Zarrinkub: it means red wine. However, neither this nor any of the other interpretations makes much sense of the rest of the couplet.

3 2 5 KH479. This ghazal is dedicated to Toorānshāh, one of the viziers of Shāh Shojā, and with its contrast between the themes of court power and pious poverty could just as well have been placed in The Age section. B7/2: *az māh bovad tā māhī*; literally from moon to fish, which is usually translated as from the moon to Pisces, although there is also a play on the second *māhī*. Iranian mythology believes that the world is balanced on the horn of a bull (which tosses it from one side to the other at the new year, producing a perceptible jolt) which in turn stands on the back of a fish: hence the meaning may be from the top to the bottom of the cosmos. I have paraphrased.

3 2 7 The final phrase reflects the Persian word *kāmel* meaning complete, ideal, perfect. As well as everyday uses, it has aesthetic and spiritual connotations. See also Chalisova (2012) and Seyed-Gohrab (2012a).

3 2 8 KH144. While this short ghazal might be placed elsewhere, the powerful final line surely gives it a mystical sense.

3 2 9 KH(158)

3 3 0 KH359. B1: Adam committed different sins in the Muslim and Christian accounts of creation, but was at fault in both. I have inserted "his" here to avoid implying the latter. B4: the treasure that Gabriel revealed is of course the Holy Koran.

3 3 1 (KH70). B9: there is a play on words in the last line *dar hīch sari nīst ke serri ze khodā nīst*. Kasravi cites this line disapprovingly as an example of Hafez' apostasy.

3 3 2 KH423. A short but complex poem. I follow Fouchécour in translating *labash* in B1/1 as referring to the lip of a cup, not a human one; otherwise we cannot make sense of what follows. The final line is an obvious reference to the famous opening of Rumi's *Masnavi*. It is striking that in a culture that placed such emphasis on language, words and writing, perhaps the most famous image in all Persian poetry is non-verbal.

3 3 3 KH334

3 3 5 Like other terms, *fanā* can have an ordinary secular meaning or a spiritual, mystical one; see Khorramshahi (1387: 381).

336 KH137. This is probably the most overtly didactic of Hafez "spiritual" poems and difficult to read in any other terms. It is based on the conceptual triangle of nature (*tabi'at*) the path (*tariqat*) and reality (*haqiqat*). The first refers not to the natural world but a mere animal-like existence, the last to the ultimate reality. B5: not finding a good English equivalent, I have translated by "experience" the Sufi term *zowq* which literally means "taste." Anvari's dictionary sets out the range of meanings of this complex word.

338 KH(50)v. This ghazal is sometimes known as the "dervishes' hymn" and recited at their ceremonies. It can however seem rather formulaic in English and I have shortened and altered it a little. Fouchécour systematically translates *darvish* as "poor" and perhaps one can recall the Biblical "blessed are the poor in spirit."

339 KH(360). I have used "gnostic" here despite my reservations about the heretical baggage it carries in the west. See Jonas (1963).

340 KH(148)v. B1: *parto* (rays) is associated with the idea of emanation discussed earlier. B3: I have translated *barq-e gheirat* as "jealous lightning." However, not only is *gheirat* a complex word, but in English "zealous" and "jealous" share the same Greek root, which makes one wonder about the Old Testament phrase "jealous God." This ghazal, along with some others, uses the imagery of light, but in general this is not as central in Hafez as it was in some forms of Sufism, in particular Sohrawardi (1999) or the subsequent "illuminationist" school.

341 KH(26).This could also be read as a courtly ghazal. The reference to washing refers to a corpse which must be ritually washed before burial. The "inextinguishable flame" is one of a number of Zoroastrian references in the Divan which are cited by those who believe that Hafez may have had Zoroastrian sympathies although it can be understood simply as an expression of undying love.

342 KH(136). First couplet. Khanlari (1387:1171) suggests that this, among several other lines in the Divan, derives from the Shirazi mystic Ruzbehān Bagli. Together with a subsequent reference in the poem to the Sufi mystic al-Hallaj it might be taken as an expression of immanence. Although the entire ghazal is famous, unfortunately I found it impossible to make it work as a whole in translation.

343 KH213. B1: I have translated *khastegān* here as weary, not wounded, because of the context. B6: '*esmat* can be translated as chastity but I think Hafez is here drawing a contrast between public, ritual purity (*tahārat*) and private domestic purity. However I am puzzled by the reference to *khānē* (home) since Hafez does not usually refer to family life, and wonder if here it is short for *khānegāh*, a Sufi hostel, in which case chastity might be right. Either way, he is expressing orthodox religious views which seem at odds with the apparently libertarian or contrarian attitudes expressed elsewhere. The Divan is, if not exactly self-contradictory, certainly variable and inconsistent in its messages.

3 4 4 KH175. The duality or plurality of meanings in the Divan is nowhere more obvious than in this ghazal which could easily be read as a courtly poem but which is equally loaded with spiritual symbolism, hence its placing here. B1: others have translated *dar enkār* as "in denial" but the contrast is surely with the preceding *kār*, so I agree here with Avery in choosing the sense of rejection or denial of access. B2: it is impossible to capture all the resonances of *pendār* which has been variously translated as reflection, brooding, even self-delusion.

3 4 6 Ambiguity (*ebhām*) and amphibology (*īhām*) are important themes in the Persian literature on Hafez: Khanlari, in an appendix, notes the ambiguity of many words and Khorramshahi (1361: 98-129) has a whole chapter on it. Mottahedeh (2009:164) argues that for many centuries such ambiguity or equivocation provided a private inner space in the face of alien and unpredictable power.

3 4 7 KH345. Tuba: see Koran 13:29.

3 4 9 KH178. There is an unsubstantiated story that this poem was written after a powerful inspirational experience in Hafez' youth, and first won him recognition as a poet. For a persuasive spiritual interpretation see Burgel (1978). Alternatively, those who hold to a worldly reading of Hafez must read this as a courtly, morning drinking song: possible, but completely against the grain of the text. It is tempting to capitalize words such as Beauty and True, but I have avoided too many capitals since they do not exist in Persian and in any case think they impede reading.

3 5 1 KH168. Khanlari states baldly that he does not understand this ghazal. The key word here—*heirat*—had a strong mystical sense in both Rumi's *Masnavi* and Attar's mystical allegory *The Conference of the Birds*, where it marks the last, negative, stage before true understanding. It is sometimes translated as "bewilderment" but I think has a more positive sense here, given the image of growth at the end. (Rightly or wrongly, I also feel that the lightness of the end-rhymes somehow lifts the poem.) Since Hafez would have been well aware of its spiritual associations, I have used a parallel from the anonymous 14th century

English mystical text *The Cloud of Unknowing*. It is hazardous to pluck things from one tradition and use them in a different context, but I think there are enough affinities between *The Cloud* and this poem to warrant it. This is usually regarded as one of the most strangely mystical of the ghazals; those who think otherwise must see it as a pastiche of such. But it is worth noting that Hafez uses the word *esteghnā* several times in the Divan and this valley of "detachment" also forms part of the mystical journey of the birds in Attar's poem (for the references see Khanlari pp. 1154-5). Clearly, Hafez knew the poem well: the question is how he regarded it. Did he want such words to carry their full spiritual weight? (Mo'in (1319) has a whole section discussing Sufi terms such as *esteghnā, 'eshq, vasool and hemmat*.) Or was Hafez merely using such terms in an eclectic, literary way, as ones which came easily to hand?

352 KH (364)

353 KH(399). I have coined the phrase "original grace" here to express the idea of divine mercy which has existed from time immemorial, to which there are references in both the Koran and the *hadith*. It is impossible in a poem to be theologically exact about complex concepts such as grace, and one cannot simply translate words from one theological context to another; there are whole systems of thought and belief involved, so a degree of imprecision is inevitable. I have omitted several couplets to maintain the continuity of the night-sky image, including the final one which is simply a familiar anti-Sufi sentiment.

354 KH(2)v. This rather schematic version of the original does I hope capture the essential dualistic message of the poem.

355 The computerized analysis carried out by Meneghini Correale (1988) shows that heart (*del*) is by far the most frequent noun in the Divan occurring 594 times. (Seddiqian (1383) who includes more derivatives, gives a figure of 618.) Apart from the proper noun Hafez, the next most frequent are *mei* (wine) with 242 and *'eshq* (love) with 230. For a discussion of the various ways in which "heart" is used in the Divan, see Glunz (1991) who *inter alia* quotes the well-known *hadith qodsi*: "My heaven and my earth contain me not, but the heart of my faithful servant contains me."

356 KH179. This is a famous and profound ghazal which I have had to condense slightly at the end. B1: *doosh*, with its long, rhetorical vowel is an important word in the Divan. It does not simply mean "last night" but evokes the realm of darkness where strange, unearthly things can happen, hence its additional meaning of "dream." The contrast is often between *doosh* and *sobh* (dawn). The reference to God's creation of man out of clay would not have been lost on Hafez' audience, but to have the angels trying to get into the tavern inverts the usual order of angelology and suggests the centrality of mankind in the scheme of things. This is further reinforced in B3 by the reference to *amānat* and Koran 33:72 where mankind alone is entrusted with the divine burden of responsibility for love. *Amānat* has a powerful resonance for Muslims which non-Muslims may not fully grasp; as well as trusteeship or custodianship it connotes fidelity and existential responsibility.

3 5 7 (KH136). While the opening couplet of this ghazal (see note 342 above) could be read as an expression of theological immanence, this second one seems to point to theological transcendence. Perhaps we need to remember that Hafez was a poet, not a systematic theologian. While I love the power and beauty of this famous ghazal, I have found it impossible to translate as a whole. Even this couplet is problematic. Alston (1996:216n3) suggests that *gomshodegān* (literally the lost ones) may refer to Ahmad Ghazāli's statement that to be on the edge of the ocean of love can give one some sense of it, but to enter it is to drown, in which case one can say nothing about it. Khorramshahi (1387: 567) says that it is not the pearl-divers who can obtain the pearl but only those who paradoxically drown in love's ocean. However, the *gomshodegān* are on the road to the sea (*rah-e daryā*) or on the shore of the sea (*lab-e daryā*) not drowning in the depths of it (I prefer the latter variant since it makes more sense and occurs elsewhere in the Divan). Thus I am pushed to the figurative sense of lost souls vainly searching where they will find nothing. Moreover I think Hafez is going even further than Ghazāli. The phrase *kown o makān* denotes everything that is and has been created, including the ocean, so even the latter image is insufficient to express the utter transcendence of the pearl. However, this is one of those couplets that generate endless debate, since Hafez is working at the very edge of language here.

3 5 8 KH470. The last line is a Koranic reference, and "he" could be capitalized.

3 5 9 KH333. B4: although Hafez' use of the word *kāfer* (infidel) is in relation to his beloved, the statement would still have been found shocking. B7: the translation of the last line is pivotal not just for the poem but the Divan. The common translation of *'āref* is "mystic" but the French scholars Corbin (1971) and

Fouchécour (2006) prefer "gnostic" as more accurate, although that has heretical connotations in the west. *'erfān* is usually understood as the Sufi term for mysticism, but Axworthy (2008:138) points out that its meaning was subsequently influenced by the Safavid religious thinker Molla Sadra, several centuries after Hafez, so it is difficult to decide quite what weight it had for Hafez. (Avery translates it as "spiritually perceptive" and Ordoubadian goes for the lower key "aware.") In the end Hafez' phrase remains inscrutable, as indeed he acknowledges in the preceding one, which plays nicely on his own name: *hāfez-e rāz-e khod* (preserver/ keeper of his own secret). But *'āref-e vaqt-e khisham* is a powerful statement and I have finally opted for Hazlitt's phrase "spirit of the age" to try to capture here both the spirituality and the public, historical claim.

IX. THE MORALIST

Iranians looked (and still look) to their poets for, among other things, moral guidance, as Fouchécour has amply demonstrated in his study of morality and politics in poetry from the 10th-13th centuries (Fouchécour, 2009a). Hafez' predecessor Sa'di is probably the most obvious example of this aspect of Persian poetry. Anglophone readers, familiar with the languorous melancholy of Fitzgerald's Khayyam, might be surprised to learn that he too can be seen as belonging to the tradition of aphoristic moralizing: the quatrains are tougher, leaner and pithier in the original (Hedayat 1339) and indeed I sometimes think that his natural translator might have been Dryden or Pope. While Hafez is not as obvious or explicit a moralist as some others, one finds overt moral injunctions scattered throughout his work, often in self-contained couplets, of which I have already translated some examples. As Khorramshahi regularly points out, many of the words that can be interpreted spiritually can also be read in moral or ethical (*akhlāqi*) terms.

Although this section contains only one ghazal, which seems to me unique in the directness of its statements, I felt it was essential to recognise and flag up this facet of Hafez. Not to do so might unbalance the overall text in the direction of the mystical; it is worth noting that Edward Browne's anthology of Persian poetry has both "mystic" and "moral" among its headings (Browne, 1927). While Hafez' ghazal here may have been written in response to a particular incident, it can be, and is, interpreted more generally.

363 KH371. B1/2: literally either blackening another's gown or dying ones own blue, the color of Sufism, and thereby enhancing ones status: I have paraphrased. B2/2: *varaq-e sha'badē*: this is obscure and might refer to documents containing dubious Sufi claims: elsewhere *varaq* has the sense of *kāghaz*. But it could also refer to conjuring or fortune-telling cards (Fouchécour translates as *"cartes de la prestidigitation."*) The Tarot was circulating in Europe by the 14th century and it is possible that it or something like it was used in the Middle East as well: Steingass gives an undated, unsourced reference to *varaq-e āftāb*, which could be the Sun card in the pack. In the absence of any hard evidence this must remain speculative, but whatever the interpretation, it is clear that Hafez was against what he regarded as trickery or superstitious practice, probably associated with certain Sufis. B3 ("it is wrong ...") is obscure, but Heravi (1378: 1565) suggests that *kam o bīsh* may refer to *māl* (possessions). Thus I think the essential point is the moral emphasis on how one acts, not what one has, whether a little or a lot.

Other specific examples of ethical injunctions, often in single couplets, occur elsewhere in my text but it is also important to distinguish between Hafez' overt moralizing and his moral message in a wider sense. He is a fearless and outspoken critic of all that he sees as sham, greedy, fraudulent, vain, superficial, arrogant or hypocritical. More than that: as Khorramshahi (1384: 29) points out, Hafez is a poet of the positive, of love, freedom and generosity of spirit, not of abstinence, fear or fanaticism. He is the poet of moral value rather than legal prescription and in a society based on and regulated by the religious law his was indeed a radical voice. That general message or tone pervades all the ghazals in the Divan and whatever issues there may be about the interpretation of particular couplets or poems surely leaves a lasting impression.

X. THE POET

In a paper on the poet and poetry in Hafez' work, Bürgel (1978) quotes another earlier, great Persian poet, Nezāmi:

> *dar sehr-e sokhan chenān tamāmam*
> *kāīne-ye gheib gasht nāmam*

literally

> In the magic of speech I am so perfect
>
> that I have come to be called the mirror of the hidden

It is an important reminder, according to Bürgel, that Persian poets including Hafez not only made great claims for their own work, as court poets competitively had to, but typically for poetry itself. They regarded it as inspired utterance, magical in its powers: unveiling, revealing reality; mirroring and reflecting the deepest mysteries; expressing the profoundest truths of the heart and navigating the differences between the *zāher* (outer) and *bāten* (inner).

It seems appropriate therefore to entitle this final section "the poet." In these notes, I have tried to indicate both the possibilities and the problems of interpreting Hafez in various ways. In the end, in my own mind, I keep coming back to the fact that he was a poet, rather than a philosopher or mystic or court servant or social critic. By this I mean not only that he wrote remarkable poetry, but that I get the sense that ultimately writing was what drove him.

There are some ghazals which evince an obvious unity of theme or purpose, as courtly odes, evocations of conviviality and friendship, or expressions of religious sentiments or mystical experience. In the majority, however, we find a mixture of themes and images, and it is this that has made the interpretation of Hafez so problematic, not only for foreign scholars but for Iranians themselves. My own view has clearly been influenced by my experience of trying to translate him and beyond that probably by the fact that I am a poet myself. That experience and perspective have privileged the poetry itself, the sheer skill and delight in language and composition that are so patent in the original. Whatever the point of departure (or arrival) of the ghazals, they typically develop in and through their own dynamics, find their own direction or trajectory, grow out of themselves. Whatever the pretext or context of the work, there is a kind of autonomy within the poetic process itself which cannot simply be reduced to or explained in terms of ideas or circumstances. To say that Hafez was a court poet or a social critic or spiritual writer is to say something, but such macro-level analysis does not fully explain the micro-movements of the actual text. For that, we have to explore the writerly process, and listen to the lines and phrases and words themselves as they unfold. Thus the answer to the "problem" of Hafez lies under our noses: he was a poet.

One might object that the idea of poetry as an autonomous or self-justifying activity is a modern one and that in the 14th century poets saw themselves in more functional social, moral or religious terms. However, as Bürgel's paper suggests, we have to recognize the peculiar potency of the Persian poetic tradition. The fact that one of the earliest poets, Rudaki, could famously move his king to return to his homeland by describing its beauties, is indicative. Poetry had immense power in itself, and indeed still has much. After religion, it constituted the main expression and determinant of the culture of the time, and was even seen sometimes as an alternative to that hegemony. The power of poetry may also stem from the language. All cultures think their language is special, and to lose your language (as has largely happened with Ireland for example) is to lose something essential. In some cases, however, there are additional factors. Arabic is extra special to Arabs because it is the language of the Koranic revelation. Persian is special for different reasons: in a land historically and geographically subject to incursion and invasion from several directions, it constitutes the thread of identity going back three thousand years (see Meskoob, 1992).

Hafez studies do not stay still and there seems to be, in some cases at least, a growing emphasis on his language in the light of a more general literary concern with language itself. It is, after all, his use of language that makes him a poet and constitutes his transactions with us as readers. In terms of the distinction drawn at the beginning of these Notes, that means attending not just to what the poems say—their exegesis—but what they do, the experience they constitute. Beyond the specific meanings of his poems, what we are left with is a sense of their movements, how they develop or re-trace, circle or spiral, point us, lead us on or surprise us. To read Hafez is to submit to, undergo, follow, live something which in the end cannot quite be paraphrased because such a paraphrase is necessarily a different linguistic event.

367 KH(249)

368 KH(34)v. B1: *tamāshā* has the sense of public appearance or show, of being seen in society.

369 Schimmel (2001: 245n152) speaks of "God's *jalāl* being manifested in the scorching sun, his *jamāl* in the gentle rain."

370 KH211. B5: Both Avery and Fouchécour translate *honar* as "virtue" but it can also mean "art" and I think here refers to Hafez' profession as a poet.

371 KH403. B7: I have translated *chaman* here as meadow. Khānlari has two possible additional couplets at the end, which I have not translated.

372 KH(218). An extract from a ghazal that may have been written in response to an invitation overseas.

373 KH344. *hemmat* has variously been translated as holy aspiration, high ambition, and spiritual purpose. As noted earlier, it can be an important Sufi term which combines the aim at and effort towards spiritual development, which I have rendered here as "endeavor": for a discussion see Fouchécour (2006:406–08). The final couplet is tricky. Sudi is surely wrong to treat *mahfel* and *majles* as synonymous: the whole point is that the first is open and the second closed. Avery translates *mahfeli* as "congregation" but I think that "public" both captures the range of occasions on which a *hafez* might be asked to perform and sets up the crucial contrast with the private gathering. I have used the older noun "divine" to translate Hafez' public role as a reciter of the Koran since there is no obvious modern equivalent in English. *shookhī* has both the sense of impudence and playing tricks, and although *khalq* could refer to all people I think the sense here relates back to the public role.

375 KH200

376 KH484. B4/2 contains the ambiguous word *harīf* (companion or rival) but the former seems right here. The phrase *bād peimoodan* (lit. to measure the wind) means to do something foolish or attempt the impossible but it is also a poetic image for a fast horse. I wondered about translating it as "go like the wind" but decided the archaic "airy steed" would do the hyperbole justice.

378 KH(165)

379 KH79. For another translation and analysis of this ghazal see De Bruijn (1997:76–81). B1: *barg-e navā* in the second line echoes *barg-e goli* in the first; *barg* can mean both leaf and sheet of paper and I have used "token" here to cover both. B2: although "manifestation" is a bit clunky, I want to give *jelvē* its full philosophical force (with echoes of Plotinus) rather than go for the easier "appearance." B6: the story of Sheikh San'an is told in Attar's *Conference of the Birds*. He was a devout Muslim who was temporarily seduced by a Christian girl, who made him do all sorts of sinful things, before returning to the faith, bringing her with him. B8: The last line is a direct quotation from the Koran (where it is a repeated phrase) here beautifully eliding the image of paradise with that of the royal garden.

381 KH312. B1: the "freedom" in the second line is that of the *rend*. Some people have translated *tā* as the preposition "until" but that has Hafez trying to overcome his *rendi*, which cannot be right. I have treated it as the conjunction "so that"; Sudi's reading is translated as "*ta ke*" (Sudi, 1341:1716). Normally this would be followed by the subjunctive but as Lambton notes in classical Persian it may be followed by the indicative, as here. It is tempting and common to treat Hafez' *rendi* simply as a literary device which would produce the appropriate frisson in court audiences, and indeed for a long time this is the way I saw it myself. However, I have come to the conclusion that we should take it much more seriously and that as with many of Hafez' images it operates on more than one level. Clearly, it forms part of a set of literary constructs, along with its opposites: e.g. the puritan, the Sufi, the judge. But I think that Hafez is also saying something about himself here. He may have been a court poet but a highly individual one. He may have been a spiritual poet but an idiosyncratic one. Wherever they take off from, his poems, like birds, make unpredictable flights. His *rendi* is real; he is a free spirit; no one owns him.

384 KH105. B6: Like others, Fouchécour (2006: 369) translates *karāmāt* as "miracles," which then entails translating *maqāmāt* as "spiritual stations," but notes that this makes the couplet seem out of place. I have read it as the plural of *karāmat* (generosity) which Anvari's dictionary seems to allow, thus maintaining the courtly theme of the ghazal.

385 KH315

387 KH(157)

388 KH318. This is a nicely-turned ghazal. It is worth noting that one finds something of the same qualities in Hafez' lesser-known contemporaries such as Khājū and Salmān, a matter not simply of word-play but syntax-play and thought-play. For example there is a line in a poem of Khājū Kermāni which goes

> *va gar gooyam ke choon zolfet parishān nīstam hastam*
> *and if I say that I am not in disarray like your hair   I am*

The contradiction at the end of the line ambushes us: and this is something that Hafez does also. Indeed Persian lyric poetry can often be read in abstract terms, in terms of the movements, patterns, twists and turns, disjunctions and rejoinings of the lines: mirroring the abstract qualities of Persian art.

389 KH30. B1: Unlike Fouchécour and Avery I think this is a court rather than spiritual poem in which the first *beyt* is a hyperbolic metaphor for the ar-

501

rival or attendence of the king at the assembly. The *ahl-e khalvat* ("initiates") are thus the king's confidants, those in his inner circle among which Hafez would like to be counted. The "Night of Power" refers to the night of the revelation of the Koran to the Prophet, although according to Avery Sufis/mystics used it also in a looser sense to mean any special, transcendent night, which is probably the case here, given that it is heretically associated with the astrological influence of the stars.

391 KH351. B4: Alexander's prison and Solomon's kingdom are thought to describe Yazd and Shiraz respectively. The reference near the end is to Persians making the *hajj* pilgrimage through Arab lands.

392 (KH483). The Alchemy of Felicity was a lengthy treatise by the famous theologian Abu-Hamid Ghazāli, here wittily reduced to a single piece of advice.

393 KH319

395 KH261. Salma is the personification of female beauty in Arabic poetry but this poem is probably addressed to Hafez' patron Shah Shoja who, leaving the poet behind, went off to conquer Tabriz in the north-west; the river Aras flows into the Caspian sea. Hafez had an additional reason to complain: the Tabriz court poet Salman Savaji (a fine composer of odes who probably corresponded with him) having long enjoyed a comfortable position under the existing ruler promptly swore allegiance to Shah Shoja when he took over: hence the reference to the parrot and the fly. A rebeck is a bowed, stringed instrument rather like a fiddle.

397 KH432

398 KH(445)

399 KH387

400 The figure is from Seddiqian (1383).

401 KH3. This is an almost complete translation of this famous but complex and disjunctive ghazal, parts of which were translated at the beginning. B1: I have tried to combine both senses of *dast* which means not only hand (including the forearm) but also influence or means. As explained in one of my interpolations, some commentators read this poem historically as relating to the conquering Tamburlane. For a structuralist interpretation see Bashiri(1979).

403 KH(264)

404 KH23. Order changed. Avery (2007: 52) notes that B3 may refer to the *hadith: He who knows himself knows his Lord.* Fouchécour (2004:164) also has a long note on seeing and knowing in relation to this couplet.

405 KH(263)

406 KH350. The negative verbal prefix *ne/na* can be quite emphatic in Farsi and its force here is enhanced by the shorter than usual line leading to the repeated *nemibinam* (I do not see). B1: *pace* Avery, *zamāné* (time, fortune) here is more general than "the time's," which would be *zamān*. *Pace* Avery, Khorramshahi and Qazvini/Ghani, I do not think "red" captures the rich depth of *mei choon arghavān*, and have followed Haïm's dictionary in going for "purple" (which is also listed in both Dehkhoda and Steingass). Since there is no proven link between the modern Shiraz/Syrah grape and Hafez' time, we cannot be sure about the color, but certainly the wine I drank in Iran was dark. I have omitted the actual name (Judas tree, of which there are several species) since the reference is distracting: *arghavān* is an ancient Persian word with royal Sassanian associations which Hafez may have welcomed. That said, he probably used it partly because of the internal rhyme with *karān* in the previous line.

407 KH(264)

408 KH454. There are a number of Arabic lines in this poem and the opening is in traditional Arabic style. In characteristic fashion the poem brings together a number of tropes and themes but is primarily an ode in praise of the ruler (probably Shah Shoja) whose beard forms the crescent shape around the moon of his face. The "mote" refers to the small black spot that Iranians believed was at the center of the heart, forming its quiddity or essence. B8: here *jalāli* means not only glorious but refers to the adoption of the solar year for the Iranian calendar following the work of Jalāl ad-din Malekshāh in 1079. The implicit comparison is with the shorter lunar year of 354 days which is the basis of the Arab and Muslim calendar.

411 KH75. The refrain of *in hamé nist* can be understood either as "this is not everything" or "all this is not." I have gone with the second because I think the phrase refers back each time to what precedes it. Even in modern Persian *nist* can be an emphatic word, and another ghazal (KH74) has the refrain *nist ke nist*, which might be rendered as "no ... that is not." B3: Others have translated *minnat* as to become beholden or obligated to, but Steingass gives *minnat keshidan* as to court favor, which I have used here. "Shore" here is *lab* in Persian, meaning lip or edge, and the next line is literally "from lip to mouth" (*ze lab tā be dahān*). I have taken mouth to be an image of the sea into which we may disappear (i.e. die) but Ordoubadian translates more sensually "from my lips to your mouth" and the lines can also be read in terms of drinking wine, from the lip of the cup to the mouth.

4 1 3 KH(156). This *maqta'* could be read as either court deference or spiritual humility.

4 1 4 KH1v. This reprise of the very first ghazal exemplifies the problem of transitions from one *beyt* to the next which permit several possible triages, seeing the poem respectively as a courtly poem addressed to the ruler, a thematic love poem or a spiritual poem:

KH1	+	?	–
Court	1,4,6,7	2,3	5
Love	1,2,4,6	5	3,7
Spirit	3,5,7	1,2	4,6

As noted earlier, such triages provide only raw data, but they do help to explain why people can arrive at different readings. Thus while Khorramshahi's *hāfeznāmē* interprets the poem in spiritual terms (which involves seeing the sea/shore image in B5 as mystical and reading *hozoori* in B7 as divine presence rather than royal audience) others see it as primarily a courtly ghazal, and I lean towards the latter. Despite these interpretive problems, I feel that now, at the end of the book, there should be a stronger sense of its unifying intensity and tone—what it *does* rather than what it *says*—which is why I have gone for this more condensed version rather than a more literal translation.

4 1 6 (KH353)

4 1 7 KH160. *shaban*: as noted above, the Iranian calendar differs from the Arab Muslim lunar one. Its new year (with various associated happy rituals) falls in the spring, as it did in pre-Islamic times, and many of the names of the months are also ancient; so it resonates deeply with Iranians. It is also much more accurate, thanks in part to Omar Khayyam, so the lunar religious calendar gradually creeps round the Persian year. B9/1 could be translated: "for your sake,

Hafez, Being came into the climes of existence"; the "seven climes" equalling the world. I think it more likely that Hafez is the subject of the verb *āmad*.

419 KH(87). Khorramshahi argues that this is the fire of love, but my interpretation of this couplet reflects the fuller analysis of it by Meskoob who makes it the title of a whole chapter and relates it to darkness and light, night and day (see Meskoob 1371:16-17).

420 This final poem is appropriately the one inscribed on Hafez' tomb in Shiraz, and has the refrain *bar khīzam:* I (shall) rise up. I have used Qazvini and Ghani's text (p. 361) rather than Khanlari's (KH328) here, since although one line is virtually repeated in the former (*kaz sar-e jān o jahān*), the latter's shorter version places what is surely the *maqta'* with the *takhallos* as the penultimate *beyt*, which does happen sometimes but is rare. B1: it is worth recalling that some Sufis adhered to the monist belief that originally God and Man were one, so *vasl* would mean not so much union as re-union. I take *az sar-e jān* as meaning the end of life; Khorramshahi notes that it has the sense of leaving behind. I have translated *mohlat* in terms of time/delay, not respite (Steingass, q.v.). B2: every other translation I know translates *be valā'ye to* as "by my love for you" but this does not connect with the rest of the couplet, and there is usually an underlying logic within each *beyt*, which in this case has to do with power. One of the meanings Steingass gives *valā'* is "the right and power exercised over one lately set free." This leads to a nice paradox i.e. having set me free, if you would make me your slave (again); so my translation is "by your leave. . . ." B3: the image of the lost speck of dust echoes the Koran 25:24.

BIBLIOGRAPHY

Note: while most of the following items are referenced in the notes, some have been included as general background reading. Where there are multiple editions, I have referred to the one I have had sight of, rather than the earliest. Bibliographic information on sources is given in the Note on Sources.

Al-'Arabi, Mohyi'ddīn ibn (1911) *The Tarjumān Al-Ashwāq: a collection of mystical odes* (trans. R.A. Nicholson). London: Royal Asiatic Society.

Al-Ghazāli, Abu-hamid (2003) *The Book of Knowledge* (trans. N.A. Faris). Lahore: Sh. Muhammed Ashraf, online edition.

Alston, A.J. (1996) *In Search of Hafiz: 109 poems from the Diwan of Hafiz*. London: Shanti Sadan.

Anvar-Chenderoff, L. (2007) The radiance of epiphany: beauty and love in the Divan of Hafiz. Paper presented at the conference on *Hafiz and the School of Love in Classical Persian Poetry*, University of Exeter, 2007.

Arberry, A.J. (1969) *A Sufi Martyr: the Apologia of 'Ain al-Qudāt al-Hamadhānī*. London: George Allen and Unwin.

—— (1993, first published 1947) *Fifty Poems of Hafiz*. London: RoutledgeCurzon.

—— (1994, first published 1958) *Classical Persian Literature*. Richmond: Curzon.

Avery, P. (2007) *The Collected Lyrics of Hafiz of Shiraz: translated by Peter Avery*. Cambridge: Archetype.

Avery. P. and Heath-Stubbs, J. (2006, first published 1952) *Thirty Poems of Hafiz of Shiraz*. Cambridge: Archetype.

Axworthy, M. (2008) *Iran: empire of the mind*. London: Penguin.

Bahrami, N. (2012) Strategies used in the translation of allusions in Hafiz Shirazi's poetry, *Journal of Language and Culture*, 3(1), 1–9.

Bashiri, I. (1979) Hafiz' Shirazi Turk: a structuralist's point of view. www. angel fire.com/mb/bashiri/Hafiz.

Bate, J. (2008) *Soul of the Age: the life, mind and world of William Shakespeare*. London: Penguin Viking.

Bausani, A. (1958) The development of form in Persian lyrics, *East and West*, new series 9, 145-53.

Bell, G.L. (1897) *Poems from the Divan of Hafez*. London: William Heinemann.

Benjamin, W. (1970) "The Task of the Translator" in *Illuminations* (trans. Harry Zohn). Edited and with an Introduction by Hannah Arendt. London: Fontana/Collins, 69-82.

Bly, R. and Lewisohn, L. (2008) *The Angels Knocking on the Tavern Door: thirty poems of Hafez*. New York: Harper Collins.

Boyce, M. (1953) A novel interpretation of Hafiz, *Bulletin of the School of Oriental and African Studies*, 15(2), 279-288.

⸻ (2001, first published 1979) *Zoroastrians: their religious beliefs and practices*. London: Routledge.

Broms, H. (1968) Two studies in the relations of Hafiz and the West, *Studia Orientalia* XXXIX, Helsinki.

Brookshaw, D.P. (2003) Palaces, pavilions and pleasure-gardens: the context and setting of the medieval majlis, *Middle Eastern Literatures*, 6(2), 199-223.

Browne, E.G. (1927) *A Persian Anthology*. London: Methuen.

⸻ (1928) A *Literary History of Persia: Vol III The Tartar Dominion (1265-1502)*. Cambridge: at the University Press.

Bürgel, J.C. (1978) Le poète et la poésie dans l'oeuvre de Hafez, in *Convegno Internazionale sulla Poesia di Hafez*, Accademia Nazionale dei Lincei, Roma, 1978, 73-98.

⸻ (1991) Ambiguity: a study in the use of religious terminology in the poetry of Hafiz, in: Glünz and Bürgel (eds) op. cit., 7-39.

De Bruijn, J.T.P. (1997) *Persian Sufi Poetry*. Richmond: Curzon.

⸻ (2003) Hafez's poetic art, *Encyclopaedia Iranica*, online version.

Carney, J.C. (1985) *Medieval Irish Lyrics*. Mountrath: Dolmen.

Chalisova, N. (2012) Hyperbole, *Encyclopaedia Iranica*, online version.

Corbin, H. (1970) *Creative Imagination in the Sufism of Ibn Arabi*. London: Routledge and Kegan Paul.

⸻ (1971) *L'Homme de Lumière dans le Soufisme Iranien*. Sisteron : Editions Presence.

Dabāshi, H. (1999) *Truth and Narrative : the untimely thoughts of 'Ayn al-Qudāt al-Hamadhānī*. London: Curzon.

—— (2003) It was in China late one moonless night, *Social Research*, 70(3), 935–980, Fall 2003.

Darr, R.A.H. (2007) *Garden of Mystery : the Golshan-i Raz of Mahmud Shabistari*. Cambridge: Archetype.

Davis, D. (1999) Sufism and poetry: a marriage of convenience?, *Edebiyat*, 10, 279–292.

—— (2004) On not translating Hafez, *The New England Review*, 25 (1,2), 310–18.

—— (2012) *Faces of Love: Hafez and the poets of Shiraz*. Mage Publishers.

Duncan, R. (1984) *Ground Work: before the war*. New York: New Directions.

Einboden, J. (2005) The genesis of Weltliteratur: Goethe's West-Ostlicher Divan and kerygmatic pluralism, *Literature and Theology*, 19 (3), 238–250.

Einboden, J. and Slater, J. (2009) *The Tangled Braid: ninety-nine poems by Hafiz of Shiraz*. Louisville, KY: Fons Vitae.

Elwell-Sutton, L. P. (1976) *The Persian Metres*. Cambridge: Cambridge University Press.

Ernst, C.W. (1996) *Rūzbihān Baqli: mysticism and the rhetoric of sainthood in Persian Sufism*. Richmond: Curzon.

Ernst, C.W. (1997) *The Shambala Guide to Sufism*. Boston: Shambala.

Farzād, M. (1978) Critical remarks on the text of Hafez, in *Convegno Internazionale sulla Poesia di Hafez*, Accademia Nazionale dei Lincei, Roma, 33–58.

Feldman, W. (1996) The celestial sphere, the wheel of fortune, and fate in the gazels of Nā'ilī and Bākī, *International Journal of Middle East Studies*, 28, 193–215.

Ferdowsi, A. (2008) The "Emblem of the manifestation of the Iranian spirit" : Hafiz and the rise of the national cult of Persian poetry, *Iranian Studies* 41(5), 667–691.

de Fouchécour, C.-H. (1996a) « nazar bazi » : les jeux du regard selon un interprète de Hafez, *kārnāmeh*, 2-3, 3–10.

—— (1996b) Une confidence de Hafez, *kārnāmeh*, 2-3, 11–14.

—— (2006) *Le Divan: Hafez de Chiraz*. Paris : Verdier.

—— (2007) Hafiz et le Sufi. Paper presented at the conference on *Hafez and the School of Love in Classical Persian Poetry*, University of Exeter, 2007.

—— (2009a) *Le Sage et le Prince en Iran Médiéval: morale et politique dans les textes littéraires persans X-XIII siecles*. Paris : Harmattan.

—— (2009b) Le siècle littéraire persan de Hafez : I 'Emad Faqih Kermani, *kārnāmeh*, 7, 5–16.

Glünz, M. (1991) The Poet's Heart: a polyfunctional object in the poetic system of the ghazal, in Glünz and Bürgel, op.cit.

Glünz, M. and Bürgel, J.C. (eds) (1991) *Intoxication, Earthly and Heavenly: seven studies on the poet Hafiz of Shiraz*. Bern: Peter Lang.

Gray, E.T. (1995, second printing 2002) *The Green Sea of Heaven: fifty ghazals from the Diwan of Hafiz*. Ashland, OR.: White Cloud Press.

Hämeen-Anttila, J. (n.d.) *Nonlinearity in Medieval Arabic and Persian Poetry*. cybertext.hum.jyu.fi/articles/85.pdf

Hedāyat, Sādegh (1339, chāp-e sevvum) *tarānehāyē khayyām*. Tehrān: chāp-khānē bānk-e bāzargāni.

Hegel, G.W.F. (1975) *Aesthetics: lectures on fine art* (trans. T.M. Knox). Oxford: at the Clarendon Press.

Heravi, Hossein-Ali (1378) *sharh-e ghazalhāyē hāfez*. Tehrān: nashr-e no.

Hillmann, M.C. (1971) Sound and sense in a ghazal of Hafiz, *The Muslim World*, LXI (2), 111–121.

—— (1972) Hafez and poetic unity through verse rhythms, *Journal of Near Eastern Studies*, 31(1), 1–10.

—— (1976) *Unity in the Ghazals of Hafez (Studies in Middle Eastern Literatures—Number Six)*. Minneapolis: Biblioteca Islamica.

Hoozhir, Abd al-husain (1307) *hāfiz-e tashrīh*. Tehrān: motbeqē majles. Second edition with added introduction by Mahdi Suahili, Tehrān: ashrafi, 1345.

Jadaane, F. (1975) La place des anges dans la théologie cosmique musulmane, *Studia Islamica*, 41, 23–61.

Jonas, H. (1963) *The Gnostic Religion* (2nd edn.). Boston: Beacon Press.

Kadkani, Shafi'i (1352) *gozidēyē ghazaliyāt-e shams*. Tehrān: sherkat-e sahami ketābhāyē jībī.

Kadri, S. (2011) *Heaven on Earth: a journey through shari'a law*. London: The Bodley Head.

Karimi-Hakak, M. and Wolk, B. (2009) *Your Lover's Beloved: 51 ghazals by Hafez*. Merrick, N.Y.: Cross-Cultural Communications.

Kasravi, Ahmad (2006) "What does Hafez say?" (trans. L. Ridgeon) in Ridgeon, op. cit., 160–190. Originally published as *hāfez che mīgūyad*, Tehrān 1322.

Khorramshāhi, Bahā al-dīn (1361) *zehn va zabān-e hāfez*. Tehrān: nashr-e no.

—— (1387) *hāfez nāmē (chāp-e sevvum)*. Tehrān: enteshārāt-e 'elmi va farhangi.

—— (2002) Hafez Life and Times, *Encyclopaedia Iranica*, online version.

Kreyenbroek, P.G. (2004) Folk Poetry, *Encyclopaedia Iranica*, online version.

Kuran, T. (2011) *The Long Divergence: how Islamic law held back the Middle East*. Princeton: Princeton University Press.

Lāhūri, abdolrahmān khātami (1384) *sharh-e 'erfāni-ye ghazalhā-ye hāfez*. Tehrān: nashr-e qatra.

Lambton, A.K.S. (1953) *Persian Grammar*. Cambridge: Cambridge University Press.

—— (1991) *Landlord and Peasant in Persia: a study of land tenure and land revenue administration*. London: IBTauris.

Lazard, G. (1978) Le language symbolique du ghazal, in *Convegno Internazionale sulla Poesia di Hafez*, Roma, 1978, 59-71.

—— (2006) The Poetics of Middle Persian, *Encyclopaedia Iranica*, online version.

Leppihalme, R. (1997) *Culture Bumps: an empirical approach to the translation of allusions* (Topics in Translation 10). Clevedon: Multilingual Matters.

Lewis, F.D. (1995) *Reading Writing and Recitation: Sana'i and the origins of the Persian ghazal*. Unpublished doctoral dissertation, Dept. of Near Eastern Languages and Civilizations, University of Chicago.

—— (2001) Review of "The Hafez Poems of Gertrude Bell," *International Journal of Middle East Studies*, 33(1), 117-119.

—— (2002) Hafez and rendi, *Encyclopaedia Iranica*, online version.

—— (2012) Hafez and music, *Encyclopaedia Iranica*, online version.

Lewisohn, L. (1995) *Beyond Faith and Infidelity: the Sufi poetry and teachings of Mahmud Shabistari*. Richmond: Curzon.

—— (2007) The Puritans and Pharisees of Islam and the Religion of Love: theosophical structures of Hafiz's anti-clericalism. Paper presented at the conference on *Hafiz and the School of Love in Classical Persian Poetry*, University of Exeter, 2007.

—— (ed.) (2010) *Hafiz and the Religion of Love in Classical Persian Poetry*. London: IBTauris in association with Iran Heritage Association.

Limbert, J. (2004). *Shiraz in the Age of Hafez: the glory of a medieval Persian city*. Seattle: University of Washington Press.

Loloi, P. (2003) *Hafiz, Master of Persian Poetry*. London: IBTauris.

—— (2003) Translations of Hafez in English, *Encyclopaedia Iranica*, online version.

Losensky, P. E. (1998a) Linguistic and rhetorical aspects of the signature verse (*takhallus*) in the Persian ghazal, *Edebiyat*, 8, 239-271.

—— (1998b) *Welcoming Fighani: imitation and poetic individuality in the Safavid-Mughal ghazal*. Costa Mesa, Ca.: Mazda Publications.

Meisami, J. (1979) Allegorical techniques in the ghazals of Hafez, *Edebiyat*, 20, 1-40.

—— (1987) *Medieval Persian Court Poetry*. Princeton, NJ.: Princeton University Press.

—— (1991) The ghazal as fiction: implied speakers and implied audience in Hafiz's ghazals, in: Glünz and Bürgel (eds) op.cit., 89-103.

—— (1995a) Hafiz in English: translation and authority, *Edebiyat*, 6, 55-79.

—— (1995b) The body as garden: nature and sexuality in Persian poetry, *Edebiyat*, 6. 245-274.

—— (2003) *Structure and Meaning in Medieval Arabic and Persian Poetry: orient pearls*. London: RoutledgeCurzon.

—— (2012) Manuscripts of Hafez, *Encyclopaedia Iranica*, online version.

Meneghini Correale, D. (1988) *The Ghazals of Hafez: concordance and vocabulary*. Roma: Cultural Institute of the Islamic Republic of Iran.

—— (1991) Quelques observations sur la structure lexique des ghazals de Hafiz, in Glünz and Bürgel op. cit., 105-136.

Meskoob, Shāhrokh (1371, chāp-e dovvum) *dar kooyē doost*. Tehrān: enteshārāt-e khārazmi.

—— (1992) *Iranian Nationality and the Persian Language* (trans. M. Hillmann). Washington: Mage Press.

Mo'īn, Mohammad (1319) *hāfez-e shīrīn-e sokhan*. Tehrān: enteshārāt-e mo'īn.

Monteil, V.-M. and Tajvidi, A. (1998) *Hafez Shirazi: l'amour, l'amant, l'aimé*. Paris: Sindbad/UNESCO.

Morris, J. (2007) Transfiguring Love: perspective shifts and the contextualization of experience in the ghazals of Hafiz. Paper presented at the conference on *Hafiz and the School of Love in Classical Persian Poetry*, University of Exeter.

Mottahedeh, R. (2009) *The Mantle of the Prophet: religion and politics in Iran*. Oxford: Oneworld.

Neisāri, Salīm (1367) *moqadamē bar tadvīn-e ghazalhāye hāfez*. Tehrān: en-teshārāt-e 'elmi.

Nicholson, R.A. (1963, first published 1914) *The Mystics of Islam*. London: Rout-ledge and Kegan Paul.

—— (1964) *The Idea of Personality in Sufism*. Lahore: Sh. Muhammad Ashraf.

Nussbaum, M. (1986) *The Fragility of Goodness: luck and ethics in Greek tragedy and philosophy*. Cambridge: Cambridge University Press.

Ordoubadian, R. (2006) *The Poems of Hafez*. Bethesda, Maryland: Ibex.

Pamuk, O. (2001) *My Name is Red* (trans. E.M. Göknar). London: Faber and Faber.

Pourjavady, N. (2007) The idea of love in Hafiz and Ahmad Ghazzali. Paper pre-sented at the conference on Hafiz and the School of Love in Classical Persian Poetry, University of Exeter.

—— (2008) *Love and the Metaphor of Drunkenness*. Presented at the Asia So-ciety, New York, May 27, 2008, online version.

Ridgeon, L. (2006) *Sufi Castigator: Ahmad Kasravi and the Iranian Mystical Tradition*. London: Routledge.

Rypka, J. et al (1968) *History of Iranian Literature*. Dordrecht: Reidel.

Saberi, R. (1995) *The Poems of Hafez: translated from Persian*. Lanham: Univer-sity Press of America.

Sa'di. (2008) *The Gulistan of Sa'di* (trans. W.M. Thackston). Bethesda: Ibex.

Safa, Z. (1961) *ganj-e sokhan (jeld-e dovvum)*. Tehrān: ibn-e sīnā.

Said, E.W. (2003, first published 1978) *Orientalism*. London: Penguin.

Schimmel, A. (1979) Hafiz and his critics, *Studies in Islam*, 16: 1–33.

—— (2001, first published 1982) *As Through a Veil: mystical poetry in Islam*. Oxford: Oneworld.

Seddīqīān, M. (1383) *farhang-e vāzhenāme-ye hāfez (chāp-e sevvum)*. Tehrān: en-teshārāt-e sokhan.

Seyed-Gohrab, A. (2007) The Erotic Spirit: Mystic vs Romantic Love in Persian Poetry from Nezami to Hafez. Paper presented at the conference on Hafiz and the School of Love in Classical Persian Poetry, University of Exeter, 2007.

—— (ed.) (2012a) *Metaphor and Imagery in Persian Poetry*. Leiden: Brill.

—— (2012b) Waxing eloquent: the masterful variations on candle metaphors in the poetry of Hafiz and his predecessors, in Seyed-Gohrab (2012a).

Shāmlū, Ahmad (1366, 2nd edn.) *hāfez-e shīrāz: bā rivāyāti-ye ahmad shāmlū.* Tehrān: enteshārāt-e morvarīd.

Shayegan, D. (1995) The Visionary Topography of Hafiz, in Gray, op. cit.

Smith, W.C. (1979) *Faith and Belief.* Princeton, N.J.: Princeton University Press.

Spicer, J. (1974) *After Lorca.* No publication details given.

Squires, G. (1968) 6 poems from the Persian, *Delos*, 2, 68–75.

—— (2010) Eight lines of Coffey: a note on prosody, in Keatinge, B. and Woods, A. (eds) *Other Edens: the life and works of Brian Coffey.* Dublin: Irish Academic Press, 38–46.

Sūdi (1341–47) *sharh-e sūdī bar hāfez; tarjomē ismat settārzāde.* Tehrān: chapkhāneh-e rangīn.

Suhrawardi (1999) *The Philosophy of Illumination* (trans. J. Walbridge and H. Ziai). Provo, Utah: Brigham Young University Press.

Tafazoli, H. (2012) Goethe, Johann Wolfgang von, *Encyclopaedia Iranica*, online version.

de Vitray-Meyerovitch, E. (1995) *Anthologie du Soufisme.* Paris: Albin Michel.

Washburn, K. and Major, J.S. (eds) (1998) *World Poetry: an anthology of verse from antiquity to our time.* New York: Norton.

Wickens, G.M. (1952) The Persian conception of artistic unity and its implications in other fields, *Bulletin of the School of Oriental and African Studies*, 14(2), 239–243.

Yar Shater, E. (2002) Homosexuality in Persian literature, *Encyclopaedia Iranica*, online version.

Yar Shater, E. (2004) Hafez: an overview, *Encyclopaedia Iranica*, online version.

Zarghāmfar, Mortaza (1345) *hāfiz va qur'ān : tatbīq-e abiāti hāfez bā āyāt-e qur'ān.* Tehrān : entshārāt-e sā'ab.

Zarrinkūb, Abdulhossein (1349) *az kooyē rendān: dar bāre zendegi va andīshēyē hāfez.* Tehrān: sherkat-e sahāmi ketābhāye jībī.

ACKNOWLEDGMENTS

This book is, in the first instance, an attempt to repay some of the many kindnesses I received from people during my three years in Isfahan, not least my first Farsi teacher, the late Khanom Ardalani. During that time, I also became aware of the great wealth of Persian literature and scholarship in this field, to which I am indebted in a different way.

More recently, various individuals and institutions have helped me. I am grateful to Hull City Library and the library of the School of Oriental and African Studies in London which I have used extensively, and to Ahmad Boroumand who obtained other books for me from Iran. Early on, Michael Craig Hillmann kindly sent me materials which helped me get started and I had valuable initial discussions with Franklin Lewis. Three anonymous readers made useful, critical comments on an earlier draft and Elham Shayegh checked my Farsi and identified several textual issues. My wife Mary was a constant touchstone and my compatriot-poet Augustus Young read and re-read the entire manuscript.

I want also to express my appreciation to Keith Tuma and Miami University Press for taking on such a large project and to Roxanne Carter for helping to see it through. Jeff Clark, the designer, has brought his own very special expertise to the process. My chief thanks, however, must go to Ali Ferdowsi and Charles-Henri de Fouchécour. Without the help, guidance and support of these two fine scholars, I would not have been able to accomplish even that which I have managed to do. It goes almost without saying, finally, that the responsibilty for what I have written is mine alone.

Front cover reproduced from a painting (2004) by the contemporary Iranian artist Golnaz Fathi, by kind permission.

GEOFFREY SQUIRES

The poet **HAFEZ** was born around 1315/17 and died in
1389/90, towards the end of what is often seen as the golden
age of Persian poetry. He lived almost all his life in the
southern city of Shiraz where he was involved in the court
circles of various rulers and played an important role in the
vibrant literary and spiritual life of the times. His poetry, which
is variously courtly, lyrical, satirical and mystical, is collected
in his Divan, which contains nearly 500 ghazals and some
other verse. Little is known about his personal circumstances.

His reputation was established in his own time and has
continued to grow ever since, to the point where Iranians and
many others regard him as one of that nation's greatest poets.

GEOFFREY SQUIRES (b.1942) is an Irish poet
who after living and working in various countries is now
retired and lives in England. His work has been collected
in *Untitled and other Poems* (2004) and *Abstract Lyrics
and other Poems* (2013), both published by Wild Honey
Press, Bray, Ireland. A translation of one book, *Sans
Titre*, was published by Editions Unes, Nice, France in
2013. He is also a translator of medieval Irish poetry.